Get the MOST for your REMODELING DOLLAR

How to Save Money, Save Time, and Avoid Frustration

R. Dodge Woodson

BETTERWAY PUBLICATIONS, INC.

WHITE HALL, VIRGINIA

Published by Betterway Publications, Inc.
P.O. Box 219
Crozet, VA 22932
(804) 823-5661

Cover design by Rick Britton

Cover photography: Top three photos courtesy of Custom Wood Products,
Roanoke, VA. Kitchen (lower left): Interior design by The Second Yard; kitchen de-
signed by Douglas Leake of Critzer Cabinet Creations. Photo by William
McChesney. Bathroom (lower right): Designed by William McChesney of Critzer
Cabinet Creations. Photo by William McChesney.

Photographs by R. Dodge Woodson
Typography by Park Lane Associates

Every precaution has been taken in preparing *Get the Most for Your Remodeling
Dollar* to make this book as complete and accurate as possible. Neither the au-
thor nor Betterway Publications, Inc., however, assumes any responsibility for any
damages or losses incurred in conjunction with the use of this guide.

Library of Congress Cataloging-in-Publication Data
Woodson, R. Dodge (Roger Dodge)
        Get the most for your remodeling dollar : how to save money, save
time, and avoid frustration / R. Dodge Woodson.
                p. cm.
        Includes index.
        ISBN 1-55870-211-3 (paperback) : $16.95
        1. Dwellings--Remodeling--Economic aspects. I. Title.
TH4816.W63 1991
643'.7--dc20   91-19495
CIP

Printed in the United States of America
0 9 8 7 6 5 4 3 2 1

Dedication

I have many people to thank for the production of this book. Kimberley, my wife, supported my efforts, and her constant encouragement and assistance allowed me to enjoy writing this book. There were numerous days and nights when she hardly saw me. When I would complete a chapter, she would inject her thoughts and experience for consideration. Over the years, she has been much more than a wife. Kimberley has been a true partner; she has soldered pipe, supervised subcontractors, and maintained my sanity. I can't thank her enough for the last eleven years.

Afton, my daughter, allowed me to work on the book without feeling guilty. There were times when she insisted I go into my office and write. She is not yet three years old, but she knows how important this book is to me. Afton, this book is for you.

My parents also played a role in the development of this book. Their support and encouragement, over the years, provided the opportunity for me to gain my experience. Without their help, I would not have enjoyed the luxury of self-employment at such an early age. Even when they have disagreed with my path, they have always helped to blaze the trail. Everyone in my family has always supported me. They all deserve credit for my accomplishments.

There are a few others I would like to thank. They are: Paul, Faye, Dave, Lynda, Harry, Joy, Bob, and Smokey. Thank you all for allowing me this indulgence. I hope you enjoy reading this book as much as I enjoyed writing it.

Acknowledgments

I would like to acknowledge the Stanley® Project Planners, Home Designer®, by Stanley Tools, a Division of Stanley Works, New Britain, CT 06050. This product was used in the illustration of a bedroom layout.

The makers of Corian® and Butcher Block® countertops are thanked for the use of their names. They provide quality products to the building and remodeling industry.

I would like to thank my wife, Kimberley, for all her help and support. Kimberley provided all the artwork contained in this book. She assisted in the final stages of preparing the manuscript and was a continuous source of support. Kimberley, thank you for your assistance and support in the production of this book and in my life.

Contents

Introduction

Congratulations! You are holding a book capable of saving you thousands of dollars. This book can also save you time and frustration. The techniques and suggestions throughout the book are based on actual field experience. I have been involved in residential construction and remodeling for more than seventeen years.

In this book, I am going to give you the benefits of my experience and my mistakes. You will be shown how to obtain the most for your remodeling dollar. There will be advice on saving money and advice on making the most of your money. These are two separate things: saving money does not necessarily mean getting the most for your money. I am going to show you how to take control of, and profit from, your remodeling ventures.

Your decision to purchase this book may be the most profitable decision you have made since buying your home. There are numerous books available on the subject of remodeling. These books are typically written for consumers wishing to do the work themselves. This book is different; it will show you how to achieve your remodeling and financial goals without picking up a hammer. Remodeling is always popular, and in today's economy remodeling is becoming more popular than ever before. With the aid of this self-help manual, you can remodel your way to riches.

This book is going to show you inside tips and tricks used by professional contractors. It will help you evaluate your ability to be a general contractor. The contents of this book are invaluable to anyone considering remodeling. Full-time general contractors can learn from this information, and the average homeowner can become a competent remodeling coordinator in the short time it takes to read this book.

Remodeling your home is a big responsibility, and this book will help you do it right. The guidance found in these pages will save you money and could keep you from losing your home and your good credit rating. There are serious risks involved with remodeling; my book will identify and defuse these risks. By the time you have finished the book, you will be better qualified than many practicing general contractors. This is not a dry and boring instruction manual, it is an aggressive guide to see you through the rough waters of remodeling.

I have been involved with the housing industry in many different ways. As a general contractor, I have been party to all aspects of residential construction and remodeling. I have worked with a hammer and with a computer. I know the importance of a job's budget and the skills needed to maintain it. Dealing with subcontractors and suppliers is difficult, but I have learned ways to reduce the problems.

I am a master plumber and have worked as a plumber, a plumbing supervisor, and owner of a medium-sized plumbing company. I have always specialized in remodeling work. I love the challenge and the reward of completing a job where others might fail. Performing the duties of a real estate broker and property management consultant trained me in other aspects of home improvements. I learned appraisal methods and those improvements with the greatest potential to sell a home. Dealing with the buying public taught me what areas of a home are most important to consumers. All of this experience has influenced my success in the remodeling business.

I made the transition from plumbing contractor to general contractor by building my first home. This was an interesting project for a newly married couple to tackle. We could not afford to buy a home, but we felt we could build our own. I knew we could save 20% of the retail value if we acted as the general contractor. I also knew that if we did much of the work ourselves, we could save much more.

The decision was made. We accepted the challenge and built our own home. Not everything went as planned, but we completed the home and saved a significant amount of money. Soon, we decided to build another home for ourselves. This was the beginning of a new career. At the peak of our activity, we were building sixty homes per year.

Remodeling remained a cornerstone of all my business endeavors; I never abandoned it. We created different companies and divisions, but plumbing and remodeling remained my primary interests. Land development, real estate sales, property management, and other related areas were explored, but nothing could take me away from remodeling. The profits were good and the work was rewarding.

Remodeling can be profitable anywhere. I have worked in very small towns and major cities. The business procedures differ, but the work is the same and the profit potential is always present. If you are planning to remodel your home, you have the potential to make serious money. This book will show you how to maximize your savings.

All of the techniques contained in this book are tested and proven. I have used them all and know they work. Your venture into remodeling is sure to be more fun and more profitable with the aid of this book. Whether you act as your own general contractor or engage the services of a professional, this book can save you a lot of money. In addition to the financial rewards, this book will make your job more pleasurable. It will teach you the methods of minimizing the common problems associated with remodeling.

How to Use This Book

This book is written to allow the average homeowner to enjoy the highest return on the money invested in remodeling projects. The terms and recommendations are on a level most consumers will understand. If you don't understand a phrase or a word, consult the Glossary in the Appendix. The Glossary is arranged alphabetically and gives clear descriptions of the words and phrases contained.

Also in the Appendix is a list of rules for remodeling. These are "Dodge's rules." They should be observed throughout your remodeling efforts. They are a compilation of years of experience and mistakes. If you obey these rules, you will not have to endure the painful learning processes I have experienced. For the small expense of a single book, you are gaining the benefit of all my remodeling knowledge. This field experience cost me thousands of dollars, but it might very well *save* you thousands in your remodeling efforts.

I have designed this book to save you money; the chapters are in sequence with your logical path into the remodeling world. The first step to saving money is evaluating your ability to act as a general contractor. Being general contractor should save you a minimum of 20% on the total value of your project. This can amount to over a year's salary and is well worth considering. As seductive as the savings are, you must make a thorough evaluation of your abilities before assuming the role of general contractor.

Some people are much better off hiring a professional to manage their job. Chapter 1 addresses this issue and enlightens you as to the responsibilities of a general contractor. There is much to consider before donning your hard hat and calling the shots. When you read this chapter, be honest with yourself. You will only be hurting yourself if you take on more responsibility than you are prepared to handle.

Designing your project is fun; it is also where the whole process begins. Chapter 2 discusses the skills needed to complete a preliminary plan. You don't have to be an artist to design your own plans. Once you have a rough draft, a professional can turn your line drawings into working blueprints. There are some aspects of the design to which you must pay particular attention. Using a consistent scale is one of the most important rules of design.

Chapter 2 teaches you to allow for wall thickness and code requirements. It will make you aware of frequently overlooked items that are crucial to your project. When you complete the chapter, you will be ready to draw your preliminary plans. The next step in your adventure will be converting your rough draft into working plans. You will also need to prepare accurate specifications for the work to be completed.

Chapter 3 educates you on the mechanics of obtaining final working plans and specifications. There are ways to have your blueprints drawn for free; these methods are examined in the chapter. Architects and drafting companies are compared. Perhaps the contractors can work from your preliminary plans. This chapter will expose the many options available in creating plans and specifications for your job.

The information describes the difference in blueprints provided by the various sources. Your blueprints could be free, or they could cost you several thousand dollars. This chapter will provide facts, allowing you to make an informed decision on the best source for your plans. Specifications will be covered in detail, as they are essential to a successful remodeling job.

What do you want from your remodeling investment? Chapter 4 delves into the reasons for remodeling. You will be asked to evaluate your proposed improvements. This chapter raises some interesting questions. Do you know when it is better to move than to remodel? You will when you have finished reading this chapter. There are times the money invested in remodeling cannot be recovered. Are you willing to spend money you will never see again?

The proper evaluation of your intended improvements can save you from financial suicide. Chapter 4 clearly describes the ways to protect your investment. You will learn how to determine the value of your improvements before they are done. This one chapter can save you more money than all your other efforts combined.

Chapter 5 builds on the foundation formed by Chapter 4. It shows you what investments are easiest to recover when your home is sold. The advice in this chapter also tells you what projects to avoid. The chapter takes you through the steps of regaining your remodeling dollar. All too often, remodeling money is invested and never fully returned. With Chapter 5, you can circumvent this problem.

Personal statements in remodeling can ruin your home's value. Most remodeling projects increase a home's value, but some improvements have the opposite effect. Being too radical can cost you plenty. Chapter 6 deals with these negative improvements. You will learn that you can invest money in your home only to *reduce* its value. Creating a non-conforming situation with your remodeling plans will devastate the market value of your home. Appraisers will label it a poor investment, and financing will be difficult to obtain. If your house is noted for functional obsolescence or non-conforming use, your sales price will plummet. Chapter 6 will protect you from these disastrous threats.

Wouldn't you like to know the most profitable project to undertake? Chapter 7 details five of the most profitable jobs in the business. If you are interested in making money with your remodeling efforts, Chapter 7 is your chapter. These five projects can all return more money than they cost.

What could be better than enjoying new living space while making money? Bathrooms and kitchens are two of the best investments you can make with your remodeling dollar. There are three other projects with similar profit potential. Read Chapter 7 and make plans to capitalize on the high resale value of the improvements discussed.

Choosing a contractor may be the hardest task in remodeling your home. The right contractor is an important part of a pleasant remodeling experience. Much of your profit can be made or lost in the selection of your contractor. Chapter 8 advises you on the techniques to use in locating and selecting the ideal contractor. It illuminates the qualities of a seasoned remodeling contractor. You will assimilate questions to ask potential contractors. These questions can save you money and trouble. Every aspect of contractor comparison will be covered in the chapter.

Chapter 9 concentrates on the subject of pricing the labor and material required for your job. Soliciting bids is a complex activity. Comparing competitive bids is a pivotal function in the success of remodeling jobs. It is easy to be blinded by the lowest bid, and this can result in disappointment and cost overruns. There are certain procedures to follow in obtaining and comparing bid prices; these procedures are explained to you in Chapter 9.

Anytime you are interested in saving money, you are interested in negotiating. Chapter 10 is dedicated to teaching you the methods required to obtain the lowest prices possible. Professionals have learned how to manipulate suppliers in the bidding process. In Chapter 10, I will expose these professional secrets to you. Following the guidelines in Chapter 10 will permit you to realize maximum savings on your project.

Chapter 11 may be the most important chapter in this book. It does not directly deal with saving money, but it can save your house. This entire chapter is built around written agreements and their importance to your security. Much of the advice given in this chapter was learned the hard way. I know the importance of written agreements; Chapter 11 will convince you of the need for them. Don't skim this chapter — study it and take notes. If you are planning to engage contractors, you must utilize these business practices.

Financing is a fact of most people's lives, and it plays a significant role in remodeling. Chapter 12 distinguishes the many sources and types of home improvement loans. Even if you don't need to finance your job, you should read this chapter. There are some inside tips here you may not be aware of.

These obscure facts may change your payment plans; there are ways to enjoy making money by financing your project. This chapter exposes everything you will need to know about home improvement financing.

One of the biggest mistakes most remodeling consumers make is paying large deposits when contracts are signed. Their money is at high risk under these circumstances. Chapter 13 proposes ways for you to stay in control of your money. It suggests risks and remedies for progress payments and deposits.

Whether you engage a general contractor or subcontractors, you will benefit from the advice in Chapter 13. Money is one of your best tools in remodeling your home; it gives you control over the contractors involved in the project. Read and heed the words contained in Chapter 13.

Will your contractors be honest? Will they complete their work in a timely fashion and in compliance with your requests? They will if you learn the routines described in Chapter 14. This chapter informs you of the ways to maintain control and respect throughout your job. These techniques will work with remodeling rip-off artists and reputable contractors. They even work with grizzly 275-pound construction workers. Before you commit to contractors, commit Chapter 14 to memory.

Can you spot a wolf in sheep's clothing? Separating reputable contractors from potential felons can be difficult. They look the same and talk the same but act very differently. Chapter 15 should prove entertaining as it takes you through some of the most common consumer abuses. Remodeling is a profession occasionally visited by some very bad characters. This chapter will give you examples of their bad intentions. It also explains how you may be taken advantage of by reasonably reliable contractors. The stories here are based on true accounts. This chapter will help keep you from becoming a victim of remodeling fraud.

How will you make your final decision? What information must you assimilate to make a sound decision? Which contractors and suppliers offer the most advantages to your project? All these questions and more are answered in Chapter 16. This chapter is filled with facts and ideas to make your decision a wise one. The summaries in this chapter enable you to make a commitment resulting in happiness and savings.

Quick decisions can spell catastrophe in remodeling. Chapter 17 is aimed at defusing the risks of quick decisions. It instructs you on the most effective means of dealing with on-the-spot decisions. All remodeling jobs have the potential of requiring fast answers to problems. You must be prepared for these situations, as the wrong decisions can be quite costly. When you've read this chapter, you will be mentally equipped to deal with the unexpected. Knowing when to act and when to think will be accurately revealed.

Some of the biggest problems in remodeling occur near the end of the job. Chapter 18 points out ways to curb these problems. There is much to be done in the last few days of the remodeling process. There are punch-lists, cleanup, final payments, and completion certificates. Negligence here can taint all your previous accomplishments. Chapter 18 guides you through this decisive stage of your job.

Chapter 19 helps you apply the final touches to your new space. It deals with decorating and getting the best results from your remodeling venture. This chapter tutors you in the steps frequently ignored by homeowners. Omitting the finishing touches will detract from your equity gain and result in lower profit. Little efforts mean a lot in the appearance of a home. These items are discussed and recommendations are made for getting the most from your finished appraisal.

Many of the chapters have sample forms and examples. These forms and examples guide you in the development of your personal contracting needs. Use them to create your own personalized forms and be sure to consult with professionals when dealing with legal issues.

Should You Be Your Own General Contractor?

1

There are projects in life that allow you to use your talents and experience. There are others you would never even consider trying. A friend knows of your culinary prowess and asks you to make her wedding cake; no problem. The den needs more shelves, and in a matter of minutes you have completed the task. It's simply a matter of the right tools for the job and a little knowledge of the basics.

Yet, suggest remodeling your house and there are usually just two reactions, "Are you out of your mind?!" and "I don't know anything about construction." Just as with the shelf installation, you will find you have experience in remodeling you never knew existed. Organization, patience, and basic product knowledge are all essential elements to any remodeling project. You need only to examine your qualifications and decide whether you have the skills required to run your own job. If not, investigate choosing the right person or people for the project. Should you coordinate the work or hire a general contractor? This question will require a great deal of thought. The wrong decision can be very expensive and frustrating. Being your own general contractor can save you a lot of money. It can also cost you more than paying professionals to do the work. Before jumping into a quick decision, consider all the factors. A little time spent now can save a lot of time and money later.

WHY REMODELING IS DIFFERENT

There are several types of qualified contractors available. They range from major corporations to individual, one-man firms. The trick is locating and choosing the right contractor for your job. Remodeling is often a complicated process and requires special talents. Matching your needs to the contractor's ability is mandatory for a successful job. There is much more to being a general contractor than hiring a few subcontractors and scheduling the work. If the role of a general contractor were easy, it wouldn't be such a lucrative business.

Remodeling varies dramatically from new construction. You will encounter problems and unexpected complications not found in new construction. Many homeowners look immediately to what they perceive to be simple aspects of a remodeling project. They think they can do much of the work themselves to save money. Don't be fooled! Even a simple alteration, like changing the bathroom faucet, can be laborious and plagued with problems. The supply lines could break or crimp, or there may be no water cutoff valves to the faucet. Entire sink tops have been know to break during a routine faucet replacement. There is a difference between coordinating the changes made by professionals and acting as a tradesman. Only consider doing work yourself in areas where you have specific experience. Keep in mind that if you will be using a plumber to replace your bathroom fixtures, you will not save much installing the faucets yourself.

SAVING MONEY AS THE GENERAL CONTRACTOR

Many homeowners discredit the idea of doing the work themselves but contemplate acting as their own general contractor. This involves more details to consider than just saving a few dollars. It is only with the right personality and ability that these savings become a significant factor. The potential savings are very tempting. The lure of saving up to 30% by coordinating your own project has a strong influence on many consumers. Some homeowners are well suited to the task. If you fall into this category, you are fortunate. Your savings overall should average about 20%.

These percentages are based on the total value of the job, not the cost of the work. This is an important detail. There is a sizable difference between the retail value of the improvement and the cost to make the improvement. Your profit will be based on the retail value. An estimated job cost indicates the anticipated cost of completing the job. The *value* is based on the appraised worth of the completed project. It is best to engage a professional appraiser to ascertain the value. A general rule of thumb: cost plus 20% equals value. When you examine your anticipated savings, use retail values. Let's assume the value of your job is $30,000. The general contractor wants this same appraised value for his work. Acting as your own contractor, the job should only cost around $24,000. You could do a lot with the $6,000 savings.

DO YOU HAVE WHAT IT TAKES?

The responsibilities of a general contractor are tedious and can be a losing proposition. If the job is not handled properly, money and time will be lost. Before becoming a contractor, consider the consequences carefully. Take the time to answer a few questions. Will you have time to arrange for blueprints and specifications? Will you be available to supervise the work while it's being done? Is special insurance needed to protect you from liability? Do you have a basic knowledge of the kind of work you are considering, such as the steps involved to replace your bathtub? These are just a small sample of the questions to be answered.

As a general contractor, you will be responsible for coordinating all the work and budgeting. Without extremely good organizational skills and a basic knowledge of construction, you can lose more than you save. This may discourage you from tackling your own project. It is not meant to deter you, rather to ensure you understand all aspects of the responsibility you are assuming.

The best way to determine your ability is to put the facts on paper. Make a brief outline of your credentials. Explore all of your experience and strong points. Compare the similarities of your abilities to the requirements of a general contractor. Be honest with yourself. It is critical to know whether you can actually handle the responsibility of a general contractor. This is your first major decision.

To evaluate your ability, you need to know what questions to ask yourself. The first question is a matter of time. Do you have time to be your own general contractor, and how much time is required? The amount of time is proportionate to the size and type of job. Small interior remodeling jobs can be handled with two hours a day or less. Large interior jobs or additions can require several hours of supervision each day. Then there is the consideration of the overall span of time the project will take to complete. It will only take a day or so of actual man hours to replace your bathroom fixtures, but two weeks of preparation may be involved in finding the right tradespeople and products.

Supervising the Work

With dependable subcontractors, you can supervise the work at the end of the day. When you get home, first, you will inspect the work. Then make a few phone calls and the job is set for the next day. With average or substandard contractors, you will need to be actively involved with the job. You'll have to be available during their work day; most problems occur during normal working hours. Many of these problems will escalate if left unattended until the end of the day. This situation is often a big problem for the working homeowner. Are you able to leave work for a few hours if necessary? Can you afford to take off from work to tend to needs at home? Depending upon your employment arrangement and your hourly wage, this can cost more than a professional general contractor would charge.

Unfortunately, many subcontractors may not be very dependable. This creates problems for even the most experienced general contractors. These subs can be difficult to motivate, even for a professional with years of experience. As a homeowner, with only one remodeling job, you are likely to find subcontractors difficult (but not impossible) to control. The demands on your personal time must be carefully evaluated. You will spend hours running the job. Much of this time will conflict with your standard work schedule. If you are not at your remodeling job, you don't know if the subs showed up. You won't know about their absence until the evening. By then, you have lost a whole day of production. Your night will be spent calling all the other contractors, because their work will have to be rescheduled. Every trade depends on another trade. When one is out of step, they are all thrown off schedule.

There are some practical solutions to these problems. Does your employment situation allow you to make personal phone calls? If so, consider arranging a check-in time with each of your subcontractors. Tell them you will call the job every day at a specified time to confirm they are there and all is going smoothly. Perhaps you have nosy neighbors who always want to know what you're doing and whose truck was at your house. Great! Let this work for you, and check with the neighbors each day for a progress report. Chances are, these neighborhood detectives will be more than happy to check your job for you.

Don't underestimate the benefit of having your older children share in the supervising process. Leave them a list each morning of the subcontractors and materials expected that day and have them call if anything is amiss. If you have a working spouse, leave both work numbers so subcontractors can call either of you with questions or problems. Take some time to consider other creative methods of controlling your project if you cannot be there personally.

Material deliveries come during business hours. Are you able to confirm deliveries from work? Unfortunately, the numerous daytime phone calls required to coordinate your project will be a distraction. Will your job allow enough flexibility to make these calls? They must be made — how will you accomplish the chore? It may be wiser to hire a professional management team or general contractor. Your regular job can suffer when your time is divided by supervising the remodeling project. Weigh your sacrifices, and don't risk losing your full-time job. The remodeling savings won't justify becoming unemployed. You will need to devote a large portion of your spare time to the remodeling project. Determine what your time is worth.

Weighing the Pros and Cons

Depending on your income, you may not save anything by supervising your own job. Consider your hourly income and compare it to the cost of a professional contractor. Don't underestimate the demands for your personal attention. There will be numerous evening phone calls to make, and on-the-

job problems will demand your personal attention. When the electrician doesn't show up, you will have to reschedule many of your subcontractors.

What will you do when your materials don't arrive? The subcontractors are there, but they have no material to work with. The subcontractors are going to request additional compensation for time lost due to lack of materials. Material acquisition is the general contractor's responsibility. If you fail to get materials on the job, it will cost you big money. Suppliers are a problem, even for the pros. Can you handle them? What will you do when the cabinets, which were going to take six weeks for delivery, are late?

Your first reaction will be one of anger. You will want to tell the supplier to take a hike, but where can you get the cabinets any quicker? This type of problem is common. You have waited six weeks already. If you change suppliers, you will have to wait even longer. If you rely on the existing supplier, who now promises delivery in two more weeks, will you wait two weeks and still not have the cabinets? The supplier did not meet the first delivery date, what guarantee do you have that they will meet this one?

These are tough decisions, even for a seasoned professional. Most contractors will gamble on the two week delivery. Sometimes they lose and the cabinets still don't show up. The contractor is a prisoner of the supplier. Making the right decision is based on unknown factors. How can you trust suppliers who do not keep their commitments? This dilemma can keep you up at night. All you can do is decide based on experience or gut reaction. In Chapter 11, we will discuss some ways to alleviate or at least minimize this problem. There are ways to protect yourself from delivery catastrophes. The point being made here is, these are the types of events involved with supervising your remodeling project.

Taking the Responsibility

As a general contractor, you are responsible for everything. You will need to produce cost estimates as part of the planning stage for your project. If you are applying for financing, you need to know if the lender will accept your estimates. Do the lender's policies allow a homeowner to be the general contractor? Will the codes enforcement office issue you the proper permits? Where will you obtain plans and specifications? Do you have the available cash to front the expenses of the job? Will your experience be adequate to keep the subcontractors honest? How much control will you have over the subcontractors? These are all key questions requiring honest, well thought out answers.

COST ESTIMATING

Cost estimating can be tedious. You can read books in an attempt to learn estimating techniques. Some books will tell you what to expect for the cost of various projects. These books can be helpful, but they are expensive. Their expense must be weighed against the money and time they can save you. A few flaws exist with estimating books. For example, the time requirements and estimates given are not universally accurate. Many of the books base their cost figures on union wages. Very few residential jobs are done by union members. Trade wages can differ by more than five dollars per hour. This factor alone can make a dramatic difference on a large job.

Another fault found in many of these books is the geographical cost differences. Prices in California cannot be compared to prices in Florida. Maine contractors and suppliers will charge different prices than the same vendors in Virginia. Some companies, like the R.S. Means Company, Inc. of Kingston, Massachusetts, publish a variety of books that include a City Cost Index to allow for geographical differences. The *Means Home Improvement Cost Guide* and the *Means Repair and Remodeling Cost Data* book are specifically geared to remodeling projects. These types of books will provide you with a rough idea of what to expect. The books are good for use as guides and reference material. They are an excellent educational tool in learning the steps of construction or remodeling. Certainly, they have value to the uninformed consumer, but don't accept the figures for costs until you adjust for your geographical location.

There is an easier way to get accurate figures. This approach won't erode your valuable time and the figures obtained will be reliable. This is the method I used when I first became a general contractor. Firm quotes from suppliers and contractors provide the best way to estimate your intended job cost. There will be much less room for error in your estimate. These quotes will guarantee many of your expenses. Written quotes can even be obtained through the mail. This is a simple process, but you need to know specifically what to ask for. If you already know what you want, you are way ahead of the game. If you don't, do some research. This is where those estimating books can be of the most help.

SPECIFICATIONS

When you embark on a remodeling project, you will need to invest enough time to create *specifications*. The specifications must be (as the word indicates) very specific. Read books, talk to suppliers, look at advertisements — all of this will prepare you for creating clear specifications. When you know exactly what you want, contact the bidders. When you ask a plumber for the price to install your bathroom, he will require details. What brand of fixtures do you want? Do you want copper water distribution pipe or polybutylene? If you decide on copper, do you prefer type "M," "L," or "K"? Would you like schedule 40 PVC piping for your DWV system, or do you prefer ABS? What grade fixtures do you want? Fixture options include Competitive, Builder-grade, Standard, and Top-of-the-Line. Will you want your bathtub to be fiberglass, acrylic, steel, or cast iron? How much do you want to spend on your faucets? Lavatory faucets start at seven dollars and run into the $2,500 range.

Is a 1.6 gallon water saver toilet suitable for your job? The principle is a good one, but will one and a half gallons of water be sufficient to flush the toilet with your old pipes? Should you have a china lavatory or a cultured marble top? Do you want an oak veneer vanity or a solid wood cabinet? Does it really make a difference? Will particle board delaminate in the bathroom moisture? Had enough of the question bombardment? All right, you get the overall idea.

These are only a few of the decisions a general contractor must make. The questions are determined by your individual situation. For example, should you invest in a temperature control shower valve? This is a very good safety feature if there are young children in your family. If you have back problems or elderly family members, an 18-inch toilet is a wise investment. Of course, unless you are clairvoyant, you will not know all the questions to ask. Remodeling is a step-by-step process. First you will come up with an idea of the changes you want to make. Then you will start to choose the accessories to make those changes a reality. How will you know what questions to ask? The same way a general contractor does. List all of your requirements and desires, then contact vendors of those products. It can be as simple as asking a plumbing supplier, "Is there any way to protect our children against accidental scalding?"

You will be amazed at the variety and usage of products available. For example, spas and whirlpools offer unlimited opportunities. You can spend $1,200 or $6,000. What is the difference between a spa and a whirlpool? Most people don't know, but you are about to learn. The big difference is, spas are designed to hold water indefinitely. You fill them, treat the water with chemicals, and they are constantly ready for your enjoyment. Whirlpool tubs are meant to be filled with water each time you use them. This can be an expensive form of relaxation. Consider the cost of producing hot water to fill the whirlpool. Many units hold 90 gallons of water or more. In most residential situations, you will empty your water heater each time the whirlpool is filled. Heating this volume of water consumes a lot of expensive energy. Whirlpools are less expensive, but spas offer more benefits.

Now let's make you a carpeting expert. Carpeting is an easy job for the homeowner to subcontract, right? Not unless you know the keys to the floor covering industry. If you buy an expensive carpet with an inferior pad, you are making a mistake. The pad is the most important part of your floor covering. An inexpensive carpet on a quality pad will last much longer than an expensive carpet on a poor pad. Do you know how to recognize a good carpet or pad? Ask the carpet representative to show you the difference in the available products.

Have the salesperson put four sample pads on a concrete floor along with four different grades of carpet. Lay the carpet samples on each pad. Now, with heavy soled shoes, walk on the carpet. Which carpet was the quickest to eliminate your footprints? Make a note of the carpet and have the salesperson move the carpets to different pads. Try the test again. Did the same carpet win? I doubt it. The proof is in the pad. This procedure allows you to determine the difference between carpets and their pads. You can easily find your best value with this procedure.

What knowledge do you have of heating systems? Can you determine the BTUs required to heat your living space? What type of heat will best meet your requirements? You can choose between heat pumps, boilers with tankless coils, electric heat, and forced hot air units. (The standard energy sources include electricity, oil, natural gas, and LP gas.) Here is a suggestion. Contact your power and utility

companies. Many power companies offer programs designed to save energy and increase your savings. You may find they can answer many of your questions regarding properly heating your improved home. Is natural gas available in your neighborhood? If possible, should you heat your hot water with your home heating system? Will it supply an adequate volume of hot water? Will your existing electrical service accommodate your new improvements? If the utility company doesn't have the answer, try asking the local codes enforcement office.

Other questions are not as easily answered. How many coats of mud will your new drywall require? Do you need to prime or seal your surfaces before painting? What thickness of insulation should you use in your new space? These are all important questions. As a general contractor, you must be able to answer them. Your only hope, if you can't find answers to these questions, is honest subcontractors. Honest subcontractors can be hard to find.

ADVANTAGES OF A PROFESSIONAL CONTRACTOR

It is unlikely, as a homeowner, that you will be fully versed in answering these technical questions. Professional general contractors have many advantages over the average homeowner. Experienced general contractors have dealt with the majority of problems commonly encountered. They know which products are commonly used versus which ones are required. General contractors use subcontractors on a regular basis. They know their subcontractors' faults. Due to the future work available from the contractor, subcontractors will respond quickly to the request of the general. Experienced general contractors know how to handle problems that arise on a daily basis. Successful generals have endured the test of time. They have paid the dues for their experience. As a homeowner, you run the risk of losing money as a general contractor. If events go as planned, you will save a bundle. If they don't, you'll lose your shirt.

How will you determine your abilities? Don't let potential savings taint your judgment. You must address your remodeling project objectively. If, after thorough evaluation, you feel qualified to tackle the job, do it. Consider all the repercussions before you make your final decision; it may be more cost effective to hire a professional remodeling contractor. Your time has value, so determine this value and compare it to the cost of a good contractor. Average homeowners are better off working with a licensed general contractor. At first glance, being a contractor looks easy. This encourages many carpenters to go into the remodeling business to fulfill their dreams of untold riches. Homeowners fall into the same trap. General contracting is not easy. It is hard work and requires special abilities. Remodeling projects rarely go as planned; the ability to make sound judgment calls is paramount. Don't force yourself into a failing situation that could doom your entire project for the sake of a few dollars. I have many other ways to show you how to save money.

Coordinating Subcontractors

General contracting is not a fountain of financial freedom. The profession is plagued with uncontrollable circumstances. General contractors are dependent on subcontractors. If the subs don't do their job, the general cannot do his. This is a frustrating and helpless feeling. A homeowner only has one job to offer a subcontractor. If a scheduling conflict arises, the homeowner loses. Subcontractors almost always respond to the people providing their primary income. This person is rarely the homeowner. Subcontractors are dependent on general contractors. When a general calls, the sub will respond. This can mean stalling a homeowner's job. The subs must look at their long-term income. A homeowner only has one job to offer; the general contractor has many profitable jobs during the year. As a self contractor, you will be faced with this problem.

General contractors are in business to make your life easier. You pay them 20% of the job's value to take care of the problems. They coordinate everything. When you have a problem or a question, you deal with the general contractor. All your problems are handled through one source, and this is a strong advantage. Simply contacting all the subcontractors involved in a change order is a time-consuming process. Almost any changes made will affect several subcontractors. For instance, the decision to move your vanity farther down the wall will result in numerous phone calls. The first call will be to the plumber. Then the electrical contractor will need to be contacted to move lights and outlets. The carpenter may need to adjust for the changes.

This simple vanity relocation may affect your ceramic tile design. When the decision is made after drywall is hung, you'll have to contact the drywall contractor. There may even be a conflict with your heating system's location. This example shows the effect of a so-called simple change. For each subcontractor involved, you will spend a lot of time on the phone and on the job site. These situations drain your personal time. A general contractor will handle all these changes after just one phone call from you. If your time is valuable, a general contractor is a good investment.

Handling Material Deliveries

The general contractor will coordinate all material deliveries. As a self contractor, would you be able to handle improper material shipments? What will happen when the material you were promised for Tuesday still isn't on site by Friday? This means down-time for your craftsmen. They will want reimbursement for lost production time or may leave to do another job. If you are the general contractor, it is your responsibility to provide for and coordinate their work. Once they have left your job, it is unlikely they will come back until their next contract is complete. If you have a full-time job, how will you get these problems resolved? Suppliers are hard to deal with and can be very undependable. They are notorious for broken promises. Paying plumbers to stand around while you locate their missing material will cost you a small fortune. You can count on this problem arising; there is no way to avoid it. If you hire a general contractor, these headaches become his or her problem.

Subcontractors can ruin your production schedule. If your heating contractor does not show up, you will have to reschedule your other subs. When the insulator lets you down, you have to rearrange your drywall contractor and painter. Everything that goes wrong creates a chain reaction. With a general contractor, the problem still exists, but you don't have to deal with it personally. If you follow the rules you learn in this book, you will have written clauses in the contract to ensure your job is completed in a timely manner. The general contractor is the one losing sleep over scheduling problems, not you.

Paying for the Work

Paying for the work is another advantage to a general contractor. General contractors will frequently bill you. For large jobs this could be on a monthly basis. On the other hand, subcontractors will want payment upon completion of their work. This can be a problem if you are financing the job. Lenders will expect you to pay tradesmen and suppliers before advancing a loan disbursement. Financing presents its own challenges and is an entirely separate consideration. As a homeowner, your financing options are limited. General contractors can open new avenues for your financing. Established contractors may offer simple "in-home" financing. Many of these loans don't require a second mortgage on your house, and the rates are reasonably competitive. There are no prepayment penalties, loan application fees, or closing costs. You may not even need a down payment. (Financing your project is discussed in detail in Chapter 12.)

Insurance

What other factors do you need to think about before deciding to be your own general contractor? There is the consideration of protecting yourself and your home. Will you need additional insurance? Acting as your own general contractor may not be covered under your existing homeowner's insurance. General contractors carry liability insurance to protect you and your property. You should ask for evidence of this insurance before signing any contract with a general contractor. There are many potential risks that make liability insurance compulsory. What happens if a carpenter drives a nail through your water distribution pipe? Your house floods! Who is responsible for the damage repair? How will you handle an electrician falling through your ceiling? It wouldn't be the first time someone was working in an attic and lost his footing. A general contractor is responsible to you for these damages. Without a general, will your homeowner's insurance protect you? Investigate your liability insurance needs before acting as a general contractor. You don't want to be on the losing end of a lawsuit. There is no money saved if that occurs.

Before making a final decision on who will run your remodeling project, read the rest of this book. The following chapters hold a wealth of information. Your decision on who should handle the contracting of the job will be easy to make when you are fully informed. It's tempting to try to get by without professional management. I encourage you to take advantage of the opportunity, if you are qualified. Evaluate what you learn from this book and make educated decisions. Take the Contractor Skills Assessment quiz below, as a tool in evaluating your potential as a general contractor. The time you spend researching your options will be well rewarded.

The information here will not protect you from *all* of the pitfalls of remodeling. It would be impossible to anticipate all the potential problems. Even after seventeen years as an active remodeler, I still learn something new with many jobs. While I can't protect you, I can prepare you for the journey into remodeling. Your project will run much smoother with the proper knowledge. This knowledge will benefit you as a consumer or a contractor.

CONTRACTOR SKILLS ASSESSMENT

For the following questions, rate your answers on a scale of one to ten. On the scale, one is very weak or not at all. Ten is very strong or a definite yes. For example, if the question was, "Do you have a full-time job?" you would indicate the numeral 10 for a full-time job, the number 5 for a part-time job, and the number 1 if you don't have a job. If the question was, "Can you make quick, accurate decisions?" and you feel strongly that you can, enter the number 10. If you are unsure of your ability, enter a number between 1 and 5. If you have average decision-making skills, use the number 5.

___ 1. Rate your ability to supervise your project during the day.
___ 2. Do you have a full-time job?
___ 3. Do you enjoy working with people?
___ 4. Do you have strong leadership ability?
___ 5. Are you comfortable around strangers?
___ 6. How often do you believe what you are told?
___ 7. Do you act on impulse?
___ 8. Are you allergic to dust?
___ 9. Do loud, repetitive noises bother you?
___ 10. Does your regular job require you to manage people?
___ 11. Do you enjoy talking on the phone?
___ 12. How willing are you to work nights, scheduling subs?
___ 13. How easily are you intimidated by people?
___ 14. Do you have a shy personality?
___ 15. Can you make confident decisions and trust your judgment?
___ 16. How much will you research remodeling principles?
___ 17. Are you sensitive to fumes and odors?
___ 18. Are you good with numbers?
___ 19. Do you have a creative mind?
___ 20. Can you visualize items from a written description?

___ 21. Do you have strong self-discipline?

___ 22. Do you get flustered easily?

___ 23. Do problems cause you extreme stress?

___ 24. How are your organizational skills?

___ 25. Are you vulnerable to sales pitches?

___ 26. Do you have time to find subcontractors?

___ 27. Do you enjoy negotiating for the best price?

___ 28. Is your checkbook balanced today?

___ 29. Do you use a household budget?

___ 30. Do you feel qualified to control irate subcontractors?

___ 31. Do you have strong self-confidence?

___ 32. Do you lose your temper easily?

___ 33. Can you react quickly to unexpected events?

___ 34. Can you make personal calls from work?

___ 35. Do you buy bargains, even when you don't need the items?

___ 36. Is your time financially valuable?

___ 37. Will you be available to meet code enforcement inspectors?

___ 38. Do you have a gambler's personality?

___ 39. Can you be assertive?

___ 40. Do you enjoy reading technical reports and articles?

___ 41. Do you retain information you read?

___ 42. Do you pay attention to small details?

___ 43. Do you know people who work in the trades?

___ 44. Can you keep accurate written records?

___ 45. Are you able to do more than one task at a time?

___ 46. How well can you prioritize your day and your duties?

___ 47. Do you feel qualified to coordinate your project?

___ 48. Can you stand to watch your house being torn apart?

___ 49. Are you capable of staying out of the way of the workers?

___ 50. Do you force your opinions on others?

Add your total score and compare it to the ranges given below to get an idea of your ability to act as the general contractor.

SCORES AND OPTIONS

If your score is 186 or less, seriously consider hiring a professional general contractor. Your answers indicate a weakness in performing the functions of a general contractor. This score may mean you do not have the right personality for the job. Technical points can be learned, but personalities are hard to change. You may be able to accomplish the task, if you do extensive research and address your weak points. Keep your quiz answers in mind as you read this book. The book will help you to identify clearly the areas you need to address. For homeowners in this scoring range, hiring a professional is the safest route to take. Before trying to coordinate your own job, read this book and evaluate what you learn. Chances are, you will decide to hire a professional to manage your job. There is nothing wrong with this. Not all people are meant to run construction crews and jobs.

If your score is between 186 and 280, you have the ability to learn how to get the job done. Most of the areas you need to work on are remodeling-related and can be learned. In this mid-range, you should be able to read enough to attempt the job at hand. Your score indicates some areas of weakness. As you complete this book, make note of your weaknesses. Spend the time needed to strengthen these areas. With enough preliminary planning, you should be able to run your own job.

If you scored between 280 and 375, you are a natural. With the right research, you can be an excellent general contractor. The higher your score, the better qualified you are. If you scored near 375, all you will need to do is polish your knowledge of the trades; you already possess the basic qualities of a good general contractor. Even with a high score, you still have a lot to learn. Complete this book, and when you feel completely comfortable with your abilities, move ahead. You will be ready to command your construction crews and save money.

Design Techniques

2

Have you ever wished that dreams could come true? Close your eyes a moment, and try to visualize your remodeled home. Are you going to finish the attic? Do you see a bathroom and a couple of bedrooms? Now look closer. The bathroom has a spa, skylights, and built-in shelves. A pedestal sink and corner toilet are the crowning touches in this fashionable yet functional space. Do you see the uncluttered, organized bedrooms? There are bureaus and closets framed into the walls. Your child's room is designed for play and includes plenty of storage. Maybe the bed slides back into the knee wall to allow for extra space. The design of your remodeling project is an exciting part of the remodeling process. If you've ever wished for something, this is where your imagination can run wild.

Anything is possible on paper. You can draw in the large bathroom you always wanted. Design the perfect family room. Create a studio loft for your hobbies. All of your fantasies can come to life on the drafting table. The options are unlimited when you start designing your new space. All the unique products, advertised in home magazines or seen on TV, can be put on paper. The design process is almost like playing make-believe or building sand castles. Have fun drawing the perfect space. Ultimately, you will have to come back to reality, but for now let your dreams start to come alive.

The design process can be done with informal methods. You don't need to be an artist or a draftsman. With a few sheets of graph paper and a pencil, you can begin to create. Before you go too far with the drawing process, you will need ideas. Coming up with creative concepts can be the most fun. Certain-ly, you have some notion of what you want. The ideas you find will enhance your rough draft.

CREATE A DREAM BOOK

Get a spiral notebook and some glue or tape. If your project will involve more than one room, use a notebook divided into sections. The spiral notebook will become your dream book. This is where you will keep all your ideas and product information. Dedicate a different section of the notebook to each room involved.

The next step is to enter your ideas into the dream book. Sit down and write all of your thoughts about the design of your home in the notebook. Write down everything you can think of. Then leave the dream book alone for a day or two. After a few days, open it and write down any new ideas you have come up with. When your ideas are getting hard to come by, go on an idea safari. Open almost any major magazine, and you will see examples of home interiors. All of these pictures will stimulate innovative ideas.

Magazines

There are many magazines catering to home improvements. Check your local magazine rack for appropriate titles. Some magazines carry extensive home design and decorating ideas. There are magazines for every type of improvement imaginable. Rustic, contemporary, traditional, kitchens and baths—they are all pictured in magazines. There will be skylights, wall coverings, plumbing fixtures, light fixtures, anything you need. When you find a product you like, cut it out and attach it to your dream book. By doing this, you are building a comprehensive product list. Be sure to include the manufacturer and model number. The dream book will be invaluable. It will help you in locating items and making your final decisions.

Newspapers and Brochures

Another source of ideas is newspapers. They contain special inserts from hardware stores and lumber yards. These advertisements feature various products for the home, and most of them will be on sale. A visit to your local building supplier can really fatten up your dream book. They have printed descriptions and photos of the many products available. These brochures can be taken home and added to your collection. Obtaining your product information in this manner offers the advantage of seeing many of the items in person. This adds a dash of reality to your dream book cutouts. Visit several stores. The more suppliers you visit, the more information you will obtain.

Suppliers and Contractors

Investigate all the brands and types of products available. Not all suppliers represent the same companies. Write down questions that come to mind, and ask the supplier for specific information. What installation and care requirements are there for the spa you're looking at? How much weight does the floor need to support? Is this a special order item? Collect promotional information on as many brands as possible. This information will help later in developing your estimated job cost.

If you elect to use a general contractor, you will find him or her a good source of information. General contractors are involved with designs on a daily basis. When they are not drawing designs, they are building them. General contractors have shelves sagging with catalogs and brochures; take a few hours to shop through these catalogs. Ask the contractor to give you photocopies of selected items to be entered into the dream book.

Another advantage of working with a general contractor is his experience. After years of working with building materials, the contractor will have comprehensive field experience with various products. You can benefit from this knowledge. Ask what brands of products he recommends. The contractor will have favorite products that install easily and don't cause warranty problems. Talk with more than one contractor; you will get different opinions on the

same products. Don't let anyone talk you into just the most basic products. At this stage you are on a fact-finding mission. The more details you have on various items, the easier your final decision will be.

MAKING CHOICES

Now that we have our dream book complete, it's time to narrow the field of options. If you have four different kitchen sinks in the dream book, you must choose your preference. This can be difficult. How will you decide what products to use? It will take some time, but you can reach a decision through elimination. The process of elimination is best started by assessing your budget. Many items will disqualify themselves by price alone. If your budget allows $150 for a sink, you eliminate the ones selling for $300. This process will thin down the dream book rapidly. If there is an expensive item you really want, move it to a special section in the back of the dream book. The money you save after reading this remodeling book will probably be sufficient to purchase that extra special item.

WORKING WITHIN A BUDGET

Every homeowner has a different budget to work with. It's important to establish your budget before you get your heart set on a plan or an item. The projected budget is up to you. Only you know what you are comfortable investing in your home. Before making a final decision, read Chapters 4, 5, and 6. These chapters will help you understand the value of your improvements and how you will recover your investment. For the time being, base your budget on what you feel you can afford, and select appropriate products. Keep the more expensive items in the special dream book section. You will be surprised how many of these upgrades you can add once your allowances are firmly established.

One way to estimate material costs and establish your budget is to take your design to building supply stores. Normally, they will do a material take-off for you. When you get the prices for the estimated material, you have half of the puzzle solved. If the supplier does not carry a particular item you want, get a separate price for it elsewhere. Add the cost to the supplier's figures. A rule of thumb: your material cost, multiplied by two, equals your total job cost. This is not always true, but it's a good starting point. Requesting multiple quotes will allow you to determine an average cost for your project. If you have three or four quotes in the same range, the quotes are probably fair.

Now begin to fit the products and material costs into your budget. Use a spa, for example. Let's assume you have chosen three spas that will suit your needs. There is one spa you really like, but the other two will suffice. With your current figures, you can easily compare costs. The product information you picked up from the suppliers will allow an equal comparison of the spas.

Mechanical comparisons are relatively easy. You look at the number of whirlpool jets, the motor size, the depth of the spa, electrical requirements, and other clinical information. This can be dull reading, but without it you may regret your purchase. It is easy to become consumed with excitement from seeing a luxurious color photograph. Buying a spa based on personal taste is fine, but be sure it will do the job. A redwood exterior and black fiberglass tub may be attractive, but it's the mechanical parts that make it work.

DRAWING YOUR PLANS

Using the logical process of elimination, you will soon know what products will be going into your home. If necessary, you can cut corners on some items to allow for the one item you especially want. Once you know what fixtures and materials will be used, begin to draw your final plans. Get out the graph paper and pencil. Use the squares in the graph paper to represent a unit of measure. Make the drawing as large as possible. Normal blueprints use a scale of ¼" equals 1'. This means every inch of paper equals 4 feet of real space in your project. You can use any scale, but keep it consistent.

A frequent mistake involves drawing a bathroom without using a scale. The space appears ample and capable of holding all of your fixtures, with room left over. This is deceiving — it's easy to make objects fit on paper. It's not so easy to make them fit when you start remodeling. There are code requirements on the spacing of bathroom fixtures. These will be quickly pointed out by plumbing subcontractors when you get quotes for the plumbing work. You may find your spacious "paper" bathroom will not accommodate the smallest plumbing fixtures. The spa that looked so good on paper is too large for the room. You *must* use a scale in designing your space, and be prepared to make changes to the final draft.

For design purposes, you can use a simple line drawing. Start with the exterior lines of your space. These lines will be measured in linear feet. A tape measure is an example of a linear foot measurement. The distance of a straight line, from one point to another, is measured as linear footage. The other common measurement you will use is square footage. To obtain square footage, measure the length and width of the room. Now multiply the two measurements by each other to get the square footage. If a room is 10' long and 10' wide, it contains 100 square feet. A proposed addition 24' long and 16' wide is 384 square feet.

Floor coverings are measured in square yards. To obtain a square yardage figure, you need to know the square footage of the space. Determine the square footage of your space, then divide the total square footage by nine. This will give you the square yardage figure. For example, if a room contains 90 square feet, it has 10 square yards of space.

Begin your design by drawing the exterior dimensions to scale, including doors and windows. Decide which way the doors will open. If the door opens into the room, it will affect the design of the interior space. When you draw in the doors and windows, be sure to draw them to scale. You will be disappointed if the shower covers up your custom window. After the exterior is drawn, start with interior partitions. Remember to include closets and their doors. Closets are often forgotten in the initial design. A room without a closet will not be considered a bedroom in the appraised value of your home. Allow enough room in the closets to accommodate the quantity of clothing you and your family will need to store. Average closets are 2 feet deep.

As you draw your interior walls, allow for wall thickness. This is another common problem for the inexperienced designer. Most interior walls will be 4½ inches thick, including drywall. A room with the outside dimensions of 10' x 12' immediately becomes 9'3" x 11'3" of workable interior space.

With all of your walls drawn, you are ready to place your fixtures. Building codes require specific placement of electrical outlets, plumbing fixtures, and heating systems. Unless you are knowledgeable about your local building codes, leave the final placement of these items to the professionals. Sketch in your fixtures and place your electrical outlets where you would like them. Indicate your preferred location of wall switches, overhead lights, and telephone outlets. If cabinets and countertops are involved, draw them in next. Remember to keep everything to scale.

One valuable design tool is a product called Stanley® Project Planners. Their Home Designer® kit contains scaled, reusable, peel-and-stick symbols for everything from fixtures to furniture. The package also includes a scaled grid board and illustrated manual, to make designing any room simple.

BATHROOM DESIGN

Designing a bathroom requires thought. The bathroom is small, and it is challenging to get the most out of a small space. There are code regulations involved here too. As an example, if your bathroom does not have a window, you will be required to install a vented exhaust fan. Codes vary from state to state. Before actually beginning work on your job, you need to confirm local code requirements and secure the proper permits. The code enforcement officer may require a set of your plans and specifications before issuing a permit. Do not be surprised if you have to make minor changes to comply with local codes. Check with the code officer before having your rough drawings made into blueprints. Changes made in the preliminary plan will be less expensive than changes made in actual blueprints.

Some bathrooms are actually bath suites, the size of a small bedroom. Others are converted from closets or the space under stairs. If you are remodeling an existing bath, begin by listing all the problem areas. Is the room dark, making it difficult to shave or apply makeup? Is it cluttered due to poor storage space? Is the toilet boxed-in between the tub and a wall? Creative alternatives exist for the smallest bathrooms.

Enlarge the visual effect of the space by replacing the mirror over the sink with one running the full length of the wall. Consider extending the vanity top along the wall to create a make-up area; be sure to install good lighting. You'll be amazed at the difference in space something as simple as a recessed toilet-paper holder can make. Open a boxed-in area at the end of the tub by reducing the full wall to a knee wall. Build storage shelves into the partial wall, and consider installing a suspended shower rod. Tired of taking turns waiting to shower each morning? Many existing linen closets are large enough to accommodate a separate shower. This

space should be at least 34" x 34". Scrutinize your bathroom, and you will discover ways to maximize the space.

Interested in a bath suite? Some attractive additions include: heat lamps, quarry tile, his and her vanities, spas, and bidets. The ideas you find in magazines for baths will quickly fill your dream book. Bath suites should focus on comfort and spacious surroundings. Frosted glass allows natural light while eliminating the need for curtains at windows. Vanities come in an array of styles, but those with drawers are the most functional. Installing separate vanities or a large top with two sink bowls will provide functional luxury to the suite. Rounding vanity top edges is both attractive and safe. Consider adding insulation around the tub and shower as a sound barrier. Some bath suites even have speakers wired to the stereo or individual music systems. The possibilities are endless.

Use your product information to get the sizes of your proposed fixtures. Suppliers can provide you with cut sheets containing this information. Consider making or buying scaled templates of your fixtures and furniture, to make sure proposed items will fit into the completed space. Then look for creative and unique ways to individualize your space.

KITCHEN DESIGN

Kitchens offer a challenge for creating productive space. Decide on the location of your major appliances first. Design your countertop and cabinets around the appliances. Window placement is usually centered over the kitchen sink. Contemplate replacing that existing hard-to-open, double-hung window with a crank-out casement style. Another option to consider is a greenhouse window, which creates an impressive effect. These windows are popular and visually enlarge a kitchen. They also offer an abundance of natural light. Lighting is important in the kitchen. Allow for recessed lighting over the sink and other work areas. Small lights under the wall cabinets are also a sensible addition to kitchen lighting. They illuminate the counter and add to the functionality of the work space. You will want as much light as possible for the kitchen. Well-designed and appointed kitchens add immense value and desirability to a home.

Cabinets and storage space are vital to a successful kitchen. Choose your cabinets prudently, and co-

This elegant bathroom's mirrored shower enclosure has tempered glass for safety, expanding look of the space. Courtesy of Century Shower Door, Inc.

This spa-type bath includes space for the whirlpool, exercise equipment, and stackable washer/dryer. Courtesy of Whirlpool Corp.

ordinate your wall colors with the cabinets. A small kitchen will appear spacious with the right lighting and color schemes. Factory cabinets will suffice in many cases. You don't need to invest in elaborate custom cabinets. Kitchen cabinets are available in many colors and designs. There are cabinets with leaded glass, stained glass, intricate carvings, and unique accessories. These are expensive but give the kitchen a look of distinction. Generally, cabinet dimensions will be the same regardless of their embellishments. Plan on corner cabinets with rotating shelves; they are practical, space-saving, and desirable. Investigate floor-to-ceiling pantry-style cabinets; these offer maximum storage of canned and dry goods. A two-section pantry offers an open space on one half for mops and cleaning supplies, and shelves on the other side.

If you're remodeling a small kitchen and storage space is a problem, consider eliminating the valance over your cabinets. This is the 10-inch or 12-inch wood front that connects the top of the cabinets to the ceiling. The valance is strictly decorative, and removing it will provide additional storage space on the top of the cabinets. Another little-known storage space is hiding right in front of your kitchen sink. The decorative panels on the sink base cabinet can be replaced with flip-out trays. These are ideal for storing scrubbing pads and sponges. Need an efficient place to store your baking pans? Install a narrow cabinet next to the stove, fitted with vertical compartments to hold those awkward pans.

Another option to consider is a movable or free-standing island counter. These units incorporate an independent cabinet with a countertop. They are available on casters, allowing them to be moved to other locations, or as stationary units. Islands add a touch of elegance to the kitchen and increase your work area. Some unique additions to your kitchen include a built-in wine rack or desk. Wine racks are made by attaching wood strips in a crisscross pattern, and they can be installed in the end of a cabinet. Attractive locations for wine racks are in the base cabinet of an island unit or over the refrigerator. A desk unit can easily replace a 2'6" base cabinet located near the kitchen phone. This becomes an exceptional place to prepare shopping lists, sort mail, or coordinate your appointments.

Countertops have an important function in the

success of your kitchen. They should be large enough to be practical, without being overbearing. One of the best tops available is made of Corian®. This is a solid (not laminated) top, able to withstand a lot of abuse. The finish can be sanded with a light sandpaper to remove burns and scratches. These tops are more expensive than standard countertops, but they are unique and extremely functional. A standard laminated top will serve you well under average conditions; they are affordable and offer a wide range of colors and patterns.

Allow for dining areas within the kitchen when possible. Breakfast nooks can consist of built-in bench seats and a small table. Adding a bay window can give you the extra space needed to create an eat-in kitchen. Extend the countertop over an island unit or base cabinet, add some stools, and you've made a breakfast bar.

If you plan to rework the entire kitchen, keep two key concepts in mind. First, limit the distance between the range, oven, kitchen sink, and refrigerator to a maximum of 7 feet. If you draw lines connecting each of these appliances, no one line should exceed 7 feet. Proper design separates the kitchen into work areas based on their function. An expression that makes this concept easy to remember is: MAKE IT, BAKE IT, and TAKE IT AWAY.

MAKE IT is the food preparation area and all its necessary components. These include: counter space, utensil storage, food processor and mixer storage, cutting boards, measuring devices, plates, and bowls. The BAKE IT section incorporates everything critical to cooking. Included in this area are: range and oven, pots and pans, counter space, seasonings, and cookbooks. Finally, TAKE IT AWAY is the cleanup area encompassing: sink, counter, dishwasher, garbage disposal, and trash receptacle. Keep the mandatory elements of each phase conveniently located to each other.

BEDROOM DESIGN

Bedrooms are often a source of frustration, and they never seem to have enough space. Try to reduce the need for furniture such as book shelves and dressers by building them into the wall. Built-in headboards can contain shelves, outlets for lamps, recessed lighting, and cabinets. Ceiling lights are very useful in bedrooms, especially in children's rooms. Closets can become utilitarian wonderlands with a few simple changes. The illustration demonstrates effective use of space by dividing the closet into compartments for shirts, shoes, suits, and dresses.

Children's rooms are difficult to keep organized and are often small. The room design shown displays an elevated built-in bed, with drawers and shelves underneath, and a closet at the end. Modifications of this design could include a pull-out desk, computer station, or toy chest. Mirrors will give a small room the appearance of more depth, and practical window seats provide storage underneath. Recommendations for customizing children's rooms are discussed in Chapter 19.

OTHER AREAS

Utility rooms can become serviceable areas with some detailed planning. Install shelves over the washer and dryer, and make sure the room has adequate lighting. Built-in ironing boards and pull-down work counters will open up the floor space. Work counters also make an ideal location for mending or sorting clothes. Add a laundry tub for pre-soaking garments, and pegs or rods to hang dry laundry.

If you are planning a new garage, keep these factors in mind. Proper storage is critical. Investigate using storage trusses in the construction, and install pull-down stairs for easy access. A floor drain will make washing cars and cleanup of various projects simple and convenient. Provide the garage with cross-ventilation, a standard entry door, and electrical outlets. Allow direct access from the garage to the kitchen whenever possible, and provide generous lighting inside the garage. A garage can be more than just a place to store your car.

In general, look for ways to remodel your home, improving existing areas with minimum change. Adding smoke detectors near the kitchen and bedrooms is an inexpensive and practical improvement. When designing closets, allow at least 5 square feet of storage for every 80 square feet of living space. Where space is a factor, consider using pocket or louvered doors — they use much less space than a full swing door. If you are working with a tight budget, think about installing a pre-fab fireplace instead of a masonry one. Close in an existing porch as an alternative to building an addition. Provide two entrances to the kitchen, one from within the home and one from the outside, near the parking area if possible. Adding a ceiling fan is both charming and

This kitchen design offers ceramic tile on floor, backsplash, and countertops. Courtesy of American Olean Tile Co.

This kitchen features the "Country French Collection," including fluted side panels on the doors, fretwork over open shelves and plate rack, and tiled floor with accents. Courtesy of Crystal Cabinet Works.

Features such as the breakfast bar at foreground, plus ceramic tile countertops and backsplash, add to the appeal of this kitchen. Glass doors in upper cabinets allow for display of cookware or collectibles. Courtesy of Quaker Maid.

This kitchen design features accessibility for everyone. Designed to be barrier-free for handicapped occupants, the kitchen is not at all institutional in appearance. Multiple work levels let the whole crowd help with meals. Courtesy of Whirlpool Corp.

energy efficient. Effective remodeling is based on maximum utilization of available space.

DRAFTING YOUR PLANS

To make your rough draft neat, you can buy a few inexpensive accessories and enhance its appearance. Drafting and office supply stores sell templates of basic building symbols. These include toilets, doors, cabinets, and other common construction items. These templates make your drafting effort easier and the symbols are easily recognized by professionals. This can save you money on your final draft. If the professionals preparing your working plans understand the sketch, their work will go faster and cost less.

For smaller projects, you may not need professional plans and specifications. A simple bathroom remodeling job will not affect the structure of your home. If you are only planning on cosmetic improvements, you can work from your line drawing. You must still draw your sketch to scale. Discuss your sketches with the general contractor or subcontractors. Ask if they feel comfortable working from your drawings. If they are experienced remodelers, they shouldn't need very detailed plans.

The design stage is one of the most enjoyable aspects of remodeling. It is your chance to change your home's physical characteristics. You can mold your environment to reflect your personality. Remodeling your home can change your life and give you a whole new attitude. The addition of a fitness room can encourage you to take better care of yourself. Adding a whirlpool can soothe those aching muscles. A well-designed kitchen can put the spice back into cooking. Be creative when you are designing your space. You are only doing this job once. Do not settle for a boring bedroom. Treat yourself to a walk-in closet. Incorporate these desires into your plans, and pay attention to detail. A small mistake on paper will create major problems when the project is started. Forgetting items you want included will be costly if you add them later.

Before you make a final commitment to your design, let it sit for several days. Read some more books and magazines; think about the rest of the project. Don't try to force design ideas into your mind. Step away from the remodeling project design completely. Let the creative side of your brain relax. After a few days, go back to your dream book and your design. You will have new ideas rushing into your head. Take the time to discover new ideas and products. Then make your final preliminary changes and get working plans drawn. Now you are ready to go on.

Plans and Specifications

3

Turning your design ideas into reality requires working plans and specifications. Depending on the project, the plans can be as simple as line drawings or as formal as architectural plans. When you deal with a general contractor, he will supply the plans for you. Some general contractors draft their own plans; many have the plans drawn by other professionals, such as draftsman. Remodeling demands a different approach from building a new house. With new construction, you might find suitable designs and specifications in a plans book. These books offer numerous house plans at reasonable rates. Unfortunately, it is difficult to mass-produce remodeling plans. No two jobs are the same, and no one can anticipate the existing conditions of your home. You will need to have custom plans drawn for your particular remodeling project.

GET HELP FROM GENERAL CONTRACTORS

General contractors can help you finalize the design of your project. Experienced contractors can provide excellent advice and are skilled in the reading and execution of blueprints. They can show you the benefits and drawbacks of your design ideas and answer your questions. While general contractors are not architects, they have much to offer in blueprint preparation. They are the people in the field with the hands-on experience. If you are contemplating a design on paper, the contractor may have already built something similar. Hands-on experience of building and remodeling is invaluable in

blueprint designing.

General contractors know firsthand what works and what only looks good on paper. Most have been in the business for some time and can give you several design ideas. Contractors will have their own designs and layouts they have built for other people. The contractors can tell you what designs cause trouble down the road. Bow windows are attractive but can cause water leaks where they attach to the house. If the window's roof is not properly flashed, your wall will rot away. Poor attic ventilation can result in structural damage. Attic ventilation is frequently overlooked by homeowners when they design an addition.

If your bedroom addition includes a cantilever, you will have a cold spot in the room. The area protruding over the foundation will be much colder than the rest of the room. Do you know how to reduce the effect of this cold spot? The contractor will know the techniques that work best. His knowledge will also be invaluable in preparing the specifications for your project. Where should the plumbing for your kitchen sink be roughed-in? If you put the water pipes in the outside wall, you could be in for an unpleasant surprise in the winter. In cold climates, plumbing should not be placed in exterior walls; pipes will freeze quickly on cold, windy days. The pipes will freeze and rupture; as soon as the ice thaws, the broken pipe will flood your home. This can ruin your day as well as your kitchen. Experienced contractors will specify the pipes to come through the floor, or into the side of the cabinets, from an interior partition. There are a great many advantages to working with contractors.

WORKING PLANS

Running the show yourself requires that you do it all. We've seen how to develop an initial plan. Now we need to get your design transformed into a set of working plans. Where shall we begin? The local lumber yard is a good place to start. Review your material quotes on lumber prices, and take your rough draft to the lumber yard with the best price. Ask the manager if the company provides design services for their customers. Most large suppliers will be equipped to draw your plans, but they may ask for a commitment to buy the materials from them. If they are low bidder on the job, this should not be a problem.

Ask them to guarantee their material prices until the job is complete. If they are willing to do this, make your commitment to buy there. The supplier will be reluctant to guarantee prices if the job will be in progress for a long time or will not start for quite awhile. Under these conditions, negotiate for a pre-arranged cost increase cap. This price cap protects you from runaway price increases, while allowing you to get your plans now. Get your material quote in writing and have it signed by the manager.

Now you have locked in material prices and free plans. Think of all the money you saved in the cost of obtaining working plans. You may be wondering where the hook is in this deal. This is just too good to be true. Is there something wrong with the plans supplied by lumber yards? How do architects survive, if suppliers will give you free plans? The hook is in the material sales. They provide the free plans to get your business. This is a practical option if they are low bidder, because you don't lose anything. You gain a big savings in the cost of the plans preparation. There are some differences in the quality of the plans. Architectural plans are much more detailed and provide extensive specifications.

The plans and specifications you receive from a building supplier will be adequate for most jobs. They will be drawn to show the basics, and a qualified contractor will not have trouble working with these plans. The specifications will detail materials, but will not be as comprehensive as architectural plans. Some contractors react in a negative way to architectural plans and specifications, especially on an elementary project. They are frustrated by countless pages of specifications. For these jobs, free plans

certainly offer some advantages.

If You Need Structural Plans

Codes enforcement offices will probably accept your line drawing for non-structural changes. If you are relocating walls or building an addition, they will want structural plans to work with. Your building supply plans should be acceptable to your codes enforcement office, because they will show all of the important structural features. These plans may not have as many elevations, detailed enlargements, or technical descriptions as architectural drawings, but they will be working plans. Do you need a detailed material legend on the plans? No, this can all be addressed in the contract and specifications sheet. You do not need it on the blueprints.

Blueprints are a reference point in remodeling. It is unlikely the job will be completed exactly as shown on the plans. There will be unforeseen obstacles and personal changes that will deviate from the original plans. Why pay thousands of dollars for extensive plans, only to change them on the job? Remodeling is in a class by itself, there is nothing like it. Even the best plans are never good enough, when dealing with unknown factors. These unknown factors will result in on-the-job decisions and modifications. You can't plan on a definite outcome with remodeling. You will need working plans, but be prepared to make on-site changes as well.

Your preliminary design might be all you need. For some jobs, all you have to do is point an experienced remodeler in the right direction. Professional blueprints are not always a prerequisite to a good job. Established remodelers are specialists, with years of experience. They have dealt with adjustments throughout their career. A clear line drawing may be all the subcontractors need. Before spending money on commercial drawings, talk with the people who will be doing the work.

OTHER OPTIONS FOR PLANS

If your plans don't come from a building supplier, you still have options. Drafting companies are a possible alternative. Drafting firms will be happy to develop your design into blueprints. Find a company specializing in construction plans by looking through the phone book or asking a contractor for referrals. All of your experienced subcontractors will be accustomed to working from blueprints. Question them about companies that provide blueprinting services. As subcontractors, they don't have plans drawn, but they do work from them. They should be able to give you names of firms that supply working prints. Your codes officer is another source of referrals. These people review plans on a daily basis. Ask them for names of companies to contact. They won't be able to recommend a specific drafting firm, but they can give you a list of places to investigate.

Take your rough draft with you when you interview various drafting companies. Show them your drawing and ask for a quote to convert your sketch into a set of working plans. For a few hundred dollars, you should be able to get detailed plans and specifications. They still won't be as extensive as an architectural package, but they will be adequate and much less expensive.

All the necessary structural information will be provided by a drafting firm. You can specify items such as bath fixtures, paint color, and other similar items in your contract or on a separate specifications sheet. The plans produced by draftsmen will include more information than those from the building supplier but less than those from an architect. These plans are a happy medium. You will have the basic building plan and other diagrams. These will include electrical, plumbing, and heating diagrams. In addition, there will be front, back, and side elevations. You will get cross-section details and any pertinent information required by the codes enforcement office. For extensive or complex remodeling jobs, drafted plans will normally be better than those available through material suppliers.

The primary difference between drafted plans and architectural plans is the detailed specifications. The drafting company plans will consist mainly of blueprints. There will not be extensive specifications to accompany them. The information on the plans will detail the basic aspects of your project. This includes size of structural members, the type of shingles to be used, siding, and other related items. There will be details of your foundation and recommendations for the footings and concrete. You can expect to see all minimum code requirements on the plans. This is an efficient, economical way to get your project off the ground.

DO YOU NEED AN ARCHITECT?

Architects are the most commonly thought of source for blueprint development. Architects are known for their ability to design outstanding projects. Another trademark of architects is their extensive specification packages. When you want the best plans and specifications, look to architects. You tell them what you want, and they will prepare a complete package for you. Consider an architect for any work requiring an engineer, such as: altering existing foundations, digging out and expanding buried basements, or raising your roof. Their services are expensive, but you get engineered plans and specs of the highest quality.

On large residential jobs and complicated projects, architects are very effective. They are responsible for the success or failure of large projects. Projects of this magnitude require architects and cannot afford to settle for anything less. Small remodeling jobs can benefit from the architect's abilities, but can rarely support the expense. Intricate residential jobs may require their expertise. If you want something unique, architects can provide it. If you want something special, they are the professionals to call. Evaluate your needs and determine which source of plans is the most logical for your job.

Architect as Consultant

If you rule out architectural drawings, due to the expense, consider retaining an architect as a consultant. You derive the benefit of his or her training, without paying for a complete architectural package. Having an architect available will make you more confident. He can answer your questions and you are assured he is giving unbiased answers. This advantage gives you an element of control over the contractors and provides you with knowledge you might not otherwise have.

Regardless of who draws your plans, he or she is dealing with pen and paper. The combination of skilled drawing techniques, experience, proper tools, and a creative mind will produce the best job. The strongest advice is to get good plans and great contractors. Your job can only be as good as the people doing the work. With a poor contractor, the best plans are only a piece of paper. Even if you act as the general contractor, you will be relying on your subcontractors. The success of any job revolves around organization and experienced tradespeople.

SPECIFICATIONS

The next requirement to discuss is specifications. These are details that ensure you get exactly what you want. When you buy a new car, you have the advantage of going for a test drive. You can see all the bells and whistles before you invest your money. With remodeling, you have to spell out every detail from the number and type of doors to paint colors. When you deal with contractors and suppliers, they will make recommendations. Examine their recommendations carefully, remembering you made a dream book for a reason. Don't be coerced into choosing expensive products you don't need or talked out of custom changes you want. Throughout the project, you will have to be cautious of camouflaged salespeople. Homeowners don't usually identify architects, contractors, and building supply managers as salesmen. Sales techniques allow them to increase their profit. Before entering into a contract, or finalizing your plans, know what you want. Be sure of what it will cost, and make sure it has been properly specified.

Be open to suggestions, but don't blindly accept recommendations that increase your cost. I have seen jobs start at $3,000 and wind up costing more than $9,000. If the additional expenses and upgrades are your idea, that's fine. Make sure they are not a decision made under pressure or out of ignorance. Regardless of the conclusion you draw, be certain to include thorough information in your specifications.

Specifying the Job Yourself

The most effective way to avoid cost overruns is to specify the job yourself. You may find that you are not qualified to coordinate the remodeling process, but you know what you want. Why pay someone to tell you what you already know? The blueprints will specify the areas beyond your knowledge. You can easily detail your desired fixtures and finishes yourself. Your estimate sheet and dream book hold the answers to your specifications. All you have to do is put them into an organized package.

Your specifications should be laid out in chronological order. At the end of this chapter, you will find a Product Identification Sheet. This form provides a simple way to list each product by phase and description. There is no big mystery here. You simply express what you want, in writing, and make it a part of all contracts. The spec sheet can be simple or complex. It depends on the type of job you are doing. The more details you include, the fewer problems you will have later. You must not forget anything. When contractors bid, per plans and specs, that is what you get. If you have omitted something

in the specifications, you will have to pay extra for it later.

When your specifications are complete, make several copies. Have the contractors initial each page and sign the last page. Refer to the specifications in your contract. This will protect you during the job. With the contractors' initials and signatures on the specifications, they can't claim a misunderstanding.

Specifications should be, as the name implies, specific. Do not leave anything to the imagination. Define brands, model numbers, manufacturers, colors, and any other descriptive information. Do not allow substitutions without your written consent. Follow the guidelines of the sample specification sheet to see where to start and when to consider your list complete. The sample refers to key points you will need to add to the actual specifications.

For example, the sample will list, "PLUMBING." It will be your responsibility to detail what your requirements are under this phase of the job. The following is an example of the correct way to prepare your specifications.

STAND BY YOUR SPECIFICATIONS

With detailed specifications and thorough contracts, you will eliminate many of the problems associated with remodeling. If you stand by your plans and specifications, you remove the threat of skilled salespeople. They will only be able to sell you what is on the plans and specs. Their attempts to upgrade your material choices will have no effect. If you don't maintain this self-control, you may ultimately buy much more than you expected.

It is very easy to get caught up in the excitement of your remodeling project. Your judgment can be overrun with desire. When this happens, you lose control. After talking to a skilled salesperson, your perspective can change. The exterior doors you loved yesterday can't compare with the ones offered by the salesperson. They will divert your attention and confuse you. Once you are not sure of your choice, selling you a different, more costly product is much easier. This is the beginning of an expensive lesson. The salespeople will capitalize on your indecision. With their skills, they will coerce you into buying their products. This type of impulse buying will destroy your budget.

If the supplier doesn't have access to the brands you specified, they will try to sell you their brand.

ROUGH-IN PLUMBING SPECIFICATIONS

The plumbing contractor shall adhere to the following specifications:

1. The plumbing contractor shall supply all required licenses and permits to complete the following work. All work will be done in compliance with state and local plumbing codes.

2. All plumbing will be installed as detailed by the plans and specifications for the job labeled "John Doe, 123 Pleasant St., Happyville, ME."

3. No substitutions shall be made without written consent of the property owner.

4. All water distribution pipe shall be type "L," rigid copper tubing.

5. All drain, waste, and vent piping and fittings shall be schedule 40, PVC.

6. Tub and shower faucets shall be single handle, chrome finish, with pressure balance control. They shall be manufactured by the "Drip-Be-Gone" company, model #1672.

7. Shower head arm outlets shall be located 6' 6" from the finished floor level.

8. Toilets shall be: 12" rough, round front, 1.6 gallon, water savers, manufactured by "Throne," in designer Sand color #THS-02, model #9001. Toilets shall be supplied with matching plastic seats from the "Throne" company, model #8001.

9. Drop-in lavatories shall be manufactured by "Dinky Sink," in Sand color #S65, model #47.

10. Lavatory faucets shall be "Drip-Be-Gone," single handle, model #2579, with a chrome finish.

11. The kitchen sink shall be a "Tin Man," stainless steel, five hole, double bowl sink, model #345.

12. The kitchen faucet shall be a "Wash-A-Lot," single handle, model #0089, with spray attachment, in a chrome finish.

13. The dishwasher, supplied by owner, will be connected by the plumbing contractor. The plumbing contractor will supply an air gap, copper hot water line, with valve, and all drain hoses and connectors.

14. The owner-supplied ice maker shall be connected by the plumbing contractor. The plumbing contractor shall make this connection and provide a valve and copper tubing.

15. The new washing machine location will be provided with a metal washer outlet box. This receptacle will be supplied and installed by the plumbing contractor.

16. All vent pipes penetrating the roof will be flashed and sealed against leakage by the plumbing contractor.

17. The plumbing contractor will be responsible for the cleanup, on a daily basis, of all areas disturbed by plumbing-related work.

18. The plumbing contractor will agree to and sign a subcontractor agreement before any work is commenced.

19. Any changes in these specifications will only be recognized if agreed to, in writing, by the property owner.

They will have supporting documentation to verify the quality of their product. Their product could be as good or better than the one you specified, but you spent extensive time researching your chosen products. Are you willing to throw that time and information away for a quick decision? Think before you act. Don't deviate from your original plans without serious consideration.

Contractors as Salespeople

Contractors can be very effective salespeople too. Once they have your confidence, you are an easy target. They may point out ways to improve on your plans. These improvements can come at a high price. They know that once they have the job, you are not likely to shop for prices on extras and changes. If they can convince you to change your plans, they can increase their profit. Some contractors specialize in upgrading customers. They come in low and leave high. These guys are dangerous to your budget.

A contractor armed with good sales techniques can sell you almost anything. If the contractor working on the job brings a problem to your attention, will you seek a second opinion? A common reaction is immediately to authorize the contractor to rectify the situation. Most contractors will treat you fairly, some won't. The bad guys know how to take advantage of you. They get well into the job before approaching you on changes or extras. By this time, you have come to trust them. If they tell you your house needs additional work, you will probably believe them. They will stress the savings of having the work done now, while they are already on the job. This is a standard sales pitch given to homeowners.

Should you get other estimates before authorizing the contractor to do the work? Get at least one other opinion. There are contractors who make a living by taking advantage of trusting consumers.

Often a subcontractor who is responsible for supplying material or fixtures will tell you the product is unavailable. Then he will offer you substitutions, which are either upgrades or items designed to make price comparisons impossible. Force him to show his hand and corroborate his statements. Ask the name of the suppliers he gets his materials from, and which of them he has checked stock with. It may be that the item is only temporarily out of stock or can be obtained through another supplier. Sub-contractors may not receive the same discount from each supplier; therefore, they may not investigate all the available options. If the contractor truly cannot acquire the item through his sources, consider omitting it from his contract price. Offer to supply the product yourself. Faced with the prospect of losing his markup on the item, the subcontractor may miraculously find the product in stock somewhere.

One of Dodge's rules is, "Don't take anything for granted, protect yourself at all times." If the cost of unforeseen work is only a hundred dollars, it probably isn't worth the time spent in getting other estimates. If contractors tell you they can't get an item, check the availability yourself. Use your own judgment, but beware of substitutions and extras. Maintain control with your established plans and specifications.

You can create a specification sheet by using your dream book. The products you have placed there will give you the information to include for the major items. For more technical information, you may need to visit the library. There are several home improvement reference books available. These books will help you detail specifications for uncommon jobs or items. These specifications tie the hands of crooked contractors. They cannot beat you when they have to play by your rules. As a consumer or a general contractor, it's important for you to maintain control. One of the best ways to control your job is with detailed written instruments.

Later in the book, we will look further into the control of contractors. Many factors give you the control and one of these factors is detailed plans and specifications. Spend the time to do these right. Don't cut corners on the specifications. Don't assume the subcontractors or suppliers know what you want. Don't consider an aspect discussed and understood unless you have specified it in writing. The time you spend now will save you frustration later. Keep the specifications clear and concise. Don't give contractors and suppliers a gap to slip through. Refer to your plans throughout the contract and specifications. If necessary, label certain areas to clarify your descriptions. In the design stage, your main concern was utilization of space. In the specification phase, focus yourself on clarity and detail. Your plans and specifications are the cornerstone of a solid remodeling job.

PRODUCT IDENTIFICATION SHEET

PHASE	ITEM	BRAND	MODEL	COLOR	SIZE
Plumbing					
Plumbing					
Plumbing					
Electrical					
Electrical					
Flooring					
Cabinet					

PRODUCT IDENTIFICATION SHEET

PHASE	ITEM	BRAND	MODEL	COLOR	SIZE
Plumbing	Lavatory	DEBA	1123	White	19" x 17"
Plumbing	Toilet	THRONE	212	White	12" rough
Plumbing	Shower	DUCKY	8765	White	36" x 36"
Electrical	Bath light	GLOW	29	Gold	30"
Electrical	Exhaust fan	ALADDIN	387	White	12" x 12"
Flooring	Vinyl floor	SURSHINE	00891	0900	8' x 9'
Cabinet	Wall Cabinet	AMBER	324	Oak	30"

Evaluating Your Intended Improvements

4

Before you sign any contracts, you should evaluate your impending decision. There are some occasions when remodeling is not feasible or practical. At these times, the benefits may not justify the expense. The motivations to remodel are as many and varied as the possible remodeling projects. For some, remodeling is done to accommodate a growing family. Others remodel to customize their homes, and many homeowners plan remodeling projects to increase their properties' value. Another reason for remodeling is to make your home more marketable in a sluggish economy. What is your rationale for wanting to remodel?

The question of selling a home versus remodeling it is common; many homeowners are confronted with the choice. Your personal situation will influence your decision to stay or go. The facts may indicate your proposed improvement is a poor investment, but circumstances may pressure you to accept this. Children make moving a difficult option. Leaving their established friends or attending school in a different district may erase moving from the list of considerations. Perhaps you prefer not to move because of job instability. When personal factors prejudice your decision, be sure to look for the most profitable remodeling projects. Is adding space to your existing house more sensible than moving? This is a question worth spending some time to answer.

REASONS FOR REMODELING

Define your reasons for remodeling before you proceed. Increasing your home's value is always a good basis for remodeling, but caution must be exer-

cised to avoid pricing your home out of the market. In some instances, you may not be able to recover your investment if you increase the home's value too much. A growing family can force you to make changes, and these often include remodeling.

Remodeling to make your house more saleable may be a mistake. It might be more advantageous to keep the sale price of the house lower. When house prices go up, the number of qualified buyers goes down. However, remodeling your home could attract a whole new group of buyers. How will you know what to do? Do you want to gamble on finding additional buyers, after you've made a large capital remodeling investment? Suppose you spend the money and still cannot sell the house? Will you enjoy and benefit from the improvements if you must continue to live there? If not, you will be paying a long time for improvements made solely in an attempt to sell the house. It is crucial to be well-informed before investing money in your home.

Before a financial commitment is made, you need to be sure remodeling is the right option for you. Many factors will influence your decision, so let's explore some of them. You must learn the principles for evaluating the effects of remodeling your home. Home improvements can be broken down into separate categories, organized by physical characteristics. These are interior improvements, exterior improvements, garages, and additions. Remodeling in these categories is done for any of three basic reasons: need, desire, and salability. *Need* means an improvement must be made for structural or maintenance reasons. A *desired* alteration deals with personal preference, and *salability* centers around selling the property.

EXTERIOR IMPROVEMENTS

Exterior improvements include all the features altering the outside of your home. Among these are siding, exterior trim, painting, roofing, windows, and landscaping. Exterior improvements deal only with the exterior condition of your present structure and the land on which it is located. Remember, additions and garages have their own category. Although exterior alterations are usually made out of need, they inevitably affect salability as well.

Homes constructed of wood need painting every few years. Weather plays a large role in the frequency of required painting. Harsh climates and moist conditions will force you to repaint the home often. Moisture is one of the largest culprits in causing your paint to peel. You can circumvent habitual painting with preventive improvements. Maintenance-reducing improvements are cost-effective and save you from major investments later. While a new paint job can sell your house more quickly by enhancing its curb appeal, it is unlikely you will recover the full cost of this improvement. Preventive improvements shelter you from spending money on maintenance.

Reducing the effect of moisture is a strong example of a preventive improvement. Moisture damage for houses on cellars or crawl spaces can be easily and inexpensively reduced. Installing a plastic vapor barrier over 80% of the ground, under the house, will reduce rising moisture. For less than $20 and a few hours of your time, you can protect your home from excess moisture. This is an excellent investment; adding foundation vents is another. Proper ventilation is necessary to reduce paint peeling and structural damage to flooring systems. Foundation vents allow moisture to escape.

Replace old foundation vents with new temperature-controlled vents. Older, manually operated vents, require you to close them for the winter. This eliminates air circulation for half the year, but is a necessary evil with the old-style vents. If they are left open, cold air permeates your home. This can cause pipes to freeze and heating costs to soar. The alternative is temperature-controlled vents that open and close automatically. As the name implies, they operate according to temperature. When the temperature is moderate, they open; when it's cold, the vents remain closed. With this system, your house is ventilated throughout the year, resulting in reduced moisture. This simple and inexpensive improvement can reduce peeling paint and structural damage.

Extensive skills are not required to install vapor barriers and vents; most homeowners can do the work themselves. These are inexpensive improvements that pay for themselves in reduced maintenance costs. When you are ready to sell, point out the features and benefits of your improvements to prospective purchasers. In fact, they should recognize the value, and it could be this difference that convinces them to buy your home rather than your neighbor's.

If your house continually needs painting, consider installing vinyl siding as an alternative. A new coat of paint will be less expensive, but will add little to the appraised value of your home. By spending slightly more, you can create a maintenance-free exterior and increase your home's market value. If you keep the house, you will never have to paint the siding again. When the home is sold, you will recover much, if not all, of your original investment. This improvement can also be the deciding influence in the sale of your home.

Should you replace your old roof? Unless it's cracking, curling, or leaking, leave it alone. The expense of a new roof will not be recovered in your home's resale value. Roofs offer a low rate of return on your investment. If an unattractive roof can be left alone, is the same true of an unsightly, cracked foundation? No, foundations should be repaired before freezing weather and before placing the house on the real estate market. Foundation cracks are commonly the result of settling. While they may not significantly affect the structurally integrity of the house, cracks should always be repaired. If nothing else, cracks are a shock to the eye and a deterrent to prospective purchasers.

We will delve into more detail on recovering your home improvement investments in the next chapter. The purpose of these brief examples is to help you understand how to evaluate your improvements. Now, we will take a hard look at what should be done with your house. What do you want from your remodeling expense and efforts? Will you be satisfied to enjoy your improvement without recovering the cost when you sell? Do you really want to subject yourself to the potential frustration of remodeling? Will you spend a huge sum of money, only to realize you should have moved to a different house?

THE IMPORTANCE OF DEFINING YOUR NEEDS

For remodeling to be effective, you must have adequate space to work with. If your family is outgrowing the house, cosmetic improvements will not solve your problem. Increasing your square footage, by finishing an attic or adding a room, can result in over-building for the neighborhood. If you over-build, you will not recover your investment and may not even be able to sell the house. Only the right remodeling decisions will result in a profit. How will you know what remodeling efforts to pursue?

Exterior improvements are commonly made out of necessity. Houses are repainted as a maintenance obligation, not just to change the color. Roofs are repaired because they leak, not because the owner wants a new shingle style. Gutters get replaced when they rust or fail to function properly, not by choice. Front steps are repaired because they are damaged or have become a safety hazard. This is not the kind of work you do for fun or profit.

Landscaping is the exception to the exterior improvement rule. It is one of the few exterior improvements that are both cost-effective and non-compulsory. Landscaping expenses can be completely recovered at the time of sale and make the home more desirable. If little or no landscaping existed before the improvement, the investment succeeds in satisfying all three remodeling motivations. Need, desire, and salability have all been fulfilled. Landscaping also allows homeowners to distinguish their property from the surrounding houses.

Interior remodeling is commonly done out of desire. A couple elects to enlarge their space to accommodate their growing family. Interior improvements require careful thought; a consumer can get overzealous when given the opportunity to expand. These alterations do not include routine maintenance. Items such as interior painting, new carpets, and other basic upkeep don't fall into this classification. It's the major remodeling ventures that you must look at long and hard. Before you build a garage or add on to your house, there is much to consider. Major capitol investments require thorough investigation.

Checking the Real Estate Market

First, compare the facts. What is the most expensive house in your neighborhood worth? What is the present value of your home? How much will your lavish improvements cost? Can you sell your house for enough to recover your investment? Real estate investors have a motto: it is best to own the least expensive house in the neighborhood. You gain all the advantages of the more expensive homes, without paying a premium price. Your house will be very enticing due to its lower price in a prestigious neighborhood. People want to live in fashionable areas, but too-high mortgage payments can prohibit them from the location of their choice.

Having the least expensive home in the area can be a real advantage. The number of people qualified to buy your home will exceed the number qualified to buy the more expensive homes. You enjoy a broader market and should see a faster sale. In real estate sales, there are three words that sell houses: location, location, and location. If you have a house in the right location, at the right price, a fast and profitable sale is almost a certainty.

Over-building for an area is a common and costly mistake. It is an easy trap for the average homeowner to fall into. When people need more space, they immediately think of adding to their existing home. Remodeling appears to be the most economical way to meet these growing demands. When the consumer calls contractors for estimates, he is prompted to proceed with expansion plans. The contractors want the work and are not concerned about the consumer's ability to recover the investment. Encouragement from contractors and exhilaration over an improved space often push the homeowner into a decision he will regret later.

Homeowners frequently decide to proceed with a project without considering its effect on the future salability of their home. If this aspect is considered, the owner often assumes the house will automatically be worth more and be easier to sell. Actually, increasing the size of a home, and the investment in it, can result in lost money. Before going ahead with extensive additions and remodeling, you need to perform some market research. This research will enable you to evaluate the feasibility of your remodeling plans, before your money is spent.

Neighborhood values can be determined in many ways. Watch the "For Sale" ads in the local paper. Get an idea of the asking prices for houses in your area or subdivision. Visit the Registry of Deeds. Real estate transfers are public knowledge, allowing you to see the actual selling prices of homes similar to your own. This is the most factual way to determine property values in your area.

Another option is to call real estate brokers.

Ask them for a free market analysis of your home. Instruct the broker to show you only confirmed sales in your area. If the Realtor belongs to a Multiple Listing Service, he will be able to show you comparable sales books. These books show all the closed transactions for the previous quarter of the year. You can easily compare your home to the others that have sold successfully. Comparable sales books provide detailed descriptions of these houses. You will know how many bathrooms were in the house. The number of bedrooms will also be listed. If the house had a finished basement, it will be in the comp book. These books detail noteworthy information about your neighborhood. Moreover, they disclose information you must know to evaluate your remodeling decision.

THREE REMODELING STRATEGIES

Consider three strategies in remodeling. The first is remodeling to increase your home's value. The second is to make your home more marketable. The third is to accommodate personal enjoyment. In some cases, you can achieve all of these goals with a single improvement; other projects miss the mark on all accounts. Personal use and enjoyment is the most common motivator for remodeling — and the most perilous. Uninformed homeowners run a heavy risk in remodeling based on purely personal desires. Some work will actually *lower* the value of your home. Making radical changes or doing unusual improvements can adversely affect your home's value and marketability. These concepts will be covered in detail in Chapter 6, but here are a few quick examples.

EVALUATE WHAT YOU WANT

Unbiased evaluation of your desired alterations is important. The type of improvement you want may not justify its cost. It is hard to deal with sound business practices when your heart wants to splurge. The impulse to go forward with your proposed improvement can be overwhelming. You might feel you must have that $700 skylight. The value will never be recovered, but it's a magnificent addition to the room. If you can afford the skylight, the decision becomes even more difficult. It's easy to eliminate items you can't pay for. It is not so easy to talk yourself out of the items you desire and can afford.

Maybe your dream has always been to own a house with an in-ground swimming pool. Swimming pools are expensive and require extensive space and upkeep. Your dream may be a prospective purchaser's nightmare. The pool has given you days of pure bliss. You taught your youngest how to paddle around in the water. You enjoyed sunbathing and refreshing swims on hot days. This improvement has provided you with unequaled personal enjoyment, how could anyone not want his own pool?

Your aquatic investment, of several thousand dollars, may hurt the resale of your home. People with children often avoid in-ground pools for safety reasons, afraid their children will fall into the pool. Another objection could be the lack of remaining lawn area, if you used all your grassy area for a cement pond. This can be a real deterrent for some home buyers. Maybe the potential buyer wants a low upkeep house. Pools require steady maintenance. The pool might immediately disqualify your house from consideration. The fencing around a pool may be visually offensive to the purchaser, and it requires maintenance as well. This means additional money and effort for the purchaser of your home.

You never thought installing a pool could hurt the sale of your property. For you, it was the ultimate home improvement. If the pool causes prospective buyers to pass up your house consistently, you will become disconcerted. Not only will you regret your original investment, you'll be stranded in a home you want to sell. At the least, this is an inconvenience. If you need to sell, it can be a financial disaster, which forces the house to sell far below market value.

IMPROVING SALES APPEAL

Remodeling to improve the sales appeal of your home makes sense. In a tight economy, the best home for the best price is the one people will buy. In a slow real estate market, you might be forced to enhance your home's appearance to sell it. This type of investment may not be recovered. Sometimes the only purpose for these alterations is to sell the property. There are two sides of this coin to consider. Should you invest money in the house to make it more marketable? Would it be wiser to keep the price low and let the buyers make their own improvements?

Different professionals will give you different answers to these questions. A good case can be made for both options. As a builder, I prefer to keep my investments at a minimum. I feel this allows for more options and flexibility. If you invest substantial money, you must get more for the property before you break even. You could force the price of the home out of a prospective buyer's range. Conversely, first impressions are important. When your home has good curb appeal, you will have more people interested in purchasing it. The odds of a successful transaction increase with every prospect who views your home. It's a proven fact: certain improvements make your home easier to sell.

My experience as a real estate broker taught me the trigger points of a sale. The first look does make a decided difference. Homes with attractive landscaping, well-kept exteriors, and paved driveways are superior. These qualities set the mood of the buyer. While these features alone don't sell a house, they keep the buyer interested longer. The longer a prospective purchaser is interested, the better the chances are of a sale.

In contrast, a rundown exterior appearance can alienate a buyer immediately. The best salesperson is helpless when this happens. The buyer will move along to another property. Real estate brokers want sales, and they don't care if it is your house or one down the street. Under these conditions, the exterior appearance of your house can make a very big difference. If your intent is to make your house more alluring to potential buyers, start outside.

Here are some simple, inexpensive ideas to increase the salability of your property. Keep the lawn well maintained, even if you have to hire professionals. Spruce up your home's exterior appearance, and clean the leaves out of the gutters. Touch up the exterior paint as needed, and clean all the windows. Trim the shrubbery — unkempt landscaping indicates a lack of home maintenance to buyers. Don't leave garden hoses lying on the lawn. Keep toys and bicycles out of the yard. Once the impression of negligence creeps into a buyer's mind, it's hard to combat. If you have a garage, keep the doors down. Add accessories to the exterior of the house. A wreath on the door makes a house a home. These small touches mean a lot.

Carry these concepts over to the interior of the house. On the inside, concentrate on the areas seen from the front door. Freshen the paint, clean the carpets, and position your furniture to convey a feeling of openness. Keep the curtains open to illuminate the rooms, and place fresh flowers in the living

and dining rooms. Place bowls of fruit in the kitchen. Put logs in the fireplace, or even a small fire if weather allows. Be sure the house is seasonably comfortable, open windows or turn on heat as necessary. A neat room looks larger, so avoid clutter. Draw attention to the home's strong points with creative decorating. Keep your capital outlay at a minimum, while achieving the maximum marketing benefits.

All of these tactics can turn your home into a buyer's dream home. You don't have to spend a lot of money to make your house desirable. All you have to do is set it apart from the competition. In a competitive market, any outstanding feature can mean the difference between a sale and a serious looker. These improvements should require minimum expense, because you will not recover the investment in the sale price of the home. If the improvements sell your home, they've done their job, and your money has been well spent.

THE ENJOYMENT/PROFIT MOTIVE

The last rationale for remodeling is the best. The foremost reason for remodeling combines enjoyment with profit. When you make big changes, you should be rewarded for your efforts. Choose your big project carefully. When you combine your desires with solid financial gains, you have played the remodeling game magnificently. Remodeling for personal satisfaction is fine. Remodeling to make your house sell faster can be necessary. Remodeling for fun *and* profit is the ultimate alternative. Done properly, remodeling can be very rewarding — you can enjoy your new improvements and make money.

Some improvements increase the value of your home beyond the cost of the improvement. This is like a gift; you spend $7,000 and, when you sell, you get $9,000 in return. The profits can increase if you act as your own general contractor. By learning how to play the game, you can save even more on your subcontractors. The profit continues to grow when you make smart product selections. Any money you save, without adversely affecting the improvement, will give you an attractive rate of return.

The Equity Gain

Building equity in your home has a cumulative effect. Traditional trends show houses appreciate by a percentage of their value each year. The amount of increase depends on location and economic conditions. A conservative figure is 5%; in some instances, 15% is not uncommon. What does this mean to you as a homeowner? The equity you gain in your house today should increase each year you own the house. In each future year, your equity builds on itself.

An improvement that increases your value by $20,000 today could be worth $23,000 next year. In another year, this same investment may be worth $26,450. Depending on the economy and your location, these numbers will fluctuate. The point is, historically, real estate gains in value each year. These gains are based on *existing* value. By remodeling, you increase the existing value and should increase your profit.

To reach the highest profit potential, you will need to know what project to undertake. The quest for the perfect project is not a difficult journey. It only requires patience and a good map of your actions. You could think of your project as buried pirate treasure. The potential money hidden in your house can be worth a small fortune. All you have to do is get to the "X" on the map. Before you can get there, you will need the map. Like any treasure hunter, having accurate directions makes your search easy.

In the search for remodeling treasures, you make your own map. This requires research from many sources. You will need to consult books, contractors, appraisers, and the Registry of Deeds. Real estate brokers can provide some of the keys to the map. Neighbors and tax assessors hold other secrets of the treasure trail. All of these sources will be used in completing an accurate treasure map.

The accumulated information will show you what constitutes a good investment. It can help you to evaluate the result of the projects planned for your house. When you know what's in demand, you have a direction to go. Knowing what to expect in the real estate market will influence your decision. Comparing value to cost will make your eyes gleam; the money that can be made with remodeling is exciting. When you project it out over five years, the profit becomes a true treasure. This is a tax-deferred financial gain. What could be a better hobby? If you have any interest in making money and living better, remodeling is worth your serious consideration.

This equity gain formula doesn't work with all improvements. Some improvements don't add much value. All you get out of them is a break-even on your initial investment. They are acceptable if you are only looking for personal enjoyment, but when you are seeking profits, they must be avoided. Some improvements depreciate rapidly; they shouldn't be done unless you have no other choice. These jobs cost you money from the day they begin.

Never spend money on known losers when you have a choice. You might as well burn your money in the wood stove. Certain improvements return more than you invest, and these are the golden rings. Concentrate your efforts on finding the right project. The challenge in this puzzle is separating the winners from the losers. Picking the winners is easier than winning the lottery, because you have control over your own success.

With the right research, you won't be gambling, and you can stack the deck in your favor. There is no real secret to finding the most profitable remodeling jobs; it just takes time and research. The answers are there for anyone willing to spend the time to find them.

Recovering Your Investment

5

Home improvements are one of the few items you can spend money on today and sell for a profit later. Unlike cars and boats, most home improvements increase in value. There are some exceptions but, overall, remodeling is a lucrative investment. Planting a rose garden or repainting the living room can become profitable pastimes. When you sell your house, those weekend projects should net you a good return. Simple improvements can equate with a higher sales price. Large projects, like additions and garages, have the potential to return thousands of dollars for your time and efforts. Whatever project you choose, make it financially feasible. Learn to look at your remodeling project through the eyes of an appraiser.

When houses are sold, they have to be assigned a value. If you have a cash buyer, this value can be determined between you and the purchaser. There are very few cash deals in the real estate market, because they tie up money that could be spread across several investments. Most buyers will seek commercial financing. Lending institutions require a professional appraisal before loaning money for the purchase of a home. This imposes a whole new set of rules on the home improvement game.

DETERMINING FAIR MARKET VALUE

The bank will be loaning a percentage of the fair market value for the purchase of the home. This value must be established before a loan amount can be determined. Lending institutions require appraisals to protect themselves. There must be sufficient value in the property to recover in the event of default. Banks do not want to be in the residential real estate business. They make their profits by loaning money, and they lose money if they have to foreclose on houses. Properties in foreclosure are sold to the highest bidder, and the sales prices are well below market value. There are legal fees involved in foreclosures, and the lender has to absorb these losses as well. Making an excessive loan is an expensive mistake for a lender.

Some banks have staff appraisers; others hire independent professionals to examine the home. These appraisers have extensive training in the art of real estate evaluation. Most are certified appraisers, with impressive credentials. Their appraisals are the last word with the lender. Most banks have an approved appraiser list, and will not accept an appraisal from other sources.

There is a common misconception pertaining to real estate brokers. Much of the public assumes real estate brokers are established appraisers. Although some are, most brokers are not qualified or approved appraisers. Have you ever received an offer for a free market analysis on your home? These free reports are a way for real estate brokers to get in the door. It gives them the opportunity to introduce themselves, hoping you will list your house with them when you decide to sell. The market evaluation is *not* an appraisal. Even if the real estate broker is a certified appraiser, there is a distinct difference between a market analysis and an appraisal.

If you are looking for a lender-approved appraisal, request a list of approved appraisers from the bank. If the broker's name is listed, consider requesting a free appraisal instead of an analysis.

Using the potential house listing as bait, the broker may provide a true appraisal. The value of this free appraisal averages about $250. These types of savings can be used to buy that extra special item waiting in the back of your dream book.

THE APPRAISAL PROCESS

To understand which remodeling efforts are the most cost-effective, you must comprehend the appraisal process. It is a wise idea to seek your own appraisal before contracting for a major remodeling project. You will be better prepared to determine the practicality of the project. Anytime you put money into your house, you should know the effect of your investment. You could be spending money you will never see again. If your house is priced in the top 20% of the homes in your area, you may not want to make a capital investment. Adding value to your home may price it out of the market; it is very difficult to sell the most expensive house in a subdivision. You should not expand your home to five bedrooms if the surrounding homes only have three. If the neighboring houses have two bathrooms, and you only have one, adding a bathroom can be a good investment.

Free Market Analysis

Before we contemplate actual projects, let's examine market value in detail. When you are ready to remodel, call a few local real estate brokers. Look around and contact the companies selling homes in your area. Ask the brokers to provide you with a free market analysis. Most firms will be glad to do this. Their purpose is to meet you and make a good impression. Brokers who are members of a Multiple Listing Service have access to beneficial information. They can show you how much neighboring properties are selling for, as well as give you information on the physical attributes of the homes. Multiple listing books contain detailed descriptions of all houses listed or sold by participating real estate firms.

When the brokers come to your house, they will fill out a Property Data Report. A blank data report sheet is provided at the end of this chapter as an example. The information will include the number of rooms, bedrooms, bathrooms, and other appurtenances of your home. Brokers place a standard value on your fireplace, deck, garage, ceiling fans, and other features of your home. The lot size, driveway, foundation type, and landscaping will all be taken into consideration. Once the form is complete, the broker will go back to her office and formulate a market analysis.

Request evaluations from at least three different firms; not all brokers will see your home in the same way. The more opinions of value you receive, the better informed you will be. A good broker will present you with a Comparable Sales Sheet. There is an example of a comparable sales sheet in this chapter. These comp sheets will include all the pertinent information on your home, as well as similar information for other houses that have sold in your area. All sales used should be current. If the houses were sold more than six months ago, the projections may not be accurate. The comp sheet should also highlight three properties similar to your home, which are currently on the market.

These comparable sales sheets can tell you much about your home. You will be able to compare your house to others in the area. The first detail to look at is price. How does your existing house compare to the others? If your estimated market value is higher than the competition, reconsider your remodeling project. If your house is priced below other sales, examine the comp sheet further. Compare the key items.

HOW TO TRANSLATE REMODELING PROJECTS INTO VALUE

Bedrooms are a good place to start because they translate into value. If you have fewer bedrooms than the comparable homes, this is an area you can improve safely. Bathrooms are one of the easiest investments to recover. Depending on your number of bedrooms, you can also recover the cost of adding or remodeling a bathroom. Two full bathrooms and a powder room (half bath) are a good balance for a three or four bedroom house.

The two rooms that sell the most homes are the kitchen and bathroom. If you want to spend money, invest it in these areas. Chapter 7 provides you with money-saving ideas for kitchen and bath improvements. The fundamental philosophy is one of serviceability and eye appeal. Money invested in conforming kitchen and bath improvements will be returned to you when the house is sold.

If garages are common in your neighborhood, you can add one without much risk. The cost of constructing a garage is minimal, compared to the return on your investment. Finished basements are a good value when you're buying, but they can be a bad investment when you are selling. Watch out for this trap. It is very tempting to finish your basement into living space, but you could lose money doing so. Recovering your expenditure in finishing a basement is unlikely.

One of the reasons converting a basement into living space is so popular is the lack of structural work involved. Many homeowners can do much of the improvement themselves. They assume if they do all the work, they can't lose. This theory has some merit, if you don't place a value on your time. If you need the space and can do the work yourself, you may benefit from the project. Be advised: finishing a basement will entail framing, wiring, heating, drywall, paint, trim carpentry, and flooring. Hiring contractors will probably result in an unrecovered investment. My experience with appraisals indicates the value placed on finished basements is lower than the cost of the labor and materials. The work is relatively easy, but the return is insignificant.

Converting a daylight basement slightly increases your earnings. Sliding glass doors and windows make the basement a better investment. Daylight basements also have a better chance of being appraised as normal living space. If you decide to finish your basement, keep the costs to a minimum. Don't invest in expensive paneling or floor coverings; keep the job simple and inexpensive. You will be playing against the odds. The less you spend, the better your chances are of recovering your costs. Basements are not a preferred investment — they just don't appraise well.

I don't know any appraisers willing to recommend finishing an underground basement. Initially, you may see your basement as a way to obtain inexpensive living space. After all, here is a chance to turn your glorified storage area into useable living space. Although basements are a way to get cheap space, their low cost is reflected in the appraisal. There is little to no money to be made finishing a buried basement. Finished basements do offer some advantages in selling a house; the extra space can make the sale. If your intent is to increase the market appeal of your home, the project can work, but don't expect great profits. When you compare basements to other projects, the profit zone is very thin.

In many cases, unfinished basements are desirable. They provide a place for storage, game rooms, and an array of other activities. Look at your basement through the eyes of a purchaser. If your house does not have a garage or attic for storage, the unfinished basement becomes a necessity.

As a remodeler, you can spend a lot of time with limited return on your investment. Think twice, or even three times, before finishing your basement. If you insist on tackling this project, do it in a intelligent way. Get an appraiser to give you before and after appraisals, based on your improvement plans. Go over the report with the appraiser. The investment may be warranted. Your area or personal situation may provide unusually good returns on finished basements. Look for specialty books on the subject. Work smart to keep your costs low; basements offer a profit only when done properly. The key is knowing how to finish the space in a cost-effective way. Talk with the appraiser and read the books dealing with basement remodeling. These two factors will give you a competitive edge.

Analyze the traffic patterns in your home. The two areas that receive the most foot travel are halls and steps. These require generous lighting and good quality carpeting. Proper lighting can transform a hall from a tunnel into an art gallery. Directional, recessed lighting can highlight paintings or photographs along the way. A light fixture with a cut glass cover produces intriguing shadows and designs. Lighting can become the ingredient that allows you to enjoy climbing the stairs or walking down the hall. These inexpensive improvements leave a lasting impression on everyone who sees them, including appraisers.

Another area for change in the hall involves interior doors. If your house has plain, flat lauan doors, consider an inexpensive facelift. Replace those dull doors with hollow core, six panel doors. This alteration will be reflected in your appraisal and will add a touch of class to the house. It is a simple project you can do yourself. The new doors will come already primed, so simply spray or brush on the finish coat of paint. Then remove the hinge pins from the old doors and hang the new ones. The replacement doors will come pre-drilled for door knobs, so changing the door handles is effortless. You have produced excellent results with minimal expense. The money spent will be returned in full with actual cash value.

New carpets, appliances, and drapes will all help sell your home, but you will not recover all these costs. Carefully studying your market evaluation will give you a good idea of your remodeling options. You can easily identify projects that will improve your home while keeping it competitive with surrounding areas. If you are interested in pursuing a questionable project, invest in a professional appraisal. It will provide you with the information necessary to put your mind at ease. With the comparative data from the free market analysis, you can adjust your remodeling design if necessary. Generate your design and specifications before engaging a professional appraiser.

GET YOUR PLANS APPRAISED

Call an appraiser when your preliminary plans and specs are ready. Ask the appraiser to determine the value of your existing house, without including any new improvements. Show the appraiser your proposed plans and request an appraisal addendum, indicating the value upon completion of the remodeling work. Appraisers are accustomed to doing proposed construction appraisals for banks. They can tell you what your finished product will be worth. Residential appraisals generally cost between $150 and $300. This is money well spent; you will know exactly what your investment is worth before your spend the money.

The procedure for a professional appraisal is similar to the market analysis. The same principles are used, but the report is more detailed. The major difference is that a certified, professional appraisal can be used at the bank. This is very beneficial if you need a loan for your remodeling job. Another distinction is objectivity. Appraisers are being paid a fee to provide an unbiased statement of value. Real estate brokers tend to be overly optimistic about your home's value. They are paid a percentage of the sales price for selling the property. If they inflate the market value, the listing price will be higher. A higher asking price, if sold, leads to a larger commission for the broker. A market analysis may reflect an overstated opinion of value. A professional appraiser will have no reason to exaggerate the value of your home. If anything, he will be conservative. This is in your favor when considering a major improvement.

It is better to base your decision on a conservative approach. If the real estate market drops, you can still recover your investment. The professional appraisal should be much more accurate than a free market analysis. Appraisers evaluate property for a living; brokers get paid to sell property. The real estate broker isn't likely to have the experience of a full-time appraiser. The broker can give you an idea of value, but trust your money to the professional appraiser. Once you receive the official appraisal, making your decision will be easy. A black and white comparison can be made.

With a professional appraisal, you have removed the guesswork and are dealing with substantiated facts. Knowing the completed value is also an advantage when shopping contractors' prices. You know the maximum amount the job is worth, and this knowledge gives you power. When a contractor tells you the job will cost $10,000, you will know whether it is a reasonable bid. You can produce the appraisal report and negotiate for a lower price. An appraisal is the best investment you can make to verify the viability of your project.

HOW MUCH WILL YOU SAVE BY ACTING AS GENERAL CONTRACTOR?

Acting as your own general contractor gives you the opportunity to increase your rate of return. When you coordinate your own job, you can save up to 30% of the total value of the work. Most general contractors charge about 20% for their services. Some charge much more; 35% isn't unheard of. This is money you can save if you have the right skills. These skills include good judgment, a mind for details, and some technical knowledge. You must already possess the organizational abilities, but the technical knowledge can be gained from books and product brochures. Time is another important factor involved in acting as your own general contractor.

You could need a lot of time. The time requirements depend on your subcontractors, suppliers, and organizational skills. If everything goes the way you have it planned, you can get by with only an hour or two each day. Undependable subcontractors and suppliers, and large projects, may demand in excess of four hours a day. Evaluate what your time is worth, and decide if you are willing to donate your time to the remodeling project.

In remodeling, events rarely go as planned; being your own general contractor is a profound responsibility. If you can meet the challenge, you can save big money. Building and remodeling profits are calculated as a percentage of the job's completed value; the bigger the job, the bigger the profit. The cash rewards are terrific when the appraisal report supports a large improvement.

Building a $40,000 addition can mean an $8,000 equity profit for you. This is a lucrative part-time venture — you win two ways. The first is the enjoyment of the new addition, the second is the financial gain. Earning $8,000 for working a few hours a night over a sixty-day period is exciting. There are no income taxes to pay until you sell, and you can reinvest your profits to defer your tax consequences. Borrowing against your new equity enables you to utilize your earnings without income tax complications. Talk with a tax expert to see how this aspect affects your personal situation.

WHEN YOU SHOULD NOT REMODEL

When your appraisal report doesn't support your remodeling plans, don't continue. Consider moving. It can be better to sell than to remodel and throw your money away. You should not spend a large sum of money on a losing cause. The appraisal is the basis for your decision. If it indicates remodeling as a poor investment, you probably shouldn't remodel. A low appraisal can stop your job on the spot. Follow my advice, and know the appraised value before you start. This saves you time, money, and regrets.

If financing is involved, an appraisal will be required from most lenders. If the appraisal is low, you will not be granted approval for your home improvement loan. If your loan is rejected because of a low appraisal, consider different options. The best alternative could be to sell your house and buy one with the features you desire. If your mind is set on remodeling your home, there is still hope for a loan. Sometimes the existing equity in your house can be used to circumvent a low appraisal.

Lenders will frequently approve a home improvement loan based solely on the equity you have in the home. They know their risk is secured by your equity. Before exercising this option, or paying cash for the project, think about your actions. Once you spend the money, you may have to live with the decision for many years. Houses being sold are usually appraised by the lenders. If the appraisal doesn't support the additional cost of your improvements now, the expense probably won't be adequately reflected when you try to sell. This represents a high risk for the loss of your remodeling investment. Your property appreciation would have to sky-rocket before you could recapture your money.

Deliberate over your plans to remodel. This is a decision with long-term effects. With a low appraisal, your investment can't be recovered for years to come. If you remodel, despite the facts, you won't have much flexibility. You may not be able to sell your house for enough to recover the money invested in it. Consider the factors carefully. If you decide to improve your home, you will be well prepared for the outcome when the time comes for you to sell. You already have your appraisal and your market analysis. This money wasn't wasted.

THE WRONG IMPROVEMENT IS A BAD INVESTMENT

Some improvements are bad investments but offer redeeming qualities in the pleasure they give you. Even with the poor economic value, they may still be worthwhile improvements to you. If you are willing to pay the price, go for it. If you can't afford to lose your investment, think before you act. Remodeling offers four types of projects when it comes to money. There are projects that break even — the money spent here will be added proportionally to the value of your home.

Then there is the snake pit. The projects in this category cost more than they are worth. Their value will not be fully recognized in an appraisal report. These jobs might provide enjoyment but offer no financial gain. They actually cost you money — you are paying for a personal preference. There is nothing wrong with this if you can afford it and understand what you are doing.

The next category is the one to avoid at all times. Wild, nonconforming changes will lower the value of your property. Can you imagine paying a contractor $3,000 to decrease your home's value by $5,000? This is a net loss of $8,000. You may not believe this can happen, but it can. Radical decisions can be very costly, so don't go crazy with unusual colors or products. Paying someone to reduce your home's value is inexcusable. Don't let it happen to you. Be sure your improvements are elevating your home's value. Research your remodeling plans, and be willing to compromise if necessary.

The fourth category is the most beneficial on a strictly business level. These improvements add more value than they cost. They also increase the marketability of your home. If you concentrate on these areas, you'll come up a winner. Read Chapter

7 for specific details; it contains five of the best projects to undertake. You will learn the principles needed to pick the best improvements. Use this information to your advantage. Remodeling for profit is an exciting opportunity.

THE RIGHT PROJECT FOR YOU

Deciding on the right project is the first step in protecting your investment. With the proper research, you can accomplish this with relative ease. Once you know what you should do, you have to decide *how* to do it. A lot can happen between the time you decide what to do and the time the project is completed. The remodeling process is filled with surprises, and some of them are expensive. What starts as a good investment can end up a loss. Your attention to detail during the project can make all the difference.

Recovering your investment depends on many factors. One of the largest variables is *you*. If you choose the wrong project, you might lose on your investment. If you pick the wrong general contractor, the results can be deflating. Bad decisions in layout and finishes can result in big losses. Straying from your original plans could reduce the appraised value or increase the estimated costs. The opportunity for a high profit exists when you make the most of the remodeling process. If you wait too long, the economy could change and labor and material prices could escalate.

THE EFFECT OF ECONOMIC CONDITIONS

When should you remodel for the highest return on your investment? Remodeling can be profitable under any economic conditions. A depressed economy offers some excellent benefits to the home remodeler. Material prices are typically lower. Labor costs are lower and there are more qualified contractors to choose from. These two factors mean larger savings on the expense of your project. Appraised values may be lower, but so are the costs of the job. If your improvement proves viable by an appraisal in bad times, you will be well rewarded in good times. Remodeling in a slow economy can mean huge profits when an aggressive real estate market returns.

There is a lot to be said for remodeling in bad times. You will have your pick of the most qualified contractors. Suppliers will cater to your needs more attentively. You are in a position of control, creating work when there aren't many projects available. You can capitalize on a weak economy. Any project that carries its own weight in a recession will soar later. If you can afford to remodel in slow times, do it. You will laugh all the way to the bank in a few years. In the meantime, you have the benefit of improved living conditions.

What about remodeling in good times? Remodeling is always advantageous, when it's done right. Stable times are geared more to new construction; this can benefit the home remodeler. In bad times, new construction tradesmen jump into remodeling. They don't have the experience to handle difficult remodeling projects. There are extreme differences in new construction and remodeling. In good times, these people are doing what they know best, building new houses. This thins the remodeling contractor selections down to the elite professionals.

Segregation of new construction and remodeling tradesmen takes some of the risks out of choosing the right contractor. It also makes finding a contractor a little harder, as there won't be as many contractors doing remodeling. This minor setback is really an advantage. You have fewer contractors to choose from, but the ones available are experienced remodelers. Remodeling during a booming economy has other advantages. Suppliers carry a larger stock of inventory, so you have more products to choose from. The prices might even be lower, due to the fast-paced competition. Getting service and deliveries from suppliers can be more difficult in good times. They are very busy and may not be as interested in a small homeowner account. This can be countered by dealing with smaller suppliers who are anxious to serve you.

Lenders are much more liberal in good economic conditions. If you need financing, this is the time to get it. Lenders will be apprehensive in a slow economy and aggressive in a fast one. Interest rates should be better and your choices in the type of loans available will be better. The financing side of remodeling is always better in a strong economy.

SELLING YOUR HOUSE

The last step to recovering your investment is selling your house. Even if relocating is not your immediate plan, it is probable you will sell your home at some point. This is undoubtedly easier in the good times. A winning strategy is to remodel in slow times and sell in fast times. This is the way to make the most profit. If you can swing your project in bad times, do the job. When the real estate cycle changes, you will be on top. Selling your house is one way to recover your remodeling dollars. The equity gain in your property is your profit, and it grows year after year. When you are ready to harvest your remodeling crop, you will have to refinance or sell.

REFINANCING

Refinancing is another opportunity to use your remodeling profits, without selling your home or suffering tax consequences. When remodeling profits increase your equity enough, you can borrow your own money. The loan is not considered income, and you have no taxes to pay while you are using the proceeds of the loan. There will be interest to pay, but this should be deductible from your taxes. When a project creates enough equity, this is an excellent way to get the use of your remodeling profits without selling. Consult with a tax expert for information on the proper procedure. The tax consequences will vary with different individuals and tax brackets.

If you sell your home, you can reinvest your profits to defer the tax bite. If you enjoyed this remodeling project, you may want to buy an older home to remodel. With the right skills, you can make serious money rehabbing old houses. Even in good times, you can buy a house in need of repair for a good price. The general public isn't interested in a house that requires investing time and money. Most people want to move in and relax. The lack of public interest keeps the sales price of older or poorly maintained houses low. If you are willing to invest a few hours and dollars, you can realize maximum profits from these diamonds in the rough.

PROPERTY DATA REPORT

Address_____

Total Square Footage of Living Space_____

Total Number of Rooms_____

Number of Bedrooms_____

Number of Full Bathrooms_____

Number of Powder Rooms_____

Number of Roughed-in Bathrooms_____

Age of the House_____

Formal Living Room Included?_____

Formal Dining Room Included?_____

Family Room Included?_____

Fireplace Included?_____

Wood Stove Hook-up Included?_____

Laundry Facilities Available?_____

Insulated Windows Installed?_____

Storm Windows Installed?_____

Window Screens Included?_____

Insulated Exterior Doors Installed?_____

Storm Doors Installed?_____

Type of Floor Coverings_____

Quality of Landscaping_____

Type and Size of Driveway_____

Type and Size of Garage, If Any_____

Appliances Included_____

School District_____

Legal Description_____

Exterior Color of House_____

House Style_____

Type of Construction_____

Lot Size_____

Type of Zoning_____

Annual Real Estate Taxes_____

Type of Siding_____

Type of Water Service_____

Type of Sewer Or Septic Service_____

Type of Heat_____

Type of Heating Fuel Used_____

Average Annual Heating Costs_____

Type of Hot Water Equipment_____

Type of Electrical Service_____

Total Amps of Electrical Service_____

Foundation Size_____

Type of Foundation_____

Age of Roof_____

Type of Roof Material_____

Type of Attic Space_____

Amount of Insulation: Attic_____

Amount of Insulation: Exterior Walls_____

Amount of Insulation: Crawl Space_____

Assumable Mortgage?_____

LIST ROOM LOCATIONS AND SIZES (example: master bedroom, 2nd floor, 14' x 16')

_____

_____

_____

_____

LIST UNUSUAL FEATURES (example: pools, spas, fencing, etc.)

_____

_____

_____

_____

COMMENTS

_____

_____

_____

_____

This will give you an idea of what appraisers will want to know. All of these factors affect the value of your home. This type of property data sheet will be used to determine the market value of your home.

COMPARABLE SALES COMPARISON SHEET

CATEGORY:	COMP 1	COMP 2	COMP 3	SUBJECT
Location				
Age				
Lot size				
Landscaping				
Style				
Construction				
Number of rooms				
Number of bathrooms				
Number of bedrooms				
Square footage				
Fireplaces				
Basement				
Garage				
Appliances				
Decks				
Porches				
Dining room				
Living room				
Family room				
Sales Price				
Adjustments				
Adjusted Value				

COMPARABLE SALES COMPARISON SHEET

CATEGORY:	COMP 1	COMP 2	COMP 3	SUBJECT
Location	busy traffic	quiet res.	quiet res.	quiet res.
Age	7 yrs.	6.5 yrs.	6 yrs.	6 yrs.
Lot size	70' x 150'	75' x 148'	65' x 150'	50' x 200'
Landscaping	good	good	good	good
Style	Cape Cod	Cape Cod	Cape Cod	Cape Cod
Construction	frame	frame	frame	frame
Number of rooms	9	9	9	7
Number of bathrooms	2	2	2	2.5
Number of bedrooms	3	3	3	3
Square footage	1,600	1,575	1,580	1,600
Fireplaces	1 brick	1 brick	1 brick	1 brick
Basement	unfinished	unfinished	unfinished	unfinished
Garage	yes	yes	yes	2-car att.
Appliances	range/retrig	range/retrig	range	range/retrig/dw
Decks	none	none	8' x 10'	none
Porches	none	none	none	none
Dining room	10' x 12'	11' x 11'	10' x 10'	10' x 14'
Living room	12' x 12'	11' x 14'	10' x 14'	12' x 12'
Family room	12' x 16'	11' x 16'	14' x 14'	12' x 16'
Sales Price	$113,000	$119,000	$117,000	
Adjustments	+ 12,500	+ 13,000	+ 11,000	
Adjusted Value	$125,500	$132,000	$128,000	

Be Different, But Don't Be Radical

6

Remodeling encompasses a wide range of endeavors, covering all enhancements to existing structures. Remodeling applies to building additions, as well as replacing worn sheet goods. The definition of remodeling is "to make over"; it implies giving your living space a new look. Structural changes, cosmetic improvements, and altering the use of space are all forms of remodeling. Even buying new kitchen appliances can be considered remodeling. When you say you are going to remodel your home, what do you think about? A new coat of paint qualifies as remodeling. Wallpaper, ceramic tile, insulation, and new plumbing fixtures all come under the heading of remodeling. Almost anything you do to your home can be called remodeling.

All these alterations affect the value of your home. Most of them increase your home's worth, but the wrong remodeling efforts can reduce the value of your home. Yes, there are some remodeling projects that hurt the resale of your house. It may not be fair, but you can spend money on your home and make it worth *less*. These negative improvements are not common, but there are enough of them to warrant your attention.

DON'T LOWER YOUR HOME'S VALUE

Something as simple as a color can devastate your home's sale price. Would you want to buy an orange house? Is purple really the preferred color for your front door? Red roofs are fine for motels, but be careful when you put one on a house. These are extreme examples, yet they provide a graphic illustration of how you could depreciate your home,

while trying to improve or customize it. The first impression a potential purchaser gets is of the exterior of a home. Having radical colors or landscaping can stop the sale of your home to potential buyers before it starts.

Paying a contractor to paint your home will cost the same, whether you paint it a shimmering chartreuse or plain old beige. You won't fully recover the cost of any paint job, and you will almost certainly lose much more money with an orange or lime green house. The dinosaur sculpture you made out of your front hedge can cost you the sale of your home. It's a great way for the pizza delivery person to find your house, but it isn't desirable to the public. This unique shrubbery sculpture will actually lower the value of your home. At the same time, it will make a bad impression on the average home buyer. I've heard people say, "I want my house to reflect my personality." This is fine, as long as it doesn't include a pink, heart-shaped tub in the bathroom.

Adding horseshoe pits in the backyard can provide hours of enjoyment. It can also ruin your landscaping value. The public may not want horseshoe pits, or well-worn paths to them, in their new backyard. Maybe you don't object to your old car dripping oil on the garage floor, but prospective buyers will have a different opinion. If you build a garage, protect the floor from oil stains and other destructive substances. Why invest $12,000 in a custom garage, only to let a few dollars worth of used oil ruin it? The point I'm getting to is one of awareness. Everyone has his or her own opinions and preferences, which may irritate others. Everything you do to your house will affect its value, so don't

Country French cabinets feature intricate fretwork and turned posts. Dish rack and hanging pot rack enhance the setting, as do the free-standing pieces such as the wall-mounted desk, the work island, and the vegetable bins at left. Courtesy of Crystal Cabinet Works.

This country kitchen includes a plate rack at right, arched valances, and decorative cutouts atop the upper open shelves. Courtesy of Quaker Maid.

This white kitchen is open and airy; its traditional styling has contemporary flair. The center island provides a second work surface. The lack of soffits above cabinets lets you use the space for display or more storage. Courtesy of Merillat Industries, Inc.

Built-in wine rack flanked by glass-door cabinets to hold cups or stemware provides easy access and a decorative touch. Courtesy of Quaker Maid.

This kitchen features work stations for two cooks. It has a baking center that doubles as a family office (see computer). Swing-up mixer is a space-saver, as is the lazy susan cabinet with shelves for condiments as well as a surface for rolling out cookies or pie dough. The cooking center has a low, under-cabinet microwave, plus a cooktop with front controls and staggered burners. Pull-out drawer has a recessed panel to hold mixing bowl and prevent slipping. Courtesy of Whirlpool Corp.

A second microwave installed in a lower cabinet area can be useful for those who must work while seated. The pull-out shelf below the oven holds hot dishes. Courtesy of Whirlpool Corp.

jeopardize one of your largest investments.

Let's take the house, room by room, and target trouble spots. The two main objectives to avoid in remodeling are *nonconformity* and *functional obsolescence*. These are appraisal terms that will have a negative impact on the value of your home. Curable functional obsolescence is a physical design or feature considered undesirable to the public. This type of functional obsolescence can be eradicated with minimal expense and remodeling. Incurable functional obsolescence represents similar problems, except they are not easily corrected and the cost of correction is prohibitive. Nonconformity refers to improvements in direct contrast to surrounding properties.

KITCHEN

The kitchen has a major impact on the value and sale of a house. It is an excellent place to direct your remodeling efforts. What should you look out for in kitchen remodeling? Walls and ceilings should be a light color, to make the room appear larger and the work space brighter. Avoid using institutional green; no one wants to feel like a cook in a correctional facility. Dark colors can be depressing; washing dishes is depressing enough, without help from the walls. The colors you pick for the kitchen are important. Your love of violets is not reason enough to paint your kitchen purple. If you insist on violets, use them as a stenciled accent, where the walls meet the ceiling.

Choose your lighting carefully; creative lighting adds a lot to a kitchen's appearance and use. If you skimp on light fixtures, you will regret it later. You will miss their benefits when using the kitchen and will feel their absence when you try to sell. Without proper lighting, your kitchen may resemble a cave with appliances. Don't let a few hundred dollars in light fixtures stand between you and gratification. Kitchen lights can make all the difference to you now and when the time comes to sell.

Harvest gold and avocado green appliances are history—these colors have been outdated for years. The safest approach to appliances is a neutral white or off-white. Appliances are a predominant part of any kitchen; their style and color dictate the entire kitchen decorating scheme. Making a profound statement with high fashion colors or specialty appliances can hurt the sales price of your home. A red refrigerator may accent the kitchen in your mind but ruin it in the public's opinion. Stick with neutral colors. They give you, and future owners, more flexibility in the decorating possibilities for the kitchen.

Specialty appliances can create appraisal and appeal problems. I have always been fond of wood-burning kitchen cook stoves. I am fascinated by the warming ovens, hot water tanks, and character of these stoves. When I was a child, they were common fixtures in many kitchens. Today, there are quality reproductions of these stoves available. They operate on various fuels and some, while maintaining the exterior appearance of the antiques, incorporate modern cooking conveniences. I must advise against their installation, however, unless it is in keeping with your kitchen's design. If your home supports the country kitchen atmosphere, these stoves seem to extend the continuity of your design.

Placing one of these high dollar stoves in your kitchen could lower your home's value. This type of stove is non-conforming and may not be well accepted by the public. Be careful when shopping for such designer items. They look terrific in promotional advertising but may have a detrimental effect on your home.

Cabinets occupy much of the kitchen's square footage; a bad decision here is hard to hide. Don't economize by installing flat, cardboard style cabinets. Buy a good quality, production line cabinet. A light-colored oak veneer is universally accepted, and white cabinets are gaining in popularity. Avoid detailed wood carvings; keep the cabinets simple. If you inject too much personal taste into the cabinets, your resale value may suffer. When the basic cabinets are attractive, a prospective buyer can simply change the doors to suit individual tastes. On fixed appurtenances, follow industry standards and don't exercise your creative genius and personal preferences.

Kitchen window treatments must be in keeping with the other decor. Intricate or busy patterns and grease-catching blinds can cause problems. Go with simple patterns and slick, easy to clean surfaces. Keep the colors neutral and light. Provide nice curtains, but don't spend a lot of money here. New buyers will often change the curtains when they move in.

Countertop selection is a serious consideration, because this is where most kitchen work is done. Corian® or authentic Butcher Block® is very desirable but very expensive. Tile countertops make a

Plan furniture purchases to enhance your newly remodeled space. The sideboard in this dining room can display china or collectibles, serve as a centerpiece for your room decoration. Courtesy of Crystal Cabinet Works.

strong statement in a kitchen, and can be attractive as well as practical. Tile can incorporate many different designs, styles, and colors. In expensive custom homes, tile countertops are extremely popular. You will not recover your investment in custom cabinets and countertops, unless other homes in the area have similar features. A standard laminated top, in an appropriate, neutral color and pattern, is suitable for most kitchens. Avoid dark colors and unconventional designs; keep the kitchen in good taste.

The floor is an area of interest to the housekeeper and prospective buyers. Typically, you will find sheet vinyl flooring in a kitchen. This is the accepted standard and is your safest investment for the average kitchen. Some country style kitchens will have wide plank, wooden flooring. These floors are unique and provide cosmetic advantages, but they are expensive. They also require extensive work to maintain. Water can stain wood floors, and kitchens are a likely place for accidental spills of every kind. Only invest in wood floors if the motif of the kitchen demands it.

DINING ROOM

Formal dining rooms are becoming popular again. There are not many remodeling options with a dining room, but you can lose big bucks fast with the few that exist. The first item of discussion is lighting, specifically the chandelier. These can be very expensive. When the value of your home is calculated, the appraiser will write, "One Chandelier," on the evaluation report. The appraiser will not know, or care, if the chandelier was imported from Europe. Regardless of whether it's made of diamonds or cut glass, it is only a chandelier. Don't get carried away at your electrical supplier. You need a dining room light, but keep it simple. You will never recover the cost of the more expensive fixtures.

Wallpaper frequently accents a formal dining room. A room with wallpaper and a chair rail will appraise for more than one with a painted surface. The problem is, you can still lose a bundle by choosing the wrong wallpaper. Remember the chandelier example; whether it is hand painted or imported, it is only wallpaper to an appraiser. Mahogany chair rail will be worth the same as pine on an appraisal report.

Crown molding falls into the same category as chair rail. It will add value, but not enough to compensate for extravagant costs. Prudent shopping will provide you with many sound, cost-effective improvement ideas for the dining room. Spend the money to add chair rails, crown moldings, and wallpaper, but don't buy imported materials. You cannot hope to regain your investment from this type of specialty purchase.

Flooring is the last major component of your

Consider making your space multi-use if possible. The room shown has durable carpeting and leather upholstery to stand up to wear; walls are durable paneling. The room has an entertainment center, an exercise area, and a conversation space. Courtesy of Plywood Paneling Council.

Zero-clearance fireplaces let you install a fireplace just about anywhere. Courtesy of Heat 'N Glo Fireplace Products Inc.

dining room. The two basic choices are carpet or wood flooring. When selecting carpet, the ideal combination is a good carpet with an outstanding pad. Purchase stain resistant carpet in a neutral color. There is nothing worse than spilling spaghetti sauce on a pure white carpet with no stain protection agent. Carpet costs run from about $6 to over $27 per square yard. A good carpet can be bought in the $14 to $18 range.

The secret to lush carpet is the pad. The quality of the pad will also increase the life of the carpet. You won't recover the cost of plush, costly carpets, so don't spend the money needlessly. Don't install a vinyl floor in a formal dining room. Vinyl is certainly practical in a room where cleaning food spills is likely, but it is not an acceptable surface in formal living space. A vinyl floor in the formal dining room could cause a functional obsolescence rating on your appraisal report.

LIVING ROOM

A formal living room is very similar to the dining room; the same rules apply. Use similar techniques in accenting a formal living room. Provide some elegant accents, but keep the expenditures under control. It would not be appropriate to install a wet bar in the corner of a formal living room. Keep this stately space in compliance with the expectations of a regal room. Formal chambers are meant for show rather than enjoyment.

FAMILY ROOM

Family rooms require special consideration and can take a lighter approach in design. The family room should be equipped to handle heavy traffic. Invest in a strong carpet pad and durable carpet. Don't concern yourself with fancy light fixtures, but provide generous lighting. Make the lower sections of the wall destruction resistant. Kids are rough on walls, and family rooms are designed with children in mind. Wainscoting or paneling is a good investment here, and the surface should be smooth and washable. Even the best-behaved children derive great pleasure from coloring the walls. A rugged surface will hold its own against paint, darts, tape, and tumbling blocks. Eliminate wallpaper and expensive trim moldings in the family room.

If you go with paint above wainscoting, the paint should be washable. Marks made by bouncing balls and hand prints will be easier to remove with a washable paint. Provide plenty of electrical outlets for televisions, games, stereos, and lighting. Overhead lights will be appreciated in the family room, so use track lighting or recessed units. There will be a lot of activity in this room; keep the area open and uncluttered. Allow plenty of space for furniture and for children to play. Built-in benches, covered with cushions, provide space-saving seating and extra storage space. Equip the benches with shelves, drawers, or flip-up tops. Overall, the room should be kept simple and livable, with an atmosphere of comfort and relaxation.

BEDROOMS

Bedrooms should offer open space and simple designs. Painted walls are fine, and light fixtures can be kept to a minimum. Closet space is of paramount importance in all bedrooms. It is not necessary for closets to be the walk-in type, or cedar lined, but they must provide adequate space. If you neglect to build a closet in the room, an appraiser will not consider the space a bedroom. Even small closets should have a light; porcelain, pull-chain fixtures are sufficient. Carpets can be of moderate quality; they will not receive heavy traffic. Still, a good pad should be used to extend the life of the carpeting. There remains a high desire for switched, overhead bedroom lighting in the real estate market. Include an attractive, closed ceiling fixture, such as a globe light (avoid the old bug catchers).

Bedrooms are personal havens. Many are appointed with cable television, a VCR, and a stereo. Consider your individual needs when remodeling a bedroom; however, limit your personality to removable items, such as bedspreads, draperies, and artwork. When searching for dream book ideas to add or remodel a child's room, beware of publications encouraging radical self-expression. You will see pictures of built-in beds shaped like trains, ceilings adorned with glow-in-the dark stars, walls painted with life-sized unicorns, and even suspended ropes and poles to swing on. Consider the idea that your daughter might outgrow the unicorn stage, or the next child to use this room might be a boy. Be realistic: remember it is very likely someone else will own this house at some point and want to change what you have done. It is completely senseless to spend money on improvements that will eventually have to be ripped out or painted over.

Sculptured armrests and adjustable air volume controls on both sides make comfortable bathing for two. Courtesy of Royal Baths.

BATHROOMS

Bathrooms offer vast opportunities for improvements. The bathroom has more potential, per square foot, than any other room in your house. Cosmetic improvements to the bathroom can include: changing plumbing fixtures, installing a new floor covering, painting, wallpapering, tile work, new cabinets, new lights, and a host of other eye-catching possibilities. These cosmetic improvements add to the appearance and value of a bathroom. Much more complex and expensive improvements involve: adding additional plumbing fixtures, enlarging the room, adding a window or skylight, increasing storage facilities, and completely redesigning the space.

Bathroom remodeling is a safe bet; it is one of the most reliable remodeling projects available for making a profit. Unless you break the rules of remodeling, you will almost never be financially hurt from remodeling a bathroom. Some of the mistakes you could make are in product selection. Free-standing metal showers are not a good investment; they cheapen a bathroom and deflate your home's

market value. Installing exotic fixtures with high fashion colors can be a mistake too. When these fixtures are installed in an average house, they are overpowering. Unless the rest of your home is modern and flashy, avoid these designer fixtures. They are expensive and their value will never be appreciated in the typical, production-style homes.

Specialty fixtures can cause financial trouble fast in a standard bathroom. If your bathroom is small and the rest of your house is built in "basic builder-grade" fashion, be careful when considering specialty fixtures. Have you seen those unique toilets with the tank hanging high on the wall? There is a chain dangling from the tank allowing you to pull the chain and flush the toilet. A decorative tube runs from the tank to the toilet, and both the tank and bowl are accented in a wood finish. These toilets are beautiful and nostalgic; they also cost more than some used cars. Making a decision to install such a classic fixture can cost you plenty. You will pay a premium price to acquire the fixture, and it may hurt the value of your home. It could be considered non-conforming, and prospective buyers may not appreciate your love of simulated antique

This frameless shower door opens up and enlarges the bath area. The ¼-inch tempered clear glass has rounded edges on all four sides for safety. Courtesy of Century Shower Door, Inc.

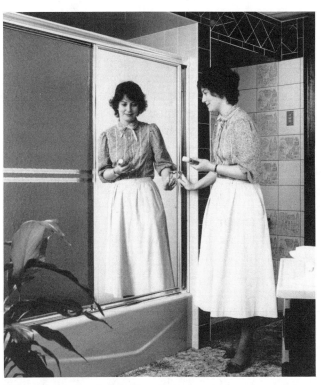

This shower enclosure has tempered glass for safety. The mirrored door makes the bathroom look larger. Courtesy of Century Shower Door, Inc.

A shower enclosure built for two offers a choice of steam bath or shower. Note the hinged transom and stationary shower ceiling, so the steam bath feature is possible with any ceiling configuration. Courtesy of Century Shower Door, Inc.

This combination of mirrors and mirrored cabinet doors not only provides storage space but serves as makeup/shaving mirrors and makes the space seem larger. Courtesy of Robern Inc.

plumbing fixtures. Ultra-modern fixtures can cause similar reactions. Corner toilets are wonderful when space is limited or in contemporary settings. These toilets could be considered odd and undesirable in the average house. Corner showers may meet with the same negative response in a typical home.

Modern soaking tubs make a fantastic alternate tub, but as a primary bathing facility, they have some undesirable qualities. Soaking tubs are very deep and have seats for the occupant to sit on. Due to design, soaking tubs are limited in their ability to provide shower facilities. If you enjoy soaking in a hot bath, these tubs are hard to beat. If you are elderly or physically restricted, they are nearly impossible to enter and exit. Their depth requires a high volume of water, and producing the hot water to fill them is expensive. Resist the urge to install this type of tub as your only bathing facility. Your home's market value and desirability can be greatly reduced by any of these expensive indulgences. Obvious extremes to avoid include: pewter or gold faucets, marble floors, hand-crafted tile, imported cabinets, and environmental control habitat units. These luxuries can only be justified in the most expensive homes.

PERSONAL TOUCHES

Think twice before adding strong personal touches to your home. Remember, your home may need to be appealing to the public in the future. Painting your favorite football team's logo on the study wall is not a great idea. If you must do it, do it so you can hide it later. Control your impulses to define your child's room as a boy's or a girl's. The new buyers' child may be older or of the opposite sex. This can reduce the market appeal of any home.

When you break the rules and customize a room with unusual effects, be smart about it. Use colors that can easily be painted over. If you have to paint a black and silver team logo on the wall, plan to wallpaper later. For children's rooms, try to keep your artistic work low on the wall. This will allow you to panel or wallpaper half the wall and paint the rest. It's your house and you should enjoy it, but do so wisely.

Hanging your photography for the world to see is rewarding, but the holes in the wall are a problem. The weight of water beds ruins carpets. Pets can leave an unmistakable odor. Wood stoves discolor walls and ceilings. Where should you draw the line? Live in the house and enjoy it, but don't abuse it. Before making extreme, nonconforming improvements, consider the price you will have to pay later for your defiance of the rules.

Wild colors and unique approaches to decorating will not be well received. For a musician, it may be perfectly normal to have carpet on the walls. It improves the acoustics but torpedoes your home's value. Having only wood heat will satisfy the pioneer in you, but the banks won't be favorably impressed when asked to make a loan. A house is more than a place to live; it is a major investment. You must recognize this fact and treat it as such. If the urge is more than you can stand, dedicate a single room as your refuge.

Hang the shiny, flocked wallpaper and install your posters and black lights. Get crazy, pretend it is your childhood clubhouse, but contain these unique personal expressions to a single room. It's easier to revamp one room than a whole house. If you have a basement, this can be the ideal area to transform into your personal expression place. Basements are separated from the primary living area and offer many benefits.

BASEMENT

Unfinished basements provide space for storage, fun, and unconventional uses. You can make an unfinished basement into your retreat from the real world. It can house a shooting range, a bowling lane, a putting green, or a year-round garden. Basements provide unlimited opportunities for hobbyists and adults with expansive collections. Electric trains can roam these open spaces, and woodworking facilities can produce a welcome additional income from craft preparation and sales. There are not many rules involved with unfinished basements; you can do just about anything you want.

Before investing money in finishing a basement, do extensive research. Depending on the type of basement you have, the money invested to complete it may never be recovered. Basement conversions are difficult to profit from, unless you do all the work yourself and shop for the lowest prices on basic materials for the completion. Instead of finishing the space, enjoy the unrestricted use of the existing space. There is a certain amount of satisfaction about being able to be as roudy as you want in an unfinished basement.

DIFFERENT VS. RADICAL

When you are planning your remodeling procedures, how will you know the difference between different and radical? Being different can produce unusually high profits, being radical can put you in line for bankruptcy. It is essential for you to be able to recognize the difference. Take a few moments to study the following words of advice, and don't forget them.

The epitome of being different is the ability to place your home on a higher plane than the competition. The differences must be subtle, cost effective, and in good taste. A one hundred dollar pedestal sink is a striking improvement over a sixty dollar wall-hung lavatory. Six-panel doors are a decisive improvement over flat lauan doors. Solid wood six-panel doors and their hollow core counterparts give the same visual impression, but the hollow core paneled doors cost half as much. Refacing kitchen cabinets gives the appearance of new cabinets at a fraction of the cost.

Herringbone wainscoting can provide your family room with a look of distinction. Attractive landscaping complements any house and is historically a profitable investment. Small decorative accessories have the ability to distinguish your home from others in the neighborhood. All of these are ways to be different without being radical.

Radical changes definitely draw attention to your home, but they are detrimental to the home's value. Installing a swinging bridge from your parking area to your front door will be different, but it will destroy the curb appeal of most homes. Extreme colors are the most common radical mistake; restrict your expressive artwork to the easel. Eliminating windows will make your addition more energy efficient, but the appraiser will not give high marks for this type of energy conservation. Lofts are popular, but don't build one requiring a ladder for access; it will not enhance your equity position.

Use common sense in evaluating your remodeling plans; there are plenty of ways to protect yourself from financial roulette. Following the advice in this book will educate you in the evaluation of your plans. Obtaining an appraisal before doing the work is the surest way to protect yourself. Reviewing and comparing your proposed plans with neighboring homes is another viable approach to making the right decision. There is no excuse for an informed homeowner to lessen the value of the home. The sources available for guidance are numerous, and with the proper research you can avoid costly mistakes.

Successful remodeling jobs are made with work, effort, and conforming standards. No homeowner wants to hear an appraiser use the two terms we spoke of earlier: "functional obsolescence" or "nonconforming." These two words can mean the end of your retirement plans. If your house is labeled with either of these terms, losing money is inevitable. You can avoid these ugly words by avoiding radical changes in your house. Follow Dodge's remodeling rules, and protect yourself from heavy financial losses. Remodeling should be fun and profitable.

The Five Most Profitable Remodeling Projects

7

Have you ever played a game of darts? It is difficult for a novice to throw a bull's eye every time. The darts may hit the wall, the floor, even your teammate. It takes skill and a little luck to hit the center of the target. Many people feel the same way about remodeling ventures. Is it actually possible to come up with a winning combination when you alter your home? Yes, you only need to know which improvements are money makers, and which are big-time losers. There really is a method to all this madness. So far, you have learned how to establish and design a cost-effective project. You have evaluated the feasibility and financial advantages of your intended changes. In this chapter, we will concentrate on the grand slam winners of the remodeling game.

Remodeling winners vary with your own personal situation. To identify a money-making project, you have to discern your home's current and future value. A home's actual value is determined by a professional appraisal. If you learn to understand appraisal techniques, you will know where to invest your time and money. Professional appraisers use more than one technique to determine a home's value. For remodeling jobs, they use two basic methods.

THE COST METHOD

The cost approach is the first system used to establish value. When working with the cost approach, the appraiser will assign estimated values to each phase of your project. The combined total of the estimated cost of each segment represents the total value of the improvement. Appraisers are concerned with the physical characteristics of your project in this approach.

The appraiser will complete a comprehensive report, based on your plans and specifications. He or she assigns a value to every aspect of your job using figures based on established industry prices. Individual appraisers may allot differing values to items, but the result shouldn't vary more than 5% between appraisals. Remodeling appraisals do not deal with site conditions, and land values aren't a factor. The appraiser must establish the value of the proposed improvement to the existing property.

THE SQUARE FOOT METHOD

One of the methods used may be the square foot method. This involves assigning a value based on the square footage of your improvement. For additions, garages, and similar projects, this is an acceptable technique. The appraiser can base an opinion of value on other comparable structures in the area. This method does not work for interior improvements to existing houses. Square footage approaches are only applicable to projects adding space to your home.

In new construction, the square foot method can be reasonably accurate. The appraiser measures the square footage from the blueprints. Each mechanical phase, such as plumbing and electrical, is then given a typical square foot cost. An appraiser's guide might suggest a value of $2.50 per square foot for plumbing; in a new home or large addition, this could be fairly accurate. With interior remodeling, it's absurd. Remodeling of this type does not allow the use of industry averages.

Frequently, the space being altered is small, and the square footage cost is high.

The square footage method is not accurate in most residential remodeling. There are too many variables. A standard family room will cost a certain amount. A family room with a quarry tile floor and a stone fireplace is much more expensive. A normal bathroom may be worth a set figure, but a whirlpool destroys the square footage pricing method. When appraisers deal with residential remodeling, they earn their money. This type of appraisal requires talent and research.

THE DIRECT MARKET EVALUATION APPROACH

The direct market evaluation approach is also used when placing a value on remodeling projects. This method compares your home to other houses in the area. The value is derived from closed sales. Appraisers judge your improvements against other recently sold homes. They compare similar features, such as age, total number of rooms, and number of bathrooms. They also compare the number of bedrooms, house style, and the home's condition. Other factors are size, location, type of construction, and any unique characteristics. This is where being distinctive, without being radical, pays off.

This is the appraisal method most often used in determining the market value of a home. The cost approach is important, but banks prefer the market approach. Lenders want to know what they could sell the property for, not how much was invested. They are only concerned with the probable sales price. Banks are eternal pessimists, always expecting the worst; this is probably justified by bad experiences. They want to loan money, not sell foreclosed properties. You can learn something from banks. If the bank doesn't believe in your project, reconsider your plans.

Bankers have been down the road; they know which cards to hold and which ones to throw away. Of course, they make mistakes; perhaps your project is the exception to the rule, but be careful. If you feel strongly about the improvement, make sure you know the consequences of your actions. Professional appraisers are right more often than they are wrong. Give close consideration to your plans before breaking the rules.

WHAT DO APPRAISERS LOOK FOR?

What factors do appraisers look for? They look at the primary features of the home and the project. These include style, construction, and the number of bedrooms. How does your house stack up against the sold properties in your neighborhood? Will your intended improvements be profitable? The appraisal report will answer both of these questions. Make your decision based on accurate information and capitalize on your appraisal report.

Now you understand how the appraiser assesses the value of your project, but which projects produce the greatest return? There are five time-tested, surefire choices. Controlling the urge to interject your personality excessively allows the Fabulous Five to put money in your pocket.

BATHROOMS

The first of these projects is bathrooms. If the plumbing is accessible, the cost of remodeling an existing bathroom will be moderate, and the profit will be above average. Converting a closet or the space under a stairway into a powder room is also very lucrative. A basic powder room will require a toilet and a wall-hung lavatory with a faucet. The rough plumbing required is minimal, as long as existing plumbing is accessible. Minor electrical wiring will be necessary to conform to local codes, and an exhaust fan will need to be installed. The work for the conversion will be insignificant compared to your profit. The value of the closet can't compare with that of a powder room.

Full bathrooms can net an even higher profit. The percentage of profit will be lower, but the financial gain will be greater. The return on the job is usually directly related to the size of the project. In total dollars earned, larger jobs net more profit. A small job can net a high percentage of profit, but that doesn't mean it will produce more money. Most remodelers are interested in the total dollars earned. If you are looking to make the big score, investigate larger projects.

Bathrooms offer vast opportunities for improvements. The bathroom has more potential, per square foot, than any other space in your house. Bathrooms and kitchens sell more houses than any other rooms. Get ready to take notes, I'm going to show you how to make the most of your bathroom. When you approach bathroom remodeling, you

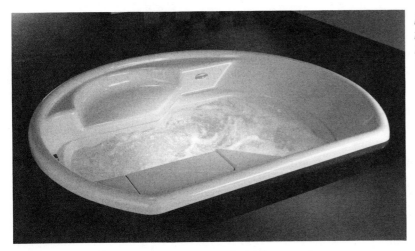

Italian bath design in this Maurea model features adjustable water jets, seat for bathside grooming, and mirrored vanity. Courtesy of Jacuzzi Corp.

This 6-foot tub is wide and deep enough to accommodate two bathers. Courtesy of Jacuzzi Corp.

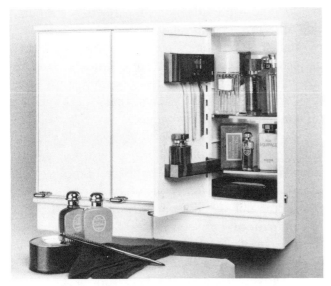

This locking bath cabinet has built-in storage for makeup, toothbrushes, and prescription medicines. Courtesy of Allibert SA Inc.

Children's bath time becomes playtime with this children's hand shower called "Nessie," after the Loch Ness Monster. Courtesy of Grohe America.

have countless options, and the possibilities are endless. You can replace your fixtures, expand the room, add lights and mirrors, or totally rehab the room.

Practically anything you do to improve a bathroom will be returned to you with a profit. I am not saying you should install $2,500 gold faucets, but this is a room you can capitalize on. Personal hygiene is high on the list of most individuals. A room conducive to making you look better is important. Statistics show women are frequently the deciding factor in the sale of a home. A designer bathroom with a makeup area is a distinctive amenity. Don't overlook the importance of a captivating bathroom.

Kitchens are important, but they are meant for work. Consumers *want* appealing kitchens, but they will *buy* unique bathrooms. What areas of the bathroom are important? All of them! Homeowners prefer a spacious room that is easy to clean. The plumbing fixtures will make a difference here. A pedestal sink, with faucets on 8-inch centers, is easy to clean. All the surfaces are smooth, and there is plenty of room to scrub around the faucets. Pedestal sinks are associated with luxury. Many people think the sink alone costs $500, and the faucets add another $200. Unfortunately, this misconception often steers the homeowner to purchase a rimmed lavatory and standard faucet.

Rimmed sinks, with 4-inch center faucets, slow the cleaning process. They are the accepted fixture for average houses, but they don't make for a memorable impression. The cost of this setup is approximately $150. With selective shopping, you can have a stunning pedestal sink and faucet for roughly $275. The additional money is minimal compared to the benefits and profits you derive. The unit will be much easier to clean, the room's value will soar, and you will have a high yield from your investment.

Now, on to the tub and shower. Fiberglass showers require less effort to clean than ceramic tile. They are also considerably less expensive than installing tile. Fiberglass units have become the industry standard and offer many advantages. There is a multitude of high quality fiberglass units designed for remodeling. The remodeling units are fabricated in sections, to allow installation in existing bathrooms. With quality fiberglass tubs and showers, you will not be bothered by water leaks in the future. Unless you have an extremely exotic home, or a love for tile, fiberglass is the best choice. The money saved will be impressive, and your full investment will be returned when the home is sold.

When ceramic tile is used, it will need extensive cleaning, to avoid mildew and staining in the grout. Periodic repairs must be performed on the grouting to prevent water damage to the bathroom walls and floors. All of this is avoided when a fiberglass unit is installed. Basic "builder-grade" ceramic tile will increase the value of your bathroom. Unfortunately, the increased value will not exceed your initial investment. At the most, it will allow you to recover only your costs at the time of sale. Money spent on elaborate tile work will not be recovered, unless it is the standard for homes in the neighborhood.

The design of the toilet can also diminish cleaning time and leave a prominent impression. One-piece toilets offer the most advantages. With their sleek design, cleaning is a cinch. There are fewer places for dirt to accumulate, and there is no gap between the tank and the bowl. One-piece toilets are a natural complement to pedestal sinks. The look of elegance is achieved.

One-piece toilets offer the disadvantage of being expensive, and they don't represent the best value in monetary terms. Like tile work, their expense will be recovered, but without a noticeable profit. For appearance, ease of cleaning, and appeal, one-piece toilets prevail. Where prudent investing is the concern, buy a standard two-piece toilet. These standard toilets will not detract from the look of the bathroom, and they offer a better rate of return on your money.

Bathroom remodeling can often be very intimidating. Many people perceive antiquated fixtures and warped drywall as a curse they must learn to accept. I'm about to show you how easy it is to make a little magic. Let's set the scene.

You have an ancient toilet, stained by years of use. There is a dull wall-hung lavatory, with a cracked rubber stopper and battered faucets. Your tub is a cold cast-iron monster, with rust stains at the spout. The acrylic tub surround, with the blue marble pattern, has seen better days. The once water-resistant walls beside the tub are done for. The tub caulking disintegrated long ago, and water is invading your walls. Hanging from a tarnished shower rod is a mildewed plastic shower curtain. The old chrome shower head spits intermittent streams of water through its mineral-clogged holes.

The floor is worn, and tiles are missing. The window trim has turned black from moisture, allowing cold air to rush past the loose glazing. The once white ceiling is a dingy gray, with evidence of moisture damage and mildew. On the wall is a horrible white enamel medicine cabinet. It has a fogged, distorted mirror and that questionable razor blade slot. (Where do those razor blades go anyway?) The one electrical outlet is part of the light fixture on the medicine cabinet and is too high to be practical. Does this sound like your bathroom? It's a common design in older homes. At one time, any bathroom was a privilege. Today, the bathroom is an integral part of the home, and old styles are no longer acceptable.

You take one look at the bathroom and wonder, what can you possibly do to improve it? No matter what you do, it will still be small. There is no practical way to enlarge it, and you assume it is hopeless. Don't be intimidated, you can conquer this bathroom battle. The options have no end. You can spend between $1,500 and $10,000 on your bathroom. The glory is, you will recover all of your expense and more. The conservative approach requires working with your existing space; this may be the best approach. Conquering this gloomy bathroom can be your biggest accomplishment.

The first step of the actual work is obtaining the proper permits from the codes enforcement office. The second step is demolition. Before beginning the demo process, remove all your personal effects from the bathroom. A good remodeler can rip out and haul away a bathroom in a single day. If you are handy and want to save money, you can do much of this work yourself. Wear safety glasses, and be careful around the plumbing. A pipe ruptured during over-zealous demolition will ruin your day. Consider renting a portable trash container to make removal of the debris simple. These containers are available on a weekly rental basis. You pay a small deposit, and the container is delivered to your site. When you are done, the company will haul away the trash bin and your demolition debris.

Complete bathroom remodeling will strip the room to the bare studs and floor joists. If you do this work yourself, be careful to avoid existing plumbing and electrical wiring. These items are hidden in the walls and must be respected. Hire a plumber to relocate pipes as needed to meet the requirements of your new fixtures. Contract an electrician to update your electrical wiring. This work will include ground fault circuit interrupter (GFCI) outlets, to provide protection from electrical shock in damp conditions. Allow for ample lighting in the ceiling, sink, and shower locations.

Carpenters will replace the plywood subfloor and underlayment. They should also replace that old, water-damaged window. The substitute should be a quality, energy-efficient window. Next, the plumber will install your new fiberglass tub and shower unit. Any old piping should be updated at this stage. Much of this work will require inspection by the local codes enforcement office. Once the rough-in inspections are complete, you are ready to hang and tape the drywall. This is a time-consuming process, requiring three separate trips to complete. If the joint compound does not dry well, it could take a full week to complete.

Once the walls are ready for paint, the job will start to move quickly again. The walls and ceilings will be painted. After the paint, your new vinyl floor will be installed. You will then be ready for the plumber to install the remaining fixtures. The new toilet will sparkle and give a whole new look to the bathroom. The oak vanity will be set in place. A cultured marble top with an attractive faucet creates an impressive sink combination. The faucet trim will be placed on the tub faucet, and your new water-massage shower head will be installed.

The carpenters will hang your oak medicine cabinet and clean the new mirror. Electricians will come in next to accent the medicine cabinet with oak light strips. Perhaps they are also installing a heat lamp/fan combination in the ceiling. This will expel moisture to the outside and warm you after a shower. The last step is the finish flooring and baseboard trim.

With a little cleaning, you now have a brand new bathroom. The cost will be between $5,000 and $8,000; the results will be priceless. Your investment is safe, and you should recover all of your expenses at the time of resale. In many cases, you will gain a noticeable profit in addition to your initial investment. Perhaps the best result is a pleasant place to spend your mornings and evenings. Your bathroom nightmare is now a dream come true.

KITCHENS

Kitchens also offer an excellent return on your remodeling dollar. Well-planned improvements in the kitchen can add thousands of dollars to the appraised value of your home. Kitchens are similar to bathrooms in their importance to appraised value. Owners spend extended time in the kitchen and the bathrooms, and they want to be comfortable.

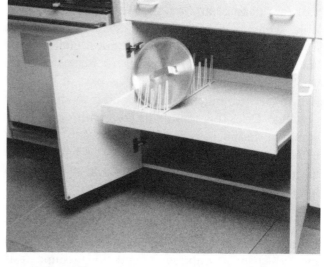

Basic cabinets can be dressed up and made more useful with the optional equipment shown. Slide-out wastebasket keeps trash hidden from sight; pull-out pan racks keep pot lids and pans close at hand; spice rack fits on the inside of the cabinet door to relieve countertop clutter. Courtesy of Merillat Industries, Inc.

An attractive custom kitchen design, featuring work island with sink, ceramic tile floor and backsplash, and granite-look countertops. Courtesy of Grohe America.

This kitchen features a work area open to the eating area, all enhanced by tall windows and a Southwestern-influenced design. Courtesy of Grohe America.

The Wine Captain displays your finest vintages while chilling them to proper temperatures. The unit can be built in under base cabinets or left free-standing. Courtesy of U-Line Corp.

Space-saving arrangement features a combination microwave/hood over free-standing or set-in range. Courtesy of Whirlpool Corp.

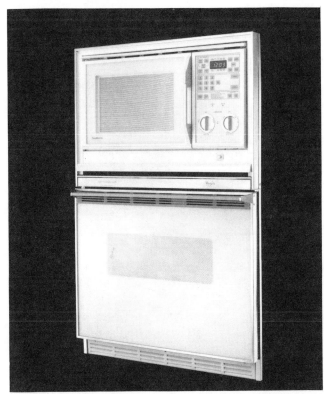

White-on-white cooking duo combines microwave speed and versatility with a self-cleaning conventional oven, sure to impress the family cook as well as the prospective owner at resale time.

This refrigerator is a refreshment center featuring a serving space with built-in counter, custom ice dispenser, and family-sized refrigerator and freezer capacity. Courtesy of Sears.

This cooktop combines four solid cooking elements with a Griddle-n-Grill feature. It has a hoodless downdraft ventilation system. Courtesy of Thermador.

Automatic ice maker can be built in under a counter or left free-standing. The unit produces up to 23 pounds and stores up to 12 pounds of ice per day. Courtesy of U-Line.

To heat food more quickly, try a quartz halogen heating cartridge in this electric downdraft cooktop. The quartz halogen unit produces instantaneous light and heat. Courtesy of Modern Maid.

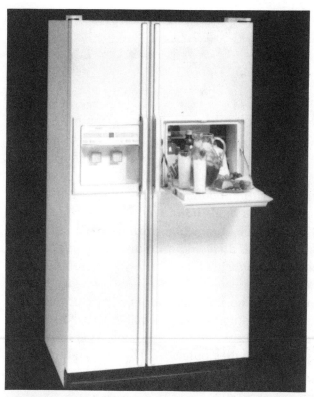

This refrigerator features side-by-side freezer convenience with custom exterior ice and water dispenser. This unit also has a Countermaker compartment for easy access to frequently used items. Courtesy of Hotpoint.

The industry's first all-gas downdraft range. Cartridges are available for a cooktop grill, griddle, or rotisserie. Courtesy of Modern Maid.

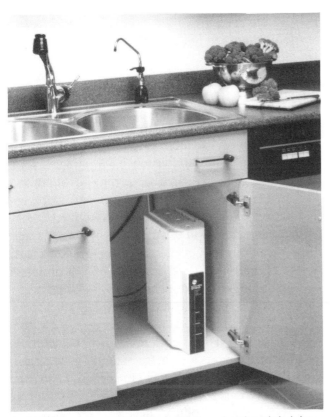

A drinking water system mounted under the sink (also available for mounting under upper cabinets). Courtesy of Kitchen Spring™.

This kitchen sink is equipped with Grohe's Ladylux pull-out scrubber. Courtesy of Grohe America.

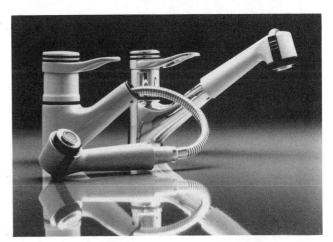

Consider these practical pull-out spray heads for kitchen faucets. Courtesy of Grohe America.

able. It's mundane to work in a dull, uninspiring kitchen. Twenty-year-old appliances are not conducive to a favorable impression, and kitchens with cramped working space are detrimental to any house. If you have limited remodeling money to spend, consider spending it in the kitchen.

You can apply many tricks of the trade to kitchen remodeling. Look at the main considerations of the space. These are food storage and preparation, cooking, cleanup, and sometimes dining. Before you tear the old cabinets off the wall, consider installing new doors and face trim. The

facelift makes the cabinets appear new. You gain the same equity from these counterfeit cabinets as you would from all new cabinetry. By investing a fraction of the money, you receive the full value of new cabinets.

Repaint flat walls with grease resistant, high gloss paint. Adding an attractive stenciled border to your walls is very popular; it updates the appearance of your kitchen at a negligible cost. Have an electrician install some decorative lighting. Lights under the wall cabinets will completely change the kitchen's work space. This is an inexpensive project;

the lights can usually be wired and installed in less than a day. Take a look at your appliances. If they came over with the first settlers, replace them. Appliances set the pace for any kitchen; invest in neutral colors to allow for creative decorating. A range with a built-in grill is impressive to appraisers and purchasers alike. If you spend some of your retained savings for this item, it will be reflected in the home's value. If the kitchen is large enough, consider including an island work area. These units can change the whole complexion of a kitchen.

Is your countertop chipped, scratched, and crying to be replaced? Before you run out and purchase a new laminated countertop, think about this. Wouldn't your counter area look fabulous with a tiled countertop? A tiled countertop will customize the entire kitchen, as well as resisting scratches and burns. In many cases, the tile contractor can even install the tile over your existing countertop. In the right neighborhood, this change will add big money to your kitchen's value and desirability. The expense of tiled countertops may not be recovered unless surrounding homes have similar kitchen amenities. Check your market evaluations before committing to a tiled top.

Converting grease-stained painted walls into attractive storage is a solid idea. Have a carpenter make the best use of your ignored wall space. Add attractive shelves, pan racks, or additional cabinets. Shelving board is a bargain. You can get up to a 100% return on your investment in custom shelves and pantries. Kitchen storage is of interest to all homeowners. If cabinets seem nonfunctional, change them. Consider converting obsolete cabinets into productive space. Install pull-out shelves for pots and pans, or remove the cabinet doors over the range to create book shelves or spice racks. Replace a base and wall cabinet with a pantry. Money spent on moderately priced cabinets will easily be returned in the sale of your home.

Window treatments are also a simple way to add to the value of your kitchen. Avoid plastic, roll-up shades, and invest in attractive, subtle curtains with valances. These cheerful accessories can be the finishing touch conveying a positive atmosphere to appraisers and buyers alike. Mental warfare of this kind will get you a better price for your efforts. Attractive decorations can be functional, while enhancing your kitchen. Something as simple as hanging baskets can provide an appealing place to store vegetables or to accommodate small herb gardens.

Be sure the accessories are in keeping with the style of the kitchen. Do not put country accents in an ultra-modern kitchen.

GARAGES

Ready to add even more value to your home? Garages offer an excellent rate of return. If most of the homes in your subdivision have garages, yours should too. The principal deterrent to building a garage is a difficult site. Extensive site work and foundation costs can reduce the effectiveness of a garage investment. Put the digging aside, and garages can be gold mines. Given acceptable ground conditions, you can see equity gains in excess of $5,000 from your long-awaited garage.

A general appraised value for garages is $15 per square foot, and a standard two-car garage contains 576 square feet. There is no real difference between an attached garage and a free-standing garage, as far as the appraised value is concerned. Using this formula, the garage is worth $8,640. There are contractors willing to produce these garages for $3,995. Does this mean adding a garage will put over $4,500 in your pocket? It is absolutely possible! By building to minimum standards, and shopping construction labor and material prices, you can take advantage of the appraisal system. The building materials used are one way of getting the most for your money from the appraised value.

Most garage appraisals deal with the total amount of dry square footage for automobile storage. They don't always specify construction materials. You could save money on a detached garage by framing it on a concrete slab, poured on level ground without a footing. Framing the walls with 2" X 4" studs, 24 inches on center instead of 16 inches on center, will also save you money. The roof system can be an inexpensive, pre-fab truss system, covered by pressed particle board. The roof felt could be omitted completely.

Exterior wall sheathing is not required by most building codes for garages, and siding can be applied to bare studs. A concrete apron isn't mandatory, and insulation and drywall are rare. Pull-down attic stairs or storage ceiling joists are not required. You don't even have to install windows or a standard entry door. Although you may opt to include some of these features, these are examples of ways to whittle away at garage costs.

Construction practices do have some effect on

The attached double garage, equipped with remote door openers, is a "must-have" in cold climates and a desirable feature in any area. Courtesy of the Genie Company.

If you thought you couldn't use your dark attic space, think again. Install skylights to bring the outdoors in; increase both light and ventilation. These skylights tilt in for easy cleaning. Courtesy of Velux-America Inc.

appraised values, but you don't have to employ expensive practices to produce the highest profit. If the garage is constructed in compliance with local codes, the appraisal will reflect average value. Adding fancy extras, or beefing up the construction, won't always increase your profit.

Attaching a garage to the house will reduce the construction cost and increase your profit. An attached garage is even more valuable due to its con-

venience. The attachment can be direct or with a breezeway. Direct attachment will cost less to build, and the resale value will be about the same. The idea of building the garage you've always wanted gets better and better. With the right game plan, you can make some serious money by building a garage.

Garages also add to the market appeal of your home. They appeal to people who don't want bad weather or tree sap ruining the finish on the car. If the garage is attached to the house, it will keep the homeowners dry in inclement weather. An over-sized garage will appeal to the individual involved in hobbies. It can provide a place, outside of the home, for uninterrupted pursuit of personal interests. Storage is another strong point of garages. They provide a place for lawn care equipment, boats, and other personal belongings.

ATTICS

Now it is time to clean out the attic, and move all the clutter to the basement. Attic expansion and completion projects convert dusty storage into usable living space. Whether finishing the attic or adding to it, attics are a much better undertaking than converting a basement. The results can be very lucrative, especially in Cape Cod-type homes. This style of home is designed with expansion in mind, and tends to offer large profits when the attic is completed. In most cases, it is relatively easy to add two bedrooms and a bathroom.

The cost of finishing an attic is substantial, but the return is even greater. Usually, finishing an attic is non-structural work, and much of it can be done by the homeowner. If you want to turn your elbow grease into cash flow, invest your time in finishing your attic. It takes about the same time and money to finish an attic as it does a basement, but the return on your attic investment is much higher. If you have the option, go for the attic.

If you are seeking an investment with enough return potential to blow the roof off your house, consider a dormer addition. Converting attic space to habitable space is like changing iron to silver. This is an excellent way to reap rich rewards. With an experienced remodeler, adding a dormer will go quickly, and the profits will be strong. Unfinished attic space is nearly worthless on an appraisal report. Changing the dead space into bedrooms will have a tremendous effect on your home's value. Add a bathroom between the bedrooms and watch your money tree grow.

If your ceiling joists will support the weight load of living space, you have the makings of an unbelievable equity gain. The right contractor can build a dormer addition in just a few weeks. In less than sixty days, you can be enjoying your new space and a large equity gain. The finished living space should appraise in the range of $50 per square foot, making the attic your ticket to hefty profits.

Dormer additions are not cheap and will require a major capital investment. If your attic has a floor space of 1,000 square feet, you might spend $30,000 to realize a profit of $20,000. Acting as your own general contractor will make these savings possible. If you can do some of the work yourself, the savings continue to grow. Most homeowners have the ability to do some of the work, such as installing subflooring and painting. If you have an eye for detail, you can do your own interior trim. This is all light work, and it's not overly complicated. The only unique tool needed would be an inexpensive miter box and saw for the trim work.

The more you can do yourself, the larger your profits will be. Even doing the cleanup will save you money. Sometimes subcontractors will allow you to work as their helper. This can be hard, dangerous work, but if you are able, it will save you even more. Know your limitations and leave the difficult work to the professionals. As with any project, weigh your time and ability against the contractor's costs. (Remember, insulation is itchy!) Trying to do work you don't understand can cost you much more than you might save.

Dormer additions don't require footings. They don't need floor joists if existing ceiling joists are large enough, and exterior wall construction is minimal. This means limited siding, sheathing, insulation, and painting. Few additional windows will be required, and your existing heating system may be capable of heating the space. The main plumbing stack should pass through the attic. This can allow access directly to tie in your attic bathroom drains. Interior partitions are inexpensive, and you won't need many. All of these factors mean less cost than the average addition. Although the cost is less, the appraised value will be about the same.

ADDITIONS

Ground level additions complete the quintet of most-profitable remodeling options. The key is making the addition large enough to allow for an adequate return. While a small, one-room addition will probably pay for itself, it will not produce significant profits. There are ways to capitalize with ground-level additions. If you own a two-story home, the easiest way to increase your profits is to make the addition two stories high. Both one- and two-level additions will require roughly the same footings and foundation. The site preparation and roof area are the same, as are roof insulation quantities and survey costs. Many of the costs are the same for either a one-level or two-level addition. This means more profit from your two-story extension, especially when the value is based on the square footage method.

Appraisers will allow around $50 per square foot for a new addition. By creating the second story, you produce inexpensive additional square footage. Your expense does not double with the second level, but the return on your dollar can. This means you spend a little more, but your profit is much greater. You make an investment and watch your profits grow immediately. These profits are compounded over the years with appreciation. This is cost-effective remodeling at its best.

To avoid nonconforming remodeling, you would not add a two-story wing onto a ranch-style home. Do you lose out if you can only build a one-level addition? No, the primary advantage of new additions is the same with both one- and two-level structures. The principle is simple. A new addition is worth more than remodeling an existing room. You are increasing the overall square footage of your property. This elevates the value of your property.

Remodeling profits are based on a percentage of the home's value. While remodeling a bathroom may increase the value by $5,000, an addition can raise the value by $30,000. Homeowners can do much of the work on an addition themselves. This provides for extra savings, which in turn increases your profits even more. If you act as your own general contractor, a percentage of the increased value goes directly into your pocket as profit.

Remodeling is not a game of chance, it is a measurement of skill. There is no reason to gamble when you learn to pick the sure winners. Remodeling for profit is a satisfying experience. It's hard not to enjoy making money while improving your lifestyle and living arrangements. These five examples represent some of the most profitable remodeling projects available. They should have you looking below the surface of every potential improvement. There is a lot of money to be made by the homeowner with a talent for remodeling and picking the right project.

Whether you are the general contractor or a consumer, you can enjoy the profits of remodeling. Investigate other homes in the area and make your decisions wisely. If you can comprehend the principles of appraised values, you can create your own wealth. Many of these projects can be done after business hours and on the weekends. This allows you to participate in the work. Your participation will save you substantial money, and saving money is the key to winning in remodeling.

Choosing a Competent Contractor

8

At this point, I must assume you are planning to go ahead with your remodeling project. Congratulations, you are about to embark on an exciting adventure. To earn your stripes, you will have to avoid the frustrations and capitalize on the advantages. Although the principles will apply to choosing subcontractors, this chapter is primarily dedicated to homeowners who feel engaging a general contractor is in their best interest. For the owner acting in the capacity of general contractor, the criteria discussed will be enlightening. Finding the right contractor can be like finding the right life partner. The search can be long and arduous, but when you find the right one, you know it.

START WITH THE TELEPHONE

Selecting the right contractor is like culling crops. You must disregard the weak, the camouflaged, and the unreliable. The first step in weeding out bad contractors is to go to the telephone. Telephones are the arteries of strong remodeling firms, and the pacesetters of weak companies. Communication is critical to a satisfying remodeling job. When you begin your search for contractors, you start with the telephone. Your phone will see a lot of use before and during the remodeling venture. There will be questions and concerns about the project. When these arise, you will want to be able to contact your contractor. The phone can tell you much about a contractor before you ever talk to him.

Answering machines are disliked by almost everyone. When you take the time to call a company, you expect to get information right away, not after the beep. Recorded messages are offensive to many people; others think it is rude to have a business phone answered electronically. If a machine answers your initial call to a contractor, what will your opinion be? Answering machines are used for many different reasons, and do not necessarily indicate a bad or disreputable contractor. Maybe the contractor spends much of his or her time supervising jobs or working on them. These are two qualities to look for in a good contractor. When the general is on the job, fewer problems occur.

A positive aspect of answering machines is that they keep overhead costs down. Receptionists and secretaries increase overhead significantly and may be unnecessary for small firms. As a customer, you pay for increased overhead, which is passed on through higher prices. The contractor with an answering machine may be less expensive.

Some contractors use answering machines to screen calls. This is not a desirable trait. Contractors needing to screen their calls usually have dissatisfied customers or hounding creditors. There is a way to distinguish between the two purposes of an answering machine. Call early in the morning and again around 6:30 P.M., and see if the contractor answers the phone. The contractor using a machine to keep costs low will probably be coordinating work at these times and will answer your call personally. The "screen machine" will answer the phone twenty-four hours a day, acting as a buffer for the undesirable contractor.

Regardless of their purpose, answering machines eliminate your ability to talk with the contractor immediately. Even if the contractor checks for messages regularly, you will not be able to reach him right away. This can be a pivotal problem if something serious goes wrong on your job. All you can do is leave a recorded message, with no way of knowing when your call will be returned. This could be reason enough to disqualify the contractor from your consideration.

Use the Phone Log

When you begin the search for contractors, keep a log. There is a Phone Log form at the end of this chapter for you to use. On the phone log, enter the contractor's name, the phone number, the date, and the time you called. When the contractor returns your call, note the time and date in the log. This may sound excessive or silly, but it can tell you a lot about a potential contractor.

You might be surprised how many contractors will never return your call. It continually amazes me that contractors can remain in business without returning phone calls. A successful contracting company is dependent on new business, and the refusal to return phone calls is business suicide. Some contractors will return the call but only after two or three days. The phone log helps you spot these red flags.

If it takes this long to contact the contractor, there is a problem. Slow response to a request for new work means no response to calls about work done poorly. Contractors should return your initial call within a few hours. If the contractor is working in the field, it may be evening before your call is reciprocated. A good contractor will tend to current clients first and then potential customers. Although your message may receive lower priority, you should not have to wait days for a return call.

Analyze Phone Response

Phone response is an important element in choosing any contractor. If a contractor uses a receptionist or personal answering service, he or she can be reached quickly. The answering service should be capable of paging the contractor or calling him on the job site. Many contractors have a mobile phone or truck radio, and will check in with the service periodically. In today's competitive market, most successful contractors utilize cellular technology. Ask the answering service when they will be conveying your message to the contractor, and how long it will be before you can expect a call. Write the information in the log, then wait and see if their

time estimate was accurate. You shouldn't base a remodeling decision on the empty promise of a rapid response.

Two hours' turnaround time is acceptable when you are not an existing customer. Once your job is started, your calls should be returned within an hour or less. There should also be a way for you to reach the contractor immediately in a crisis situation. An answering service can promptly relay your call for help; an answering machine cannot. Overhead costs for the contractor remain low with an answering service, and the phones can be tended twenty-four hours a day. For the small contractor, this is the sensible solution to the phone challenge. For the consumer, it is an acceptable arrangement, combining fast phone responses with lower contract prices.

Contractors with administrative personnel and offices offer consumers a sense of security. The customer can go to an office and speak with the contractor or his office staff. Unless the contractor is doing a high volume of business, you will pay more for these conveniences. This secure, professional appearance can also be misleading. Offices and administrative assistants don't make good contractors. Do not be lulled into a false sense of security by outward appearances. It is possible the office rent hasn't been paid in months or the administrative staff is from a temporary service. The office furniture and equipment could be on a monthly lease. You can't judge contractors on appearance alone.

Finding the right contractor requires attention to detail and a well-conceived plan. The phone log is only the beginning — it allows you to eliminate some contractors right away. If they don't perform well in your phone test, they won't perform well on your job. Delete contractors who don't promptly return your call — they obviously don't want or need your job. If they don't care enough to return your calls, forget them. You are looking for a good contractor with a desire to do your job.

The right contractor will understand your needs and strive to meet them. There are good contractors available, but finding them can be a challenge. Like any good thing in life, locating the right contractor takes time. You will have to look hard to pinpoint exceptional contractors, and inducing them to do your job may take some creative maneuvering. These high demand contractors have plenty of work. Don't despair, Chapter 10 will give you some pointers to make your job desirable to the busiest contractor.

USE THE YELLOW PAGES

Where should you start your contractor quest? The yellow pages of the telephone book are a logical answer. Here you will find contractors who have been in business for awhile. It takes time to get into the yellow pages, and the advertising rates are steep. If you really want to do your homework, check the phone company for back issues of the yellow pages. You can chronicle a contractor's business history by noting the size and style of his ad over a period of time. The general contractors in the yellow pages cover every aspect of construction and remodeling. Many of the ads will list the contractor's specialties. You must sift through the list to find suitable contractors for your job.

LOOK AT CLASSIFIED ADS

Advertisements in the classified section of your paper are another good resource for names. These contractors are probably either hungry or starting in business. Cross check to see if the contractor is also listed in the phone book and yellow pages. Here is a quick tip on telephone advertising. If the contractor advertises in the paper as "John Doe Building," he should also be listed as "John Doe Building" in the phone book. If you find a listing in the white pages for "Mr. John Doe," and no yellow page listing, you can assume he operates from home, without a business phone number. If you don't find "John Doe Building" in the line listings, he is probably a rookie or a part-timer.

This isn't always bad. John Doe may have years of field experience with other contractors. This background can override the lack of business experience, and you might get your best deal from John Doe. If Mr. Doe tells you he has ten employees and has been in business for fifteen years, be cautious. The phone company is not in the habit of allowing people to operate a business from home without paying additional fees. Official businesses are customarily given a free line listing in the phone book. A little research can go a long way in testing the validity of a contractor.

LOOK FOR JOBS IN PROGRESS

Another effective way to find contractors is by doing some undercover work around your neighborhood. Look for jobs in progress on other houses. When you see a contractor's sign or truck, write down the name and phone number. Jot down the address of the house where the work is being done. Jobs under construction often yield easy access and allow you to see the contractor's work. If you like what you see, call the contractor, and ask if he is interested in bidding your job.

Explain that your house is close to the one he is working on; ask to walk through the job in progress with the contractor. Finished jobs are much more difficult to gain access to, because homeowners don't appreciate a parade of people going through their recently renovated house. During the remodeling process, homeowners expect a lot of traffic. Take advantage of your timing, and go see the work while you can. If you get the opportunity, ask the homeowners if they are satisfied with the contractor.

ASK YOUR FRIENDS

Do you know anyone who recently had work done on his home? Friends and acquaintances are a reliable resource, because you get the names of tradesmen who have done satisfactory work for people you know personally. Do not take this information as the absolute solution to your contractor search. Before running out and signing a contract, ask yourself a few questions. Was the work done for your friend similar to the work you want done? If they had their bathroom remodeled, it doesn't automatically qualify the contractor to build your dormer addition. A contractor capable of building exquisite decks isn't always the best candidate for extensive kitchen remodeling.

CHECK WITH OTHER CONTRACTORS

Make sure the contractor is qualified to complete the work you want done. If not, make the most of your efforts by asking the contractor for references of other tradesmen he might know. Good contractors do not associate with unprofessional amateurs, who might tarnish their reputations. Networking among reputable contractors increases the chances of finding a good contractor for your job. Mentioning that you were referred by a fellow tradesman or a satisfied customer also carries a lot of weight with a contractor.

ESTABLISH YOUR NEEDS

The first step in finding the right contractor is

establishing your needs. Make an outline of the type of work you want done. Do you plan to build a garage? A competent contractor in bath and kitchen remodeling may not be the best choice to construct your garage. The bath contractor works with existing interior conditions, as opposed to footings, site work, or rafters. Check out your contractors carefully, and compare their qualifications to your specifications.

Many remodelers are specialists in their field. Remodeling has become increasingly complex and can be compared to medical services. Would you go to a pediatrician for advice on a heart condition? A dormer addition requires a specialist who is experienced in cutting open a roof and the many structural changes involved. The knowledge required for work of this magnitude is different from the experience needed to finish a basement. The company that did a great job on your neighbor's basement could prove a disaster for your dormer addition. Whenever possible, you want to compare apples to apples, to differentiate the knowledge and skill needed for the job at hand.

There is almost no comparison to building a dormer and finishing a basement. Basement work doesn't usually require any structural expertise. A contractor doesn't have to contend with inclement weather or rafter cuts. Finishing a basement has its own challenges, with support columns and altering existing conditions. Proper care to control moisture is another skill necessary in finishing a basement. With a dormer, contractors have to know how to deal with rain, wind, and snow. Most of the work is new construction, and existing conditions only play a small role in the dormer construction. The contractors who execute these jobs can be as different as the two types of work performed. A comparison will show both types of contractors are professionals in their field.

There may be a few contractors capable of doing both types of work well, but this is the exception rather than the rule. Finding a well-rounded, fully experienced contractor is rare. The majority of contractors specialize in closely defined areas of remodeling, which are determined by several factors. Some contractors concentrate on the jobs offering the highest profit, and others specialize in work they enjoy. You must determine a potential contractor's weaknesses and strengths. Usually, the work a contractor does the most often is the work he does the best.

CONTRACTORS OFTEN SPECIALIZE

The fields of specialization can cover any aspect of remodeling. Garages can be a specialty. Sunrooms are a common specialty, and dormers or additions offer the opportunity for specialization. Kitchens and bathrooms meld together well for a remodeling trademark. With so many possibilities, how will you know which contractors to call?

Some companies stress their special talents through advertising. The bulk of newspaper ads consists of newer businesses. Many haven't been established long enough to get in the yellow pages. Newspaper ads and fliers are easy sources of effective advertising for young businesses. Contractors just starting out can be an inexpensive alternative to get your job done. With the right precautions, new businesses can result in exceptional values.

SHOULD YOU TRY A NEW BUSINESS?

New businesses need your work, and will try very hard to win your job. Your negotiating power is stronger with these contractors. While they are new in business, they may be extremely good at what they do. They may have years of experience working for another company, and experience is what you are looking for. It doesn't matter where they learned to do the job, as long as they do it right. The contractor who sits behind a desk for five years could have less experience than the tradesman just starting a business. Your interest is in remodeling experience, not a business degree.

There is some risk to a new company, since it is more likely to fail. This will result in trouble when a warranty problem arises. You could get well into the remodeling process, only to have the company close its doors. Getting another contractor to come in to finish someone else's work isn't easy, and it *will* be expensive. To reduce this problem, stay in control. Be prepared for the worst, and never let the contractors have more money than has been earned. If you follow the guidelines of this book, you will greatly decrease your risk.

Do not be afraid to use a new company, as the savings often offset the risks. Maintain control; don't give the contractor a large cash deposit; tie everything down in writing; and inspect all work closely before advancing any money. Insist on lien waivers when any money is paid. Ask for original certificates of insurance before any work is started, and these should be provided to you without delay.

If a copy is furnished, call the insurance company to confirm the coverage dates and information.

Ask for three credit references and several job references. Follow up on the references, and ask to see actual examples of the contractor's work. It's easy to give friends and relatives as job references, so check them out personally. Request evidence of the contractor's state and local license numbers. Ask for the contractor's physical address — this will make a bad apple squirm. Validate and investigate all the information to protect yourself against the unforeseen.

These basic rules should be used with any contractor. A company in business for ten years can be out of business in a day. The longer a company has been in business, the more time it has had to get into financial trouble. Businesses that grow too fast sink even faster. From the outside, a company can look extremely successful, even when it is in deep trouble. Shiny new trucks, fancy offices, and large management staffs are impressive but expensive. A company with these expenses must compensate for its overhead with volume or higher prices. Any company with extensive overhead is a potential bankruptcy case.

A contractor may have been successful for the last several years and still get in trouble fast. A growing business, with heavy overhead, can be derailed by a slow economy. If the company's volume of business declines, it can't afford its overhead. Items like a fleet of trucks and expensive offices quickly consume any reserve capital. When this happens, a once successful company fails. Don't be fooled by an impressive exterior appearance. Keep your guard up, and make all contractors play by Dodge's rules. You can be hurt by either an established company or a new one. You have to protect yourself at all times.

BE SELECTIVE

If you find a contractor from newspaper or yellow page ads, be selective. Call enough contractors to get a fair assessment of the talent available. Evaluate each contractor and use Dodge's rules of remodeling. Ask questions, get everything in writing, and don't assume anything. It is important to establish a position of control from the beginning. Reputable contractors will respect you for your knowledgeable business practices. The experienced contractors will be happy not only to answer your questions but to put their answers in writing. They know this process will eliminate much of the competition, and contractors appreciate an informed consumer. If you know enough to ask the right questions, the quality contractor will get your job. He doesn't have to worry about the fast-talking, hard-selling low bidder.

Good contractors constantly fight the price war battle with questionable contractors. They have to survive without using the slick tactics of less honorable companies. Regardless of the game, playing by the rules is the hardest way to win. In the remodeling arena, there are a lot of people looking to win at the customer's expense. The best contractors are in business for the long haul, and your satisfaction will mean more business down the road. They know you will call again for future work, or you will refer them to your friends. Word of mouth advertising is the best a contractor can have. It is inexpensive and produces a consistent flow of good work.

IDENTIFYING THE "BAD" CONTRACTORS

Contractors living on the dark side will not carry these concerns. They are looking to make a fast buck. They aren't building a business, they're making money. Their objective is to get your money, and they operate on a one-shot basis. In larger cities, they survive because of the turnover of residents. In many urban areas, a contractor can get to you before his reputation does.

Large cities are a perfect breeding ground for shoddy work. The environment allows renegade contractors to run rampant. They know their present customer isn't likely to affect future business. All these contractors concentrate on is getting the job, so they can get the customer's money. Many contractors have refined this approach into an art. They utilize good advertising and trained salespeople to thrive in the city. They know all the ways to stay one step ahead of you. Unfortunately, their methods are legal, and their tactics are well defined.

These contractors prey on uninformed homeowners. With demographic studies, they can attack the people of their choice. These are not contractors, they are professional sales forces. When selling to first-time homeowners, they may arrive in a compact car so as not to appear overly successful. The objective is to appear on the same financial level as the consumer.

When working a different neighborhood, the

vehicle of choice may be a four-wheel-drive pickup truck. This is the "Good Ole Boy" approach, designed to assure you the contractor works just as hard as you do for his money. He will wear jeans and a flannel shirt with boots and a tape measure. He will take notes on a metal clipboard to give the illusion of a working contractor. Some people respond better to a general contractor who works on the job himself. These camouflaged salespeople prey on a homeowner's weaknesses. They know how to do it, and they make their living selling jobs. I have seen these people in action; they often sell more jobs than the workmen can complete. Then it's up to the scheduling department to juggle irate homeowners like hot potatoes.

In the upper class neighborhoods, these birds of prey arrive in a luxury car, wearing a three-piece suit, and carrying a leather briefcase. Laptop computers and gold pens will be part of their arsenal of sales tools. This is the "Dress For Success" method, giving the contractor the image of a dynamic, prosperous businessperson. He acknowledges that your time is valuable and points out that his is, too. He suggests he can squeeze you into his busy schedule, if you sign the contract tonight.

Is this the kind of game you want to play? It shouldn't be, unless you are willing to lose. These sales-oriented professionals seldom have any field experience in remodeling. It is likely they use subcontractors for all the work. Their prices will be inflated to allow a hefty profit for their time; you are probably paying them a commission to sell you the job. Why should you keep them in thousand dollar suits and luxury cars? Cut them out and enjoy the money yourself; you probably know as much about remodeling as they do.

Calling a contractor you know nothing about is risky. A business card picked up from the community bulletin board could produce a good deal or a remodeling rip-off artist. Advertisements in free newspapers deserve a phone call, but be wary. Use common sense, and never allow yourself to be pressured or persuaded into a commitment. There are unlimited possibilities to finding good contractors. The tricky part is finding a suitable contractor for the type of work you want done. Not all contractors are created equal; some are better than others in specialized areas.

PROTECT YOURSELF

Follow Dodge's rules of remodeling to protect yourself from the unknown. Don't sign anything without thinking and without reviewing the documents. Ask about material and work guarantees, and be sure to get them in writing. Requiring the contractor to use your contract will immediately weed through many of the sharks. Remove their fancy clauses and legal rhetoric and you pull their teeth.

Swing the pendulum to your side in every way possible. Read books and research your project before dealing with any contractors. Try to get a referred contractor, if at all possible. Do your homework before having work done on your home. A call to the Better Business Bureau or Contractor Licensing Board can tell you if the contractor has been reported for adverse or illegal business practices. Dodge's remodeling rules can bring the unreliable and inexperienced contractors to their knees. If you follow my advice, you will avoid the majority of the contractors wearing black hats, and find the contractor who is right for your job.

PHONE LOG

Date/Time	Company Name	Contact Person	Remarks

Putting the Job Out to Bids

9

Remodeling requires two things: materials to work with and people to perform the work. These two factors account for most of the costs incurred in a remodeling project. To stay on budget, you have to control both of these expenses. The most effective way to control job costs is with written quotes. Your goal is to expedite accurate quotes and compare the information to establish the best value for your investment dollar. Collecting quotes allows you to establish conclusive budget figures and finalize your plans and specifications. This is not a complicated process, but it requires an eye for details.

CALCULATING COSTS

You began to establish your remodeling budget in Chapter 2. This aspect of cost estimating dealt primarily with product selection and costs for tubs, cabinets, flooring, and so on. Now you will begin to calculate the project's total costs. Hard costs consist of footings, foundations, carpentry, plumbing, and electrical labor, and other mandatory construction phases. At the end of this chapter there is a Cost Estimates form, which lists the primary areas of costs to be incurred in a job. The form will show you how to make your own cost estimate sheet.

It is easy to overlook the smaller aspects of a remodeling job. These oversights can be expensive. Trash removal, permit fees, and cleanup costs are good examples of frequently missed expenditures. By using the Cost Estimate form, you will see these classifications and know if you need an item included in your quotes. The categories will provide you with the information necessary to test the in-

tegrity of labor and material quotes. For example, does the contractor's quote include rip-out, clean-up, and removal of all debris? It should be spelled out clearly in the quote.

ESTIMATES VS. QUOTES

Soliciting bids for labor and material is a very important step in starting a project. The success of your job hinges on solid quotes. When remodeling costs get out of hand, the job suffers, and corners must be cut to save money. Careful planning eliminates compromises and allows your dreams to become reality. Estimates give you a monetary range to work within, but quotes are needed in the final budgeting phase. *Don't confuse an estimate with a quote.*

The difference between an estimate and a quote can mean thousands of dollars to you. Estimates are like a hypothesis; they are educated guesses. Prices listed in an estimate can fluctuate greatly, and some contractors use low estimates as a sales tactic. They plan to get into a job by being the low bidder and then add to their price with extras. Work you thought was included in the original price suddenly becomes an additional expense. This procedure allows a contractor to be the low bidder initially and ultimately leave your job with more money than the competitors.

How can contractors get away with this? The *estimate* is their escape path. Estimates only include a vague description of the work to be done, leaving much room for interpretation and problems. I once took my truck in to be serviced. I was careful to ask for an estimate of the repair cost, and it seemed like a reasonable price. The final bill included additional parts, extra labor, and freight charges! "The first price was only an estimate," replied the manager, "Once we got into it, we found more problems." It is risky to allow anyone to work with only an estimated cost projection.

Estimates may contain a lot of words, but they might not mean much. There is an example of a Painting Estimate from Worthless Paint Works at the end of this chapter. How does this estimate compare with a quote? There are many differences. The painting estimate only contains a few specific details, such as the room to be painted, the color of the paint, and how the paint will be applied. Detail will be reserved for the payment schedule, which will be very clear and require a deposit upon acceptance of the estimate. The next payment could be due when the material is delivered to the job, with the final payment due upon completion.

Does this appear to be an acceptable estimate? After all, the location, color, and type of paint have all been clearly specified. What other considerations exist in a painting proposal? Visualizing the painting process will allow you to discover the omissions. Interior painting will involve moving furniture. Whose responsibility is it? Will protection from spillage be provided by you or the contractor? You can bet an estimate will not address these matters.

Does the estimate say how long the job will take? Will primer or sealant be used before the paint is installed? Most estimates will not answer these questions. What hours of the day will the work be done? Maybe the contractor has a full-time job and only paints in the evening. When an estimate says the contractor will paint the walls and ceiling of your family room, what is actually included? Are they going to paint the baseboards and window and door trim as well? Are the holes and dings in the wall going to be patched before the walls are painted?

Another unanswered question involves the type of paint. Will it be flat or semi-gloss? The contractor agreed verbally to allow your choice of paint, but paint prices vary with quality and type. What will you do when the contractor charges extra for the paint you selected? What happens if he tells you, after the fact, that the price was for a builder-grade paint, and your selection was a more expensive custom color? Do you have to pay the additional cost? The contractor will say yes, you will say no, but ulti-

mately it may be up to a judge to decide. The bottom line in an estimate cannot be compared to, or considered, a quote. You will have a difficult time suing someone for a guess, but a quote is an absolute commitment.

MAKE THE QUOTE WORK FOR YOU

Even though contracts are more specific than quotes, not all contracts are created equal. Make sure the quote addresses all of the pertinent concerns. The sample proposal at the end of the chapter, from Presto Paint, says the contractor will supply plastic for the floors, but whose responsibility is it to put it down? There is also no mention of protecting lights, outlet covers, and doors from overspray. The contractor may assure you he will take care of this, but his contract specifically voids any verbal commitments. Empty promises cannot be proved in court.

The description of the work states that the walls, ceilings, and trim will be sprayed to allow proper coverage. How many coats are required, and what is proper coverage? Similar language mentions timely completion, in a workmanlike manner. Who is to say what is timely or workmanlike? When you receive a quote, it is necessary to analyze the information and look for discrepancies. What first appears to be a reasonable quote may turn out to be a nebulous, one-sided proposal. At the end of the chapter is a comprehensive contract from Paint All Painting, Inc. Compare this proposal to the contract supplied by Presto Paint for the same job. This provides an obvious example of the differences between a mediocre quote and a thorough, detailed, binding proposal.

AVOID TIME-AND-MATERIAL BILLING

Some homeowners are influenced by a contractor's low hourly labor rate, and accept a proposal to do the project on a time-and-material basis. Whenever possible, avoid time-and-material agreements. Costs can skyrocket in these situations, and you have no control over the final cost of the work. If you agree to have the work done in this manner, you are responsible for paying whatever the final bill may be. Labor rates can be very deceiving, even among honest contractors. Contractors work at different speeds and skill levels, and this distorts the view of hourly rates.

The total charge for time and material billing will be related to the speed of the contractor. If Mr. Carpenter only charges $25 per hour but does all the work alone, he can cost you more than Zippy Carpenters, who charge $35 per hour for a crew of men. Material prices in this type of billing can also have wide variances from contractor to contractor. One contractor may only charge 15% above his cost, while another could charge 35% above cost. When you are not protected by a pre-established firm quote, these costs are uncontrollable and add up quickly.

Crooked contractors love T&M jobs; they can drag the job out and bleed the consumer. They are masters in the art of working without getting anything done. To the untrained eye, they appear to be working hard, every hour of the day. In truth, they are going through the motions, putting on their best performance, to impress the consumer and collect as much money as possible. These contractors will meticulously unpack and clean up their tools and materials each day. There will be numerous daily trips: first to purchase extra nails, then to get one more stud, then to the hardware store. You pay for all of this extra time needlessly.

Without a quoted price and a contract, a contractor can set you up before you know what happened. The job may start smoothly but won't stay that way for long. At first, extra charges will be minor; this is the feeling-out stage for unscrupulous remodelers. They bill you for the first phase of completed work, according to your understanding, and include only a few small extra charges. Then the job suddenly develops unforeseen problems, like my truck did, and the next bill is laden with extra costs. When the final stage arrives, the contractor refuses to patch cracks he created in the living room ceiling from excessive hammering, until you pay his outrageous bill in full.

Many contractors will try to convince you that a time-and-material job will save you money. After all, you pay only for what you get. They can't hide exorbitant profits, the way a contract price can. Just remember, no one does remodeling work without financial reimbursement. There are very few jobs competent contractors cannot give you a firm price on. Once work is started, a contractor has potential lien rights against your property. You cannot compare time-and-material estimates, and they do not give you any information to finalize your budget. Avoid potential problems by keeping a tight leash on the contractor, with a firm contract and quoted price.

DEALING WITH MATERIAL SUPPLIERS

Avoid dilemmas; remodeling comes with enough challenges, you don't need to add to them. Stop the problems before they start. Subcontractors aren't the only people who use low bids as a ploy. Material suppliers can be guilty of similar tactics. Envision going to a building supplier to order your kitchen cabinets. After looking at the displays and catalogs, you make your choice, and the company gives you a written estimate. The price looks good, and you order the cabinets. The salesperson tells you the cabinets should be available for delivery in four to six weeks. You rush home to get the remodelers going. In just a few weeks, your dream kitchen will be a reality.

There are already many potential problems in this example. You ordered your cabinets and the remodelers are working. A few weeks later, the old cabinets, countertop, and kitchen sink are ripped out. This doesn't bother you because the new cabinetry will be installed next week. A couple of days without kitchen facilities is tolerable; it gives you a good excuse to enjoy dining in restaurants. Acting as the general contractor, you've successfully coordinated the remodeling effort flawlessly, to this point. You feel great, and the money you've saved being the general contractor allows some extra features in the new kitchen. You can envision that beautiful, decorative sink and faucet you craved gracing your kitchen ensemble.

The big day arrives. Your new cabinets will come today and by tonight, you can do dishes again. By late morning, you are getting concerned. By mid-afternoon, you're getting angry. Where are those cabinets? The carpenter and the plumber are waiting for the delivery, and paying them to stand around is eating up your profits. You call the supplier, and a counter person gets on the phone. When you ask about the status of your cabinet delivery, you are put on hold; the counter person has to check with the shipping department. The longer you are on hold, the higher your blood pressures gets. This is ridiculous, how hard could it be to give you a delivery time? When the counter person finally comes back to the phone, you wish she hadn't.

Your cabinets had to be back ordered and won't be in for a few more weeks. That's the breaking point, now you lose your temper! You demand to speak to the manager. She is on a break and not available to the phone. You hang up and rush out of the house, leaving the plumber and carpenter waiting for your return. You race to the supplier with your estimate in hand, and go straight to the administrative offices. The manager is on the phone. You wait, your anger building to a dangerous level. Finally, she invites you into the office. You're so upset that when you show her the estimate sheet, it is shaking in your hand. Trying to maintain composure, you explain what is happening to you.

The manager reviews the estimate. You notice a strange expression on her face. When you ask what she intends to do about this, you are astounded. She explains that this estimate is all she has to work with. The details in the estimate are not very good, and tracking the order could be a problem. She goes on to apologize for the present problem, and offers to do whatever she can to find your cabinets. In the meantime, you have a carpenter and a plumber waiting at your house. The clock is running, and these subcontractors are expensive. When you ask what can be done about the cabinets, the answer is not what you want to hear.

The estimate is ambiguous, it doesn't state a delivery date. The design of the cabinets isn't detailed in the paperwork. Was a countertop ordered as well? The hardware for the doors and drawers is not included with this brand of cabinets. The hardware is a separate order and will take another week or so to get. Were you going to pick up the cabinets? There is no reference to delivery in the estimate. Delivery is available, but there is an additional charge for the service. Freight charges are not included in the estimate and they are extensive — the cabinets are coming from 1,800 miles away.

This is where the supplier turns your adversity into their advantage. The manager reviews the situation, and offers you a deal on cabinets she has in stock. She wants to make amends for your inconvenience. The cabinets in stock retail for 45% more than the units you ordered. As compensation for your trouble, she offers you the more expensive cabinets at a discount, and will give you free delivery, today. The total cost will only be 30% more than the original estimate. Since you must incur additional expenses and time delays for the original cabinets, you will save money and time with this type of deal.

If you order cabinets from another supplier, you may have to wait for another month, or more. If you wait for your original order, the additional costs will push your losses over the price of the special of the day. What are you going to do? Don't forget about the carpenter and plumber waiting for you and the cabinets at home.

Believe it or not, some companies make their profits from scenarios just like this. Normally, if the building supply manger is a good salesperson, you will take delivery of the higher-priced cabinets. This is a prime example of the pain that can result from working with loose estimates. Don't do it, get firm quotes. Use detailed contracts with enforceable clauses, and leave nothing to speculation. As my wife once said, "There is never a problem, until there is a problem."

ALWAYS GET A WRITTEN QUOTE

Now you know the problems with estimates. You *must* recognize the need for written quotes. Even with a general contractor, you will need a written quote. If your agreement is in writing, you know what you are paying for and how much it will cost. This is a crucial aspect of any remodeling project. If you allotted $2,300 for cabinets, and they wind up costing over $3,000, your out-of-pocket expense has increased by 30%. Where will the additional $700 come from? You will be forced to take shortcuts and reduce the quality or quantity of the work. Getting into this difficult situation can be avoided with detailed quotes.

This document, which will save you time, money, and frustration, is called many things. Quote, bid, proposal, or contract; regardless of the term, this is the written instrument you're looking for. Quotes contain much more information than estimates. Contractors know a quote is a firm price, so they will be much more specific in their description of labor and materials. The intent of a quote is to guarantee a fixed price. The cost of the service or material cannot exceed the amount specified in the quote. This makes your budget balance. When you are dealing with quotes, you can be sure of your costs.

CREATING YOUR BUDGET

Establish your budget based on the average bid price from several bidders. This will protect you from a low quote that can't be performed. To establish the average price of five different bids, add the total of each proposal together. Now divide the grand total by the number of bids (in this case five), and you have the average job cost. Quotes that are way below average should arouse suspicion. There has to be a reason why one price is so much lower than the others. Perhaps you will be unable to get the contractor to do the work when you need it, or the material may not be available during your timetable. These complications force you to consider the next lowest bidder. By using the average quoted price, you won't be placed in a financial bind. If one quote is much lower than the others, don't include it when averaging the bids. It will throw the true average off.

BID REQUESTS

When requesting quotes, give all bidders the same information. You cannot expect competitive proposals if the bidders are working with different information. Your bid request needs to include specific details. There is an example of a Bid Request form included at the end of this chapter. Your complete plans and specifications should accompany the bid request. You want to establish consistency, so the prices you get from five contractors should be for exactly the same work. Bidders may notice something you left off your plans or specifications. If so, ask them to note any items you omitted as an addendum to the bid. Without using this procedure, the bids will not be equal.

A contractor who includes code requirements you overlooked will be more expensive than the contractor bidding strictly by your plans and specs. In the end, you will have to pay for the code requirements. The difference is in knowing the cost before the job is started. You can use the bid process to locate superior contractors. Make note of who mentioned your omission and who did not. The contractor who considers aspects and requirements you did not specify exhibits the extra effort and knowledge to give you a thorough job.

Preparing your bid requests deserves a lot of attention. The bidders will only be obligated to provide costs for the work you specify. This is where all the time and effort you put into your plans and specifications will pay off. Following a few rules in the bidding process will increase your savings. Don't allow suppliers to substitute materials in their bids. Specifications lose their purpose when substitutions are made. If substitutions are mandatory, have them placed on a separate bid addendum. There is a sample Bid Addendum at the end of the chapter. Uniformity in the bids is essential to comparing competitive bids.

Specify the grade of lumber to be used. Studs come in several grades. You don't have to require the best, but specify the grade. There is a great deal of difference in the cost between lumber grades. The same is true for other items. If your specifications simply call for sheathing behind your siding, what will your bids be based on? One contractor will bid plywood for sheathing. Another may plan to use particle board. The third contractor might base his quote on fiberboard, and a fourth contractor may quote insulated foam sheathing. All the contractors included a price for the sheathing, but the prices are all different. It will be easy to tell which bid is lower, but which one is the better value? You have to specify everything to get truly competitive bids.

PUTTING YOUR SPECIFICATIONS TO WORK

Now you might be wondering how you can create comprehensive specifications if you don't know the differences in materials. You can read one of the many books available on the subject, or you can ask professionals for suggestions. Call various suppliers and ask them for recommendations on the materials you should use. Consult your dream book and compare the qualities of different materials. During your initial conversations, ask contractors what they normally use in projects similar to your job. Then make your decision and stick to it. If a contractor or supplier says you have made a poor choice, request their recommendations on the Bid Addendum. If the price is right and the reasons are valid, you may decide later to change your plans and specs.

The specifications will take a long time to complete and will feel like a waste of time. You will get bored and you will get confused. After hours of writing specifications, you'll know why architects charge so much. This part will not be as much fun as designing the job. The specifications are as important or even more important than the design. Spend time at your desk solving problems before they happen. As unpleasant as this job is, it's better than the potential problems you will encounter without dependable specifications.

The result of detailed plans and specifications is a quality quote. You can easily compare all the prices equally and know, without a doubt, what is included in each bid. Compare all bids on a step-by-step basis. If you use a form like the Bid Request form, this is an easy task. All the elements of the quotes are broken down on the bid request sheets. You can scan the page and see every expense to determine who has the best prices on which items. This is another area with strong potential for saving money.

DECIPHERING MATERIAL QUOTES

Many contractors and homeowners prefer to deal with one supplier. This is definitely the easiest way to buy, but not always the best. Putting your job out to bids can be done several ways. The most common is to request a lump sum price. This method indicates who has the lowest overall price, but it doesn't show you the items that could be bought cheaper elsewhere. Using a detailed bid sheet will expose these savings. Some suppliers will be resistant to detailed bids; they want to mask their prices in a bulk figure. If they want the sale badly enough, they will comply with your request. If they are unwilling to show you all of their prices, you should not deal with them anyway. They are all but telling you they are hiding something.

When you go to a grocery store, everything is priced individually. Hardware stores price their items, so why should a building supplier be any different? Just because they deal in larger items and higher volume doesn't give them the right to hide their prices. Be firm on this point. Insist on knowing what all the components of your job will cost. It's very easy to hide excessive profits on volume sales. It is not feasible to price every screw, hinge, and nail, but you can price all the major items. Break the items down into bid phases. Phase breakdowns are bargaining chips and can hold hidden treasure for you.

CHALLENGING QUOTES

Contractor's quotes can be challenged in much the same way. Request a breakdown of labor and material. Some contractors will not give this information, knowing it could expose excessive hidden profits. If you are suspicious, demand a breakdown. This is the only way to verify quotes and control your costs.

A common trick of the trade is to camouflage material substitutions. This is done by including vague language in a quote, which specifies your product or "an equal" will be used. Who is to determine what is equivalent to your product? Your satisfaction may not be met with these so-called equal products. Require the bids to be based on specific names, model numbers, colors, and other pertinent information, and you will eliminate these sneaky substitutions.

When you get your prices back, lay the bid sheets beside each other and scan the categories. You are sure to find some interesting differences. The bottom line will show the overall low bidder, and the phase prices will expose ways to increase your savings. Look at the framing lumber section. Who is the overall low bidder on the framing prices? How do the window and door prices compare with other suppliers? Does their insulation price beat the other bidders? What do their numbers look like for the roofing phase? By now, you will have found areas to investigate. The overall low bidder won't be the lowest in all phases. It would be very unusual if one supplier had the lowest prices for every aspect of the job.

SHOP CAREFULLY

Selective shopping saves money. You don't have to buy everything from one supplier, but it is best to buy each complete phase from the same company. Don't spend a lot of time buying a little here and a little there. Concentrate on the phases, and buy from the lowest bidder in each category. Use your bid sheets as a negotiating tool. Show the other bids to the supplier you prefer. When you put his competitor's price in front of him, he may offer you a better price. Suppliers price their material in different levels and have room to offer additional discounts.

You won't get a better price if you don't ask for it. Laying your bid sheets on his counter proves you are serious. The supplier knows you can, and might, buy from his competitor. When you get to this stage, you will have his attention. Don't deal with a sales associate; ask to talk with the manager. Only the manager has the ability to give you the lowest price. When the prices are close, you will almost always win. The supplier has invested time and money in preparing your bid, and knows the only way to recover that money is by making a sale. You are the buyer and you have power in this negotiation. Use your power to save on your material costs. The slower the economy, the better your chances are of winning. Don't be intimidated. It's your money and your decision where to spend it.

Similar tactics work with contractors, especially general contractors. Ask them to segregate their bids into phases and compare the different areas with opposing contractors. When you find specific areas with inflated prices, start your negotiations. If a general contractor believes he will lose the entire job because his flooring price is high, he will lower the price to secure the work. The general contractor may ask his subcontractor to lower the price of the work, or he may absorb the loss to be awarded the job. In either event, you benefit from additional savings.

CONDUCTING THE BID PROCESS

Putting your work out to bids will require time, so allow several weeks for the process. Many contractors and suppliers will be slow in responding to your request for quotes. Some will refuse to bid the job under your terms and conditions. To get the most for your money, you may have to shop in other areas. Large cities can afford you lower prices. In some cases, you may find out-of-state prices are lower. Maine's material prices are high. I can buy the exact same products in Massachusetts for up to 35% less. You may find similar savings with your exploratory bid requests. Take the time to conduct the bid process properly — it is your best shot at saving money.

You need to formulate a plan to have as many bidders compete on the job as possible. The more quotes you get, the better your chances of saving money. Seek prices from every available source. To save time, solicit bids by mail and include a complete bid package with each request. To save on copying and postage costs, start with a letter. Send a letter to each prospective bidder to see if he or she is interested in bidding your work. When you get favorable replies, mail the complete package. You will be surprised at how much you can save with aggressive shopping.

When you get into serious negotiations, watch your step. Don't be fooled by low prices based on substituted materials. Confirm, in writing, the delivery and completion dates. Beware of any bidder beating all the others by a large margin. All the bids should be within the same range. If one is substantially lower, something is wrong. Double check your plans and specifications before requesting quotes. Once you receive the quotes, you can begin to eliminate contractors and suppliers, and then you will be ready to negotiate for the best possible deal.

COST ESTIMATES FORM
COST PROJECTIONS FOR BATHROOM REMODELING

ITEM/PHASE	LABOR	MATERIAL	TOTAL
Plans			
Specifications			
Permits			
Trash container deposit			
Trash container delivery			
Demolition			
Dump fees			
Rough plumbing			
Rough electrical			
Rough heating/ac			
Subfloor			
Insulation			
Drywall			
Ceramic tile			
Linen closet			
Baseboard trim			
Window trim			
Door trim			
Paint/wallpaper			
Underlayment			
Finish floor covering			
Linen closet shelves			
Closet door & hardware			
Main door hardware			
Wall cabinets			
Base cabinets			
Countertops			
Plumbing fixtures			
Trim plumbing material			
Final plumbing			
Shower enclosure			
Light fixtures			
Trim electrical material			
Final electrical			
Trim heating/ac material			
Final heating/ac			
Bathroom accessories			
Cleanup			
Trash container removal			
Window treatments			
Personal touches			
Financing expenses			
Miscellaneous expenses			
Unexpected expenses			
Margin of error			
TOTAL ESTIMATED EXPENSE			

COST ESTIMATES FORM
COST PROJECTIONS FOR KITCHEN REMODELING

ITEM/PHASE	LABOR	MATERIAL	TOTAL
Plans			
Specifications			
Permits			
Trash container deposit			
Trash container delivery			
Demolition			
Dump fees			
Rough plumbing			
Rough electrical			
Rough heating/ac			
Subfloor			
Insulation			
Drywall			
Baseboard trim			
Window trim			
Door trim			
Paint/wallpaper			
Underlayment			
Finish floor covering			
Hardware			
Wall cabinets			
Base cabinets			
Countertops			
Plumbing fixtures			
Trim plumbing material			
Final plumbing			
Light fixtures			
Trim electrical material			
Final electrical			
Trim heating/ac material			
Final heating/ac			
Appliances			
Kitchen accessories			
Cleanup			
Trash container removal			
Window treatments			
Personal touches			
Financing expenses			
Unexpected expenses			
Margin of error			
TOTAL ESTIMATED EXPENSE			

COST ESTIMATES FORM
COST PROJECTIONS FOR GARAGE

ITEM/PHASE	LABOR	MATERIAL	TOTAL
Survey			
Plans			
Specifications			
Permits			
Site preparation			
Dig footings			
Concrete for footings			
Pour footings			
Concrete for slab			
Wire mesh			
Gravel			
Plastic ground cover			
Pest control			
Pour slab			
Pour apron			
Finish slab			
Framing lumber			
Roof trusses			
Attic vents			
Sheathing			
Framing labor			
Siding			
Siding labor			
Shingles			
Roof labor			
Trim material			
Windows			
Small door			
Garage doors			
Garage door openers			
Overhead door labor			
Nails & misc. material			
Pegboard			
Shelving			
Pull-down attic stairs			
Misc. carpentry labor			
Rough electrical material			
Rough electrical labor			
Light fixtures			
Final electrical labor			
Insulation			
Insulation labor			
Drywall			
Drywall labor			
Paint			
Paint labor			
Trash container deposit			
Trash container delivery			
Dump fees			
Hardware			
Landscaping			
Cleanup			
Trash container removal			

COST ESTIMATES FORM
COST PROJECTIONS FOR GARAGE CONT'D

ITEM/PHASE	LABOR	MATERIAL	TOTAL
Personal touches			
Financing expenses			
Miscellaneous expenses			
Options:			
Heating/ac			
Plumbing			
Interior trim			
Floor sealant			
Driveway repair or extension			
Unexpeceted expenses			
Margin of error			
TOTAL ESTIMATED EXPENSE			

COST ESTIMATES FORM
COST PROJECTIONS FOR ATTIC CONVERSION

ITEM/PHASE	LABOR	MATERIAL	TOTAL
Plans			
Specifications			
Permits			
Demolition			
Repairs to existing ceiling			
Framing lumber			
Framing labor			
Dormer material			
Dormer labor			
Nails & misc. material			
Misc. carpentry labor			
Plumbing fixtures			
Final plumbing labor			
Rough heating/ac material			
Rough heating/ac labor			
Heating/ac equipment			
Final heating/ac labor			
Rough electrical material			
Rough electrical labor			
Light fixtures			
Final electrical labor			
Insulation			
Insulation labor			
Drywall			
Drywall labor			
Paint			
Paint labor			
Interior doors & hardware			
Interior trim			
Interior trim labor			
Underlayment			
Finish floor covering			
Wall cabinets			
Base cabinets			
Countertops			
Window treatments			
Trash container deposit			
Trash container delivery			
Dump fees			
Cleanup			
Trash container removal			
Personal touches			
Financing expenses			
Miscellaneous expenses			
Unexpected expenses			
Margin of error			
TOTAL ESTIMATED EXPENSE			

COST ESTIMATES FORM
COST PROJECTIONS FOR ADDITION

ITEM/PHASE	LABOR	MATERIAL	TOTAL
Survey			
Plans			
Specifications			
Permits			
Site preparation			
Dig footings			
Concrete for footings			
Pour footings			
Foundation wall material			
Foundation wall labor			
Pest control treatment			
Foundation backfill labor			
Demolition			
Repairs to existing wall			
Framing lumber			
Roof trusses			
Attic vents			
Sheathing			
Framing labor			
Siding			
Siding labor			
Shingles			
Roof labor			
Exterior trim material			
Exterior hardware			
Windows			
Doors			
Nails & misc. material			
Shelving			
Pull-down attic stairs			
Misc. carpentry labor			
Rough plumbing material			
Rough plumbing labor			
Plumbing fixtures			
Final plumbing labor			
Rough heating/ac material			
Rough heating/ac labor			
Heating/ac equipment			
Final heating/ac labor			
Rough electrical material			
Rough electrical labor			
Light fixtures			
Final electrical labor			
Insulation			
Insulation labor			
Drywall			
Drywall labor			
Paint			
Paint labor			
Interior doors			
Interior hardware			
Interior trim			
Interior trim labor			

COST ESTIMATES FORM
COST PROJECTIONS FOR ADDITION CONT'D

ITEM/PHASE	LABOR	MATERIAL	TOTAL
Underlayment			
Finish floor covering			
Wall cabinets			
Base cabinets			
Countertops			
Window treatments			
Landscaping			
Trash container deposit			
Trash container delivery			
Dump fees			
Cleanup			
Trash container removal			
Personal touches			
Financing expenses			
Miscellaneous expenses			
Options:			
Concrete for slab			
Wire mesh			
Gravel			
Plastic ground cover			
Pour slab			
Finish slab			
Gutters			
Decks			
Unexpected expenses			
Margin of error			
TOTAL ESTIMATED EXPENSE			

ESTIMATE

WORTHLESS PAINT WORKS
189 HARD TO FIND PLACE
SKIPTOWN, OH 65478
(101) 555-2341

DATE: June 10, 1991
CUSTOMER NAME: Mr. & Mrs. J. P. Homeowner
ADDRESS: 192 Hometown Street, Moneytown, OH 65478
PHONE NUMBER: (101) 555-9876

DESCRIPTION OF WORK

Worthless Paint Works will supply all labor and material to paint the above referenced job as follows:

(1) Supply and install off-white latex paint in the living room, dining room, and family room.
(2) Paint all walls and ceilings.
(3) Paint to be sprayed on wall and ceiling surfaces.
(4) Owner may select any off-white builder-grade color from paint charts supplied by contractor.
(5) Contractor will remove excess paint from window glass.
(6) All work will be completed in a workmanlike manner.

PAYMENT FOR WORK AS FOLLOWS:

PRICE: One thousand, eight hundred dollars ($1,800.00), payable:
one-third $600.00 due at the signing of the contract,
one-third $600.00 due when materials are delivered,
one-third $600.00 due when work is completed.

If you have any questions, please don't hesitate to call. Upon acceptance, this becomes a binding contract between both parties.

Respectfully submitted,

R. L. Contractor
Owner

ACCEPTANCE

We the undersigned do hereby agree to, and accept, all the terms and conditions of this proposal. We fully understand the terms and conditions, and hereby consent to enter into this contract.

Worthless Paint Works   Customer

By _____   _____
Title _____   Date _____
Date_____

PROPOSAL

PRESTO PAINT
170 SHADY PLACE
NOGO, OH 65478
(101) 555-2341

DATE: June 12, 1991
CUSTOMER NAME: Mr. & Mrs. J. P. Homeowner
ADDRESS: 192 Hometown Street, Moneytown, OH 65478
PHONE NUMBER: (101) 555-9876
JOB LOCATION: 192 Hometown Street, Moneytown, OH 65478

DESCRIPTION OF WORK

Presto Paint will supply, and or coordinate, all labor and material for the above referenced job as follows:

(1) Supply and install off-white latex paint in the living room, dining room, and family room.
(2) Paint all walls & ceilings, and window, door, and base trim.
(3) Paint will be sprayed onto wall and ceiling surfaces, in a manner to properly cover these areas.
(4) Owner may select the off-white color of his/her choice, from and of contractor's suppliers.
(5) Contractor will supply plastic to cover the floor in work areas.
(6) Contractor will prepare all surfaces for paint, and scrape all areas, as needed, before painting.
(7) Contractor will remove excess paint from window glass.
(8) All work shall be completed in a timely and workmanlike manner.

No other agreements, whether implied or made verbally, shall be binding.

PAYMENT SCHEDULE:

PRICE: One thousand, eight hundred fifty dollars ($1,850.00), payable:
one-third $600.00 due at the signing of the contract,
one-third $625.00 due when materials are delivered,
one-third $625.00 due when work is completed.
All payments shall be made, in full, upon presentation of each completed invoice.

If payment is not made according to the terms above, Presto Paint will have the following rights and remedies. Presto Paint may charge a monthly service charge of two percent (2%), twenty four percent (24%) per year, from the first day default is made. Presto Paint may lien the property where the work has been done. Presto Paint may use all legal methods in the collection of monies owed to Presto Paint. Presto Paint may seek compensation, at the rate of $30.00 per hour, for attempts made to collect unpaid monies. Presto Paint may seek payment for legal fees and other costs of collection, to the full extent the law allows.

If the job is not ready for the service or material requested, as scheduled, and the delay is not due to Presto Paint actions, Presto Paint may charge the customer for lost time. This charge will be at a rate of $30.00 per hour, per man, including travel time.

If you have any questions or don't understand this proposal, seek professional advice. Upon acceptance, this becomes a binding contract between both parties.

Respectfully submitted,

B. D. Contractor
Owner

ACCEPTANCE

We the undersigned do hereby agree to, and accept, all the terms and conditions of this proposal. We fully understand the terms and conditions, and hereby consent to enter into this contract.

Presto Paint   Customer

By _____   _____

Title _____   Date _____

Date _____

PROPOSAL EXPIRES IN 30 DAYS, IF NOT ACCEPTED BY ALL PARTIES

PAINT ALL PAINTING, INC.
111 BUSINESS WAY
CLEARVIEW, OH 65487
(101) 555-4322

QUOTE

This agreement, made this _10th_ day of _June_, 1991, shall set forth the whole agreement, in its entirety, by and between PAINT ALL PAINTING, INC., herein called Contractor, and _Mr. & Mrs. J. P. Homeowner_, herein called Owners.

Job Name: _Homeowner - paint_
Job location: _192 Hometown Street, Moneytown, OH_

The Contractor and Subcontractor agree to the following:
Subcontractor shall perform all work as described below and provide all material to complete the work described below. Subcontractor shall supply all labor and material to complete the work according to the attached plans and specifications. The work shall include the following:

(1) Scrape all painted surfaces in the living room, dining room, and family room.
(2) Fill all cracks and holes with joint compound.
(3) Sand painted surfaces as needed and prepare all painted surfaces for new paint.
(4) Provide protection from paint or other substance spillage.
(5) Prime all surfaces to be painted.
(6) Paint all existing painted surfaces with two rolled coats of Latex off-white paint, color number LT1689, made by NoDrip.
(7) Remove any excess paint from window glass or other areas not intended to be painted.

SCHEDULE

The work described above shall begin within three days of notice from Owner, with an estimated start date of 6/20/91. The Contractor shall complete the above work in a professional and expedient manner within fifteen days from the start date.

PAYMENT SCHEDULE

The Contract Sum is: _Two thousand dollars ($2,000.00)_, payable as follows:
CONTRACT DEPOSIT OF: _$500.00_ due at signing of contract, with additional payments of: _$750.00 due when job is started_, and _$750.00 due at time of completion_.

This agreement, entered into on June 10, 1991, shall constitute the whole agreement between Contractor and Owner.

_____   _____
Contractor   Owner

BID REQUEST

CUSTOMER NAME: Mr. & Mrs. J. P. Ownit
CUSTOMER ADDRESS: 192 Home Street
CUSTOMER CITY/STATE/ZIP: Calico, MA 05022
CUSTOMER PHONE NUMBER: (001) 790-7632
JOB LOCATION: Same
PLANS & SPECIFICATIONS ATTACHED: Yes
PLANS & SPECIFICATIONS DATED: June 10, 1991
BID REQUESTED FROM: Mid Range Suppliers
SUPPLIER ADDRESS: 42 Supplier Street
CONTACT PERSON: Liz Materialwoman, Manager
DATE: July 25, 1991
TYPE OF WORK: Remodeling

DESCRIPTION OF MATERIAL TO BE QUOTED:

ALL QUOTES TO BE BASED ON ATTACHED PLANS AND SPECIFICATIONS. NO SUBSTITUTIONS ALLOWED WITHOUT WRITTEN CONSENT BY CUSTOMER.

PLEASE PROVIDE QUOTED PRICES FOR THE FOLLOWING:

- [ ] Framing lumber
- [ ] Roof sheathing
- [ ] Roof shingles
- [ ] Masonry products
- [ ] Nails
- [ ] Siding
- [ ] Insulation
- [ ] Exterior doors

BID ADDENDUM
REQUEST FOR SUBSTITUTIONS

CUSTOMER NAME: Mr. & Mrs. J. P. Homeowner
CUSTOMER ADDRESS: 192 Hometown Street
CUSTOMER CITY/STATE/ZIP: Yooho City, MA 00001
CUSTOMER PHONE NUMBER: (001) 756-3333
JOB LOCATION: Same
PLANS & SPECIFICATIONS DATED: June 10, 1991
BID REQUESTED FROM: Mid Range Suppliers
SUPPLIER ADDRESS: 42 Supplier Street
CONTACT PERSON: Liz Materialwoman, Manager
DATE: July 25, 1991
TYPE OF WORK: Remodeling

THE FOLLOWING ITEMS ARE BEING SUBSTITUTED FOR THE ITEMS SPECIFIED IN THE ATTACHED PLANS AND SPECIFICATIONS:

Roof shingles — The brand specified is not readily available. Our proposed substitute is product number 2246 from WXYZ company. The type, color, and general characteristics are very similar.

Siding — The brand requested is not available through our distribution network. It can be special ordered, but this requires payment prior to order placement. A proposed substitute is product number 4456 from ABEC company. The color and general features are essentially the same as the requested siding.

How to Negotiate for Big Savings

10

At the end of the last chapter, we looked at ways to save money by comparing bids. In this chapter, I am going to expose the secrets professionals use to obtain the lowest prices possible. You can save big money with the right techniques. These savings are especially evident on larger jobs. The more you are buying, or contracting for, the more you can save. Contractors and suppliers rarely give you their lowest price. They are in business to make money and will not voluntarily give any more than necessary to win the job. Getting to the bottom line will take time and planning on your part. Your efforts will be compensated with meaningful savings.

As a consumer, it is difficult to recognize inflated prices. You have very little to compare prices with, and most comparisons come from the same type of sources. All of these sources are looking to make money and increase the list price of their material accordingly. How will you know when you have reached your best deal? Getting to the lowest price is a matter of trial and error. You have to keep negotiating until you are at a standstill. By using special tactics, you can be more successful than most consumers. These strategies will be explained, in detail, throughout this chapter.

SAVINGS FROM SUPPLIERS

Suppliers offer you the most opportunity for savings. They price materials in different levels, and as a homeowner, you will be given the highest prices of all. The average homeowner accepts this and pays the premium price. If you work on this area, you can save a minimum of 10%. The savings can be much larger, because various items carry different percentages of markup.

Understanding Markups

Some of the items with the highest markups are the ones you are most likely to use. These products include kitchen cabinets, plumbing fixtures, light fixtures, and other finish items. Lumber and basic construction materials fluctuate in the percentage of markup, as do windows and doors. Almost any expensive item will have a large profit built into the sales price. Wholesale prices vary as much as 30%, and average consumer markups run from 10% to 50%. This means there is a big spread in the prices you might pay for identical materials. Buying from the right place can reduce your costs by an average of 15%.

The products with the highest markups are frequently light fixtures. Lights carry price increases of up to 100% above what the electrical contractor pays. Why do light fixtures support a 100% markup, compared to plumbing fixtures, at a 25% markup? Most light fixtures are low dollar items, allowing for a larger retail markup. Excessive markup on an already costly whirlpool would reduce its market appeal. No one questions the $20 price of a light fixture that wholesales for $10. Ten dollars seems a small expense when compared to the $5,000 it will cost to remodel your bathroom.

As a contractor, I have seen the contractors' prices and compared them to retail price tags on light fixtures. They frequently carry a 75% or higher markup. Obviously, if an electrical supplier wants to make a sale, there is room to negotiate a lower price. Sometimes, all you have to do is ask for a lower price, but there are occasions when you must be a tough negotiator.

Now, we know light fixtures carry a large markup and are a good target for price savings. The next phase to look at is plumbing. Plumbing fixtures are a good category to scrutinize. In some areas, only licensed plumbers can buy direct from wholesale dealers. In other locations, you can buy from wholesale dealers, but only at retail prices. Try to get prices from both your plumber and a supplier for the same products. There is no way of knowing who will give you a better price, until you compare them side by side.

Some plumbing contractors sell their fixtures considerably above the suggested list price. Others let you have the material at 10% above their cost. They do this to win the overall bid and make a profit from their standard hourly labor rate. On items over $200, the average markup to you, from a plumber, will be between 10% and 35%. On less expensive items, the percentage may be as high as 100%.

Plumbing fixtures purchased directly from a supplier will carry average markups from 20 to 50% above wholesale. The brand and price range of the item are the determining factors in the markup. A toilet will have a markup of about 75%, and a standard bathtub will carry a profit percentage of about 45%. Inexpensive wall-hung lavatories can be marked up 65%, and well pumps can have profit margins of 100%. The kitchen faucet you pay $95 for will cost the plumber around $58. More expensive items, like whirlpools, carry markups in the 25% range. Armed with this knowledge, you can whittle away at plumbing profit margins during the negotiation process.

Heating systems carry markups in the 40% level. Don't overlook heating accessories while campaigning for a lower price on the main heating unit. HVAC accessories can be sold at profits as high as 100%. As a savvy consumer, work all the angles in achieving the lowest prices possible. Furnaces and boilers are worth negotiating for, but the big savings are in the accessories. The contractor may sell the main heating system at only 20% above his cost, but will undermine your budget with the parts that go with it. The thermostats, valves, and similar items may be marked up by 75% or more. Ask for a detailed breakdown of all labor and materials.

Getting Price Breakdowns

Most contractors will try to avoid giving itemized breakdowns of their prices. The first strategy might be to show you the actual invoice on the product. They will explain that they are only marking the unit up by 20%. The contractor will try to justify the need for this with overhead expenses. These expenses include delivery, paperwork, and insurance. All of this will make sense and sound reasonable, which is the whole purpose for showing you the figures. The contractor's attempt is to justify the profit margin and get you to agree his markups are fair.

Most strict investigation from consumers ends here. The ploy is to convince you that the prices are fair. Once you see the actual invoice on a product, you are expected to admit the price is rational. While the markup on the main unit is fair, they can fleece you with little items. The majority of contractors will not be trying to take advantage of you. Only a few will resort to these unsavory sales tactics. They put your suspicions to rest with the big ticket item and empty your wallet with the accessories. Most homeowners stop asking questions after seeing the actual invoice on the most expensive item. This is where they make their big mistake. Don't accept evidence of one or two items; require a detailed breakdown on all labor and material.

WHERE CAN YOU FIND THE SAVINGS?

Basic construction products are the hardest to save on. Drywall, paint, lumber, and related items offer markups in the 10 to 20% range. These percentages are lower, but the volume of materials used will justify negotiating. You will use more of these items than anything else. Do not be blinded by the relatively small percentages of profit. Spend enough time shopping to be sure you are getting the best deals available. Saving 5% on all the lumber and drywall used to build your addition will make a huge difference in the price.

Floor coverings are an excellent place to save big money. Carpet and vinyl are marked up by as much as 75%. All the subtle little extras — stain resistance, no wax, and associated terms — add to the price. There are several grades and types of flooring from which to choose. Ceramic tile floors give contractors a hefty markup on materials. You can beat these prices at tile outlet centers and through negotiations.

Kitchen cabinets and countertops are another area to attack. The profit percentage here can easily exceed 60%, with markups on custom cabinets being even more. Kitchen appliances cost the contractor 10 to 15% less than the typical consumer. These items may not be worth your time and trouble, depending on what your time is worth. Special kitchen items carry the largest markups. Objects like garden-style windows have absurd profits built into the sales price. The same is true of unusual sinks and faucets. With any of these items, save money with thrifty shopping and supply the product yourself. Research your costs and compare them to the contractor's material quote. Remember to allow for delivery charges if you supply the materials yourself. By investing your time, the savings can mount up.

Insulation isn't worth your time. The markups are low and the savings are minimal. Hire subcontractors to supply and install the insulation. In some cases, you cannot buy the material for the price a contractor charges to supply and install it. Many people experience skin irritations from insulation. Unless you enjoy working for minimal savings and getting very itchy, avoid doing your own insulation. It is just not worth the effort.

Windows and doors are a different story. Depending upon brand, the markup can hit 65%. This amounts to a lot in an addition full of windows. Make the supplier sharpen her pencil on the window and door prices; there is plenty of room for discounts here. Beat the supplier to her lowest price and supply your own windows and doors. You'll be glad you did.

Standard trim lumber does not offer much room for savings, but custom-milled trim material does. If you are going with standard trim, let the subcontractor supply it. Most of what you lose will be headaches. On the other hand, wallpaper is an excellent source of savings. It carries a profit ranging from 45 to 100%. By now, you're getting the picture. There are certain areas to aim your efforts at, when seeking lower prices. Now that you know what to save on, you must learn how to achieve those savings.

NEGOTIATING WITH SUPPLIERS

I have found the best approach with material suppliers is to put numbers in front of them. I mentioned this method in Chapter 9. To get the lowest price, you need to have your facts together and be ready to make a commitment. After collecting several bids from suppliers, you're ready to play the game. This is like playing poker but, because you already hold the winning hand, you show your cards to the other players. Use your bid request sheet, which breaks down the different phases of the job, to enter various suppliers' prices. Listing them side by side creates a strong graphic impression. When a supplier sees the competition's prices, it has a hard-hitting effect.

Sit down with the manager of the building supply store and show her where her prices are too high. Stress your interest in buying all of your material from her company. Then ask her to reconsider the store's original quote. The odds are good you will be offered reduced pricing. If you aren't, pack up your bid request sheet and visit the other suppliers. Don't be haughty or rude to any of the stores—you may have to deal with them later.

If you live in a small town, branch out with your savings effort. Call suppliers in nearby larger cities. Pricing is often more competitive in an area with more competition. Cities provide higher populations and higher demand. They also support more building supply outlets. These factors contribute to lower prices. Many out-of-town suppliers will deliver to your job at no additional cost. It requires extra time to investigate the options, but the savings can be outstanding.

I have priced my material 20% below my competitors, and still made more money than they did. This was possible because of aggressive shopping. A savings of 20% on materials amounts to a lot of money, and homeowners have the same option to save money through serious shopping. If you act as your own general contractor and find a discount supplier, you could save 30% on the total cost of your job. On a $40,000 job, this is a savings of $12,000.

SUPPLYING MATERIALS YOURSELF

If you find a contractor with inflated material prices, offer to supply the material yourself. Be prepared for a battle. Many contractors will tell you they don't work with owner-supplied material. Some of their reasons have merit. Frequently, owners make mistakes ordering materials, costing the contractor time and money. When a contractor sends a full crew to your house, they are expected to work.

If you make a mistake with the material acquisition, the crews may not be able to work. The same is true if the material you receive is the wrong material or damaged. Either way, the crews cannot work. This is disappointing to you and devastating to the contractor. Your slip-up on material can cost the contractor $1,200 a day. These events happen often enough to make experienced contractors apprehensive.

Offer to Pay a Penalty Fee

When they hit you with this objection, take it away. Tell the contractor you will pay extra for any time lost due to your failure to have the correct materials on the job. When you make this offer, be prepared to volley back and forth for control. You have just agreed to put a special clause in the contract to protect the contractor; don't make this agreement completely one-sided in favor of the contractor. The remodeler may request to be compensated an hourly rate for all lost time. If so, this rate should be reasonable and should have an established maximum daily limit.

The contractor might try to require a daily penalty for every mishap you make. While you can understand why contractors must protect their income from your inexperience, you must remain in control at all times. The contract provisions should not include excessive penalties or compensation. After all, if the shoe was on the other foot, would the contractor agree to pay you $1,000 for every day his material delivery was delayed? Do not create a situation where a contractor looks for reasons why his crews cannot work. Keep the contractor motivated to complete the job, rather than giving him an opportunity to abuse your bank account.

You can protect yourself by scheduling your material deliveries to arrive two days before they will be needed. Agree to pay the contractor a delay fee only if you are unable to give him twenty-four hours' notice of a scheduling change. With this much time, he can change his schedule and not lose money from lack of work the next day. You want to propose a fair agreement to both parties. If the contractor still balks at your offer, you have exposed a greedy contractor. This remodeler is either trying to hide excessive profit in his material prices or wants to milk penalty fees out of you. You may reach a standoff, with no satisfactory solution. If the contractor refuses to price the job, based on installing your materials, find another contractor.

When the remodeler is working on a contract price, he can't afford lost time. The quicker the job is finished, the more money he makes. If you supply the material, he doesn't have control of the job production time. Your offer to compensate for any lost time removes the contractor's risk of loss. Any continued resistance from the contractor indicates definite trouble. No reputable contractor will refuse to use your materials under the proper conditions. Conversely, be suspicious of a contractor who insists you supply all the materials. These may be remodeling bandits, setting you up to steal your materials and disappear into another state. Stick to your guns and keep the contractor leveraged into the job. Never pay retail prices for materials, and cover all the bases.

Getting contractors to lower their prices is difficult. Contractors can be very independent and stubborn. If you try to supply your own material, some contractors won't do your work, because they want the extra profit from material markups. If the contractor you choose is a small operator, he might appreciate your supplying the material. He will not have to tie up money in materials and won't have to worry about getting paid on time for his materials. Supplying your own material is a great way to cut costs, if you can coordinate punctual, accurate deliveries.

NEGOTIATING LABOR RATES

Negotiating for lower labor rates is the hardest part of the bidding process. Good people won't work cheap — they don't need to. There is a shortage of quality contractors, and superior tradesmen know they are in demand. These contractors know they can maintain their prices and still stay busy. In most cases, it is possible to shave up to 7% off the labor quotes without sacrificing the best contractors. Most good remodelers factor in this much to allow for problems.

If this buffer amount is the pivotal point, the contractor may forfeit it to secure the job. If he refuses to drop his prices, chances are you have found a good contractor. These expert tradesmen rarely take a job with the intent of breaking even or losing money. Keep this in mind: contractors have overhead expenses and need a fair wage to survive.

Labor is different from material; it doesn't carry the same kind of profit latitude. Material is easy — a supplier buys a sink for a fixed price and sells it for a profit. Labor doesn't work that way. A contractor can never be absolutely sure of the labor cost to do a job. He can't look in a catalog and determine his exact cost. All he can do is draw on his experience to estimate the total labor needed for the project. With remodeling, this guesswork is especially difficult. How can you calculate the exact time required to replace kitchen cabinets? Determining the amount of time needed to raise a roof or add a dormer is an exacting process.

When a contractor is dealing with new construction, such as additions, estimates are much easier to make. There are no existing conditions to contend with. The contractor knows what to expect when building a garage, and can be comfortable with the man-hours needed to complete the job. Stripping an existing bathroom to the bare studs and joists is a different story. Estimating the labor in this situation is risky. The best a remodeler can do is to rely on his years of experience, and allow for the unexpected by padding the price.

There is no way to know what will be found when the wall coverings are removed. Suppose the floor joists are rotted? Will the existing conditions allow for a satisfactory finish, without unplanned, additional work? Warped walls or floor joists require additional preparation before the finished products can be applied. On one remodeling job, we opened the wall to do a simple sink installation and discovered a swarm of bees. Working in a beekeeper's suit slows your work down quite a bit! A seasoned contractor will have some money loaded into the quote to allow for these unforeseen problems. You can extract this money from the bid and enjoy the savings.

Guarantees and Contingencies

How can you persuade the contractor to eliminate his buffer zone and drop the extra money figured into his price? You can offer guarantees, and you can make your contract contingent on certain circumstances. This technique can save you money, and it may put the contractor at ease. When a reputable remodeler pads a bid, it is to protect against unknown conditions. You can act as an insurance company and play the odds. How often will bathroom floor joists be rotted? Normally, there will be evidence to suggest a problem with the floor structure. The floor will slope, the toilet will be unstable, or the baseboard trim will be discolored. Contractors look for these warning signs and you can too.

In the remodeling game, the odds can favor an informed homeowner. This is a strategic, mental battle, like chess. When the contractor has given you his best price, make your first move. Ask the contractor what he can do to reduce the price. The contractor will probably claim he cannot go any lower on the price. Ask if he has included an allowance for unforeseen problems. If the contractor says he doesn't allow extras for problems, find a new contractor. This one is either inexperienced, or he is lying to you. When the contractor admits to an extra cushion in the bid, make your next move. Explain that you understand his need to allow for unexpected problems. Offer to remove this risk from his contract, by inserting a clause regarding existing conditions. The clause will protect the contractor from the unexpected.

Compare with Other Contractors

You can try to lower a contractor's price by comparing it to that of other contractors. In slower economic times, this will be an effective tool. If there are more quality contractors than there is work, you are in the power position. In strong economic times, you lose this leverage against the remodelers. Even in a poor economy, good remodelers are in demand. Slow economic conditions force people to remodel, because they can't afford to buy or sell. These factors make it tough to get a reduced price from remodelers; good remodelers' rates are usually firm. If you can get any discount, you've done a good job.

Make the Job Attractive

Making your job attractive to the contractor is the key to bargaining for a lower price. Every time a contractor bids a job, he is asked the same question, "Is this the best you can do?" Don't begin your negotiations with this obvious lead-in. Go around to the back door and offer to increase the contractor's benefits. Are you dealing with subcontractors in various trades? Here are some tidbits to whet their appetites.

General contractors rarely offer contract deposits to their subs. The accepted business practice is to pay for the job within thirty days of completion. If you are willing to pay promptly, you can demand a lower price. Giving a deposit when materials are delivered is another way to make your job appealing. Now the sub doesn't have to pay for that $2,000 spa out of his own pocket. Your ability to keep a subcontractor's cash flow at high tide is a powerful motivator.

Creative scheduling is another trump card you can play. Evaluate your timetable and production needs, then consider allowing the subcontractor to use your job as fill-in work. If your job allows for such latitude, this is a powerful option to exercise. For the subcontractor, a fill-in job means steady work. You provide him with the opportunity to be productive and earn income when problems occur on other jobs. It is not uncommon for a contractor to plan a full day's work, only to wind up with nothing to do.

In the construction business, weather has a major influence on production schedules. If a carpenter is planning to work on exterior framing and it rains, what are his options? He could go home, but that doesn't put food on the table. Your fill-in job can save the day. Don't overlook this advantage in your negotiations.

Did you find your subcontractors by looking at other neighborhood jobs? If so, try to get a price break for being conveniently located to an ongoing job. Contractors like to have several jobs in the same area for two reasons. It affords them more exposure and reduces their operating expenses. Business builds on business. Contractors recognize yard signs as effective, low-cost advertising. The more signs they have in a subdivision, the better their chances are of getting more work. The contractor can also juggle workmen and material deliveries between neighboring jobs. If you point out these opportunities, you certainly will open the door to lower prices.

When you start to talk with subcontractors, ask questions about their willingness and availability to do your work. Try to establish their true motivations. If you learn enough about them, you can uncover areas for focusing your negotiations. Most general contractors try to beat subcontractors down to their lowest price. Acting as your own general, you can pay the sub more for the job and still make money. You can't compete with the volume offered by established general contractors, but you can successfully win subcontractors away. Your job can offer more money and added benefits. You can negotiate for low prices without sacrificing quality.

DON'T SACRIFICE QUALITY FOR PRICE

Cutting corners on contractors can become very

expensive. Choosing a contractor with the lowest bid could be a major mistake. You have to evaluate the quality of the contractor's work and the caliber of each contractor. When you find the right one, he may be expensive. Jockey for the best position possible, but keep in mind his abilities could be well worth the price. Don't pay a premium price for substandard work, and avoid paying full-time rates for part-time production. Beware of part-timers who only do this kind of work for extra money.

Part-timers

Moonlighters often work for a fraction of the cost of a full-time contractor. In some rare circumstances, this is good value. More often than not, it is trouble. These occasional contractors seldom have the proper insurance, and many are not licensed. If they were truly good at the trade, they would probably be working for themselves full-time. Part-timers fall into two categories.

The first group is working for extra money, and they have no intention of building a business. These contractors are dangerous. You will have no recourse for warranty claims, and they can disappear overnight.

The second group is interested in starting a full-time business. To go into business, you must set aside operating capital. The transition period between full-time employee and full-time business owner is arduous. A delicate balance must be maintained until the change can be made. These would-be contractors can represent your best value. They will give you excellent service, because they want to establish references to build their business.

Offer to allow the contractor to use your job as a reference, and request a lower price for the privilege. This helps both of you. Your reference provides the contractor with new work, which benefits his business growth. If the contractor is successful in business, he will be there for your future needs. If he is seriously gearing up a business, the contractor will have licenses and insurance. If he doesn't, don't use him. All the savings in the world are not worth the damages caused by an unlicensed contractor with no insurance.

REALISTIC SAVINGS

Concentrate your savings efforts on material. When you are shopping for specific brands and model numbers, it is easy to recognize a good deal.

If the two products are identical and delivery is available, the lowest bidder should win. You don't have to use judgment in evaluating the differences in identical materials — there aren't any. With contractors, you cannot be so sure of your decisions. Don't bargain yourself into a bad deal.

Your goal is to obtain prices that are competitive and realistic. This requires detective work, determination, and the ability to gain the upper hand. Once you sit down at the bargaining table, judge the circumstances, and play all of your cards. Increased savings is your reward for mastering the challenging game of negotiation.

Get It
in Writing

Get it in writing! These four words convey the most important message in remodeling. The significance of having everything in writing cannot be stressed enough. Written documents eliminate confusion and solve problems before they happen. Concise written agreements protect your investment and assure your satisfaction. Without these agreements, you are exposed to a variety of uncontrollable, potentially devastating problems. At the end of this chapter, you will find examples of forms that are vital to the success of your remodeling project. After reading this chapter, you will understand the function of each form, as well as the importance of getting everything in writing.

THE OUTLINE

The first form you will use is the Outline. This form gives you the ability to document and organize your intended improvements in writing. No signatures or legal jargon are required on this form. It is simply an orderly list of your desires. A good outline should be designed in chronological order. The categories create an overview of the scope of the work to be done. The information should focus on the types of work you want done, not the products you intend to use. If you want to convert a closet, or make room for a whirlpool tub, this is where you define the project. Two sample outlines for each of the five major projects can be found at the end of the chapter. The first style, Outline of Work to be Done, shows examples of considerations for the construction of each project. The second, Categories of Work to be Done, simply lists each stage

of construction in order. Either of these methods is effective.

Keeping a written report of your remodeling interests will make your life simpler. You won't forget to have work priced in the bidding stage, because the outline reminds you what to request quotes on. Put everything in the outline. Include the faucets you want replaced, the location of carpets to be installed, and the skylight you are considering. This is not a bid sheet, so put everything you want on it. You can edit the list later; it is only for proposed work. Listing specific products will complicate the form and make it less effective.

CONTRACTOR SELECTION FORM

When your outline is complete, move on to the Contractor Selection Form. This form is designed to help you during the contractor selection process. All the major groups of subcontractors are listed on the form, and you should note those you will need on your job. When you get to the bidding process, this list will be very helpful. Knowing which subs to call will be obvious, and omissions are less likely. The contractor selection form can also remind you of a phase of work previously forgotten.

You will know if you need to call a plumber, an electrician, an insulator, or other tradesman. This form serves as a reminder, to tell you what trades will be needed to complete the work. You will need competitive bids for each phase of the job to plan your budget. A budget loses its effectiveness if you forget you will need a tile contractor for your bathroom remodel. There are spaces on the form to list the name and phone number of the company you choose to do each phase of work. This allows you to use the form as a quick reference sheet during the project. You may think you could never forget to get prices from all the necessary subs, but it can happen in a flash. When you are deeply involved in a project, details can slip through the cracks. The more you have in writing, the less you will forget.

PROFESSIONAL SERVICES DIRECTORY

Now you know the work you want done and the type of contractors you need to complete the job. The next document to use is the Professional Services Directory. This form is similar to the contractor guide, in that it lists all the services you will require. An example of this service directory is located at the end of the chapter. Surveyors, architects, draftsmen, attorneys, and other professionals should be indexed on this form.

Your mind is on the physical aspects of the job. Are you likely to recognize the need for a surveyor? If you're adding on to your home, or building a new structure, you will need one. There have been times when a garage or addition was erected on a neighbor's land. This is a big problem. In these cases, you may be required to move the structure. Using a certified surveyor helps you avoid such expensive miscalculations. The professional service directory tells you whom to include in your arrangements.

If a problem comes to light after a professional survey, you will have someone to blame. The problem is a result of the surveyor's mistake. The expense of moving the addition will still be incurred, but the surveyor will be responsible for the additional costs. Although this will not make the move any easier, it will soften the financial blow to you. The huge cost of relocating your new structure could put you into bankruptcy; the small cost of a survey is good insurance.

Don't trust vague descriptions of your land. Know where you can build and where you can't. Check with local authorities to determine setback requirements in your community. Just because you own the land doesn't mean you can build on it. The utility company may have an easement across your property, which prohibits building. Review the list of professionals on the sample form, and see which ones you might need. All of this paperwork will pay off in the long run, by reducing your problems and your exposure to trouble.

QUERY LETTER

Your next written tool will be the Query Letter, which requests prices and the availability of services. Mailing this form letter to all the professionals you anticipate needing will save you time and money. The letter saves hours of phone calls to answering services. All you have to do is customize the form letter provided at the end of the chapter, make photocopies, and send them to prospective professionals. Mailed requests for information are an effective way to cover all the bases. You can send a letter to every surveyor in the phone book and eliminate days of phone calls. An example of a completed query letter is also included at the end of the chapter.

Form letters allow you to achieve maximum results with minimum effort. They are effective with professionals, contractors, and suppliers alike. Written requests for service rates, material prices, and availability will eliminate uninterested parties. Some companies will not respond to your requests, and others will be afraid to put anything in writing. Scratch them off your list. A form letter saves you untold time in wasted phone calls. The companies who respond to your letter will be anxious for your business. These companies offer the best opportunity for good service and low prices.

PRODUCT IDENTIFICATION SHEET

The next form you will need is the Product Identification Sheet. This sheet is broken down into construction phases. It will detail all the specifics of the products you are interested in. An example of this form was provided at the end of Chapter 3. The sheet lists information such as: brand name, model number, color, size, and other pertinent information. This breakdown can be included with your specifications and used in conjunction with your bid request. It guarantees you are getting prices for the right material. You can make the form as explicit as you think is necessary, to remove any doubt about the products to be priced. Don't allow substitutions without your written consent, in the form of a change order. (The change order form will be discussed later in this chapter.)

Do you feel like you are being buried in paperwork? These forms don't have to be used, but the results, without them, are unpredictable at best. At this point, you know what work you want done and the people required to do it. You even have your product list ready for bids. Are you ready to start the job? No, there is still work to be done in the office, before the field work is started.

ESTIMATED COST SHEET

Review the information you have assembled. Create files for all the suppliers and contractors. These files will help you during your negotiations and final decision. Using the Estimated Cost Sheet from Chapter 9 is the next logical item to approach. This worksheet will give you a rough idea of the costs required to complete your remodeling project. The estimate sheet will be divided into phases of work such as: framing, siding, trim, electrical, hvac, plumbing, and the other trades. These phases are considered hard costs. In addition, your estimated cost sheet should include soft costs. These are professional fees, loan application fees, interest charges, and other broad-based costs. Soft costs can add up to a staggering figure, so be on the ball and do not overlook them.

The estimated cost sheet should include all expenses. You have to know what the total cash requirements will be before committing to a project. Without including soft costs, you could run out of money before the job is finished. Review the sample cost sheets and add categories as needed. Some hidden expenses could be related to a home improvement loan. These loans can require points, title searches, loan application fees, closing costs, and other finance-related expenses. Be aware of these potential costs, and allow for them in your estimate.

SPECIFICATIONS SHEET

With your estimating done, you can move on to the next step. This involves fine-tuning your preliminary design. Refer to the specifications sheet you have created. It should detail all of the proposed materials required for the job. This is where you begin to cross-reference the information in the stack of paperwork you have generated. The specifications sheet should be accompanied by a revised contractor list. Perhaps you found you cannot afford a stone fireplace or quarry tile floor. These changes need to be reflected in your spec sheet. Adjust the estimated remodeling costs in accordance with your proposed changes. At this stage, you are getting ready to go for final quotes.

The changes you make within the specifications sheet may affect your contractor selection list. Changing the scope of the work may eliminate the need for some subcontractors. Make these notations on your contractor selection form. Don't waste time contacting contractors you won't need. The purpose of all this paperwork is to simplify your remodeling project once it is started. Keeping current, accurate records will achieve the intended goal. The planning stages of a remodeling job set the pace for the whole project.

If you have endured this onslaught of forms, you are on your way to a successful job. Every job should start with good written agreements and a strong production plan. Predicting an accurate financial budget is vital to completing a successful job. By this time, you have a good idea of the extent of the project you are embarking on. The next forms will take on a new level of importance. Up until now, the paperwork has been for your reference only. Now we will be dealing with forms creating commitments between you and the people involved in your remodeling project.

BID REQUEST FORM

The bidding process is the financial backbone of your job. Chapter 9 addressed the procedure for requesting and obtaining the best quotes. The Bid Request Form (found in that chapter) is an intricate part of the bidding process. Without it, you are dealing with ambiguous bulk numbers.

CONTRACTOR QUESTIONNAIRE

When you are ready to start making commitments, you need to tie down the details. The Contractor Questionnaire at the end of this chapter can help with this important procedure. Do the contractors you plan to use have liability insurance? Do they provide worker's compensation insurance for their employees? Are their workers properly licensed? Does the contractor have the required business licenses? Is the contractor licensed to do the work you are requesting? Will the work performed be done by employees or subcontractors? Is the contractor bonded? Has he ever had complaints filed by other customers?

These are questions you should answer before signing a contract. The questionnaire is designed to ask these questions without embarrassing you.

When a contractor is asked to complete a form, he knows you are requesting the same information from other contractors. This competition will provide the motivation for the contractor to answer the questions. The form gives you the opportunity to get a contractor's answers in writing.

It is easy for a remodeler to side-step your verbal questions or even to answer the questions with lies. Questionable contractors will think twice before answering with lies in writing — they could be charged with fraud. This is a proven way to cull the crop of bad contractors. Don't feel bad about asking them to complete this form. If they are good contractors, they will have no problem answering the questions in writing. The bad contractors will disappear and save you a lot of trouble.

SUBCONTRACTOR AND SUPPLIER AGREEMENTS

Once you find the right contractors, you are ready to proceed with your contracts. There is no reason to limit written contracts to tradespeople. There is an example of an owner-supplied subcontractor agreement at the end of Chapter 9. While it not a routine business practice to contract with suppliers, it is a good idea. You can achieve additional assurances of your prices and delivery dates with a solid contract. Don't be afraid to ask for a contract from everyone involved in the project. Everything you have in writing reduces your risks.

I once asked a subcontractor to sign a foundation contract. This man was about 6'6" tall and tipped the scale at 320 pounds. He told me he had never signed a contract during his fifteen years in business, because his word was his bond. At that point, I had two choices. I could risk insulting this gentleman by insisting on a contract, or I could take him at his word. Being an experienced builder, I decided to take my life into my hands and pursue the contract.

I approached the subject again, but from an inoffensive angle. Explaining I was confident the contractor was a man of his word, I subtly pointed out the benefits of a written contract from his standpoint. First, I asked if the homeowners could pick any brick they wanted, from any supplier in town. No, he responded, it must be builder-grade material from XYZ Supply. His price to me was to build the foundation of the house, did that mean it would be five courses high or ten? When he replied five, I explained I had estimated seven courses when I bid

the overall project. I was assuming his price was based on seven courses of material. If he submitted a bill charging extra for those two courses, bad feelings and disagreements would ensue. Finally, I explained the contract was not intended to tie him down, but rather to protect him from any misunderstandings. At that point, we amicably signed my subcontractor agreement, and the project proceeded smoothly. By the way, the job required seven courses of brick.

THE WRITTEN CONTRACT

A written contract with your general contractor or subcontractors is absolutely necessary. Contracts are an accepted requirement in building and remodeling. The contract should be strict but fair. If you slant the contract too heavily to your advantage, contractors will not sign it. Most contractors will want you to sign their proposal or contract. They will have pre-printed forms, with the information regarding your job filled into the blank spaces. Contracts ultimately protect those who write them, so try to avoid using a contract supplied by others. Contractors may be resistant at first, but they will sign your contract if it is fair.

The written contract is the last word in your job. It answers all the questions and calls all the shots. Legal documents, such as contracts, should be prepared by attorneys. Attorneys have the skill and knowledge to write contracts capable of standing the test of the courts. The contract is for your benefit, and you should have some input as to its structure. Don't leave the contract preparation in the hands of a lawyer without your personal input. Lawyers know law, but they don't necessarily know remodeling. When you get to Chapter 14, you will find an example of an owner-supplied contract, which includes important language and clauses. This example will be explained and the purpose of various clauses defined. You can offer this sample to your attorney as a guideline for your contract.

Now, it's done. You have all your contracts signed. For awhile, you thought you would never see the end of the paperwork. Well, you haven't, the job is only about to begin. There are reams of paper yet to be used. A successful job runs on paper. Without it, you will suffer in the end. What else could you possibly need to put in writing? Some suggestions include change orders, lien waivers, and completion certificates.

CHANGE ORDERS

Once the job is started, it is sure to produce unexpected results. When these problems arise, you need to adapt your plans and agreements to accommodate any necessary changes. Use a written Change Order for every deviation from the contract. There is a Sample Change Order, as well as a Blank Change Order Form, provided at the end of this chapter. You must maintain consistency in your construction management. Written change orders reinforce your dedication to have every aspect of the work clearly defined in black and white.

During the job, you will be tempted to avoid all of this paperwork, especially change orders. You will gain a comfort level with your contractors, which will make change orders seem unnecessary. So far, the contractors have been great to work with and have done what they said they would. If you get a phone call at the office regarding mandatory alterations, you will be tempted to give verbal authorization for changes over the phone. Resist these urges. If the situation demands immediate verbal authorization, follow it up with a change order as soon as possible. It is important to maintain continuity. If you start making exceptions, your paperwork will become almost useless.

Contractors will be less likely to take advantage of you when change orders are used, and there will be fewer misunderstandings. Requiring the use of written change orders prevents unexpected price increases. Your contract should state that change orders will be required for any changes or additional work. In this way, a contractor is not entitled to payment for extra work, unless you first authorize it in writing. By requiring written change orders, you will be better prepared if you find yourself in court.

Going to court is never a planned part of remodeling. It is an activity you want to avoid. The best way to bypass the courts is to maintain clear, concise written agreements. When you follow the rule of requiring written agreements, your position will be stronger if a contractor causes you trouble. A judge will consider your use of written agreements. Showing a judge your piles of paper will prove you only authorized changes in writing. A contractor making a verbal claim will have little chance of prevailing, if you maintain a strong management posture. Under these circumstances, the contractor will be unlikely to triumph without a signed change order. Do not make exceptions. No matter how inconvenient it is, get everything in writing.

CODE VIOLATION NOTIFICATION

As work progresses, contractors will want to be paid. In most cases, local code enforcement inspections will be required on the work done. Don't advance any payments until these inspections are completed and accepted. The codes office will provide written evidence of satisfactory inspections. Insist on a copy of each inspection certificate from the contractor. This protects you from code violation problems. If a codes officer turns down an inspection, complete a Code Violation Notification, and give it to the appropriate contractor. A sample notification letter can be found at the end of Chapter 13. This notification gives the contractor a specific period of time to have the work corrected and approved by the codes officer. In this way, you avoid delays that may affect other trades and throw your project way off schedule. Stipulate, in the contract, your desire for a photocopy of all permits and inspection results. Never advance money to a contractor until the work passes the inspection of the local codes officer.

LIEN WAIVER FORM

Before paying anyone, you should complete a Lien Waiver form. These forms should be signed by any vendor receiving money for services or materials related to your job. Require the lien waiver to be signed at the time you make payment for the service or material. The lien waiver is like your receipt for issuing payment, and will protect your home from mechanic's and materialman's liens. There are detailed explanations and examples of lien waivers in Chapter 13. For now, know that these should be signed every time money is advanced for services or materials. Any experienced contractor will be familiar with lien waivers and will not resist signing the form when he is paid.

PUNCH LISTS

A Punch List is a written notice, to contractors, of items left to be completed or repaired. These lists come into play at the end of the job; a sample punch list can be found at the end of Chapter 18. When the contractors are finished, you should inspect all the work before final payment is made. Use the Punch List form to note all unsatisfactory or incomplete workmanship or materials. After your inspection, and before final payment, present a copy of the punch list to the contractor. Have the contractor agree to the list by signing it, and allow a reasonable time for corrections to be made. When the punch-out work is done, inspect the job again. If there are still deficiencies, complete another punch list. Continue this process until the work is done to your satisfaction.

Here is some advice about the proper use of the punch list. Remember, throughout the remodeling process we have stressed the need to be fair. Be realistic about the work you demand on the punch list. Don't require the contractor to replace an entire roll of wallpaper just because there is a tiny wrinkle down by the floor. By the same token, do not allow a contractor to bully you into accepting work with obvious or offensive flaws. Be very thorough when you make the first punch list. Contractors will be quickly angered if they repair everything on your list only to have you find additional items you missed in your initial inspection. The only items added to the list should have been *caused* by the punch-out work.

For example, during your initial inspection you discover the hot and cold water are reversed on your kitchen sink. This is not uncommon, especially with some brands of single-handle faucets. After the plumber repairs the situation, you notice the sink drain is leaking. Many times, the drain seal will be disturbed during work on a sink, causing it to develop a leak. You do not have to accept problems that arise as the result of fixing defects. When everything is complete to your specifications, make your final payment according to the terms of your contract. These terms should allow a retainage for unknown defects.

RETAINAGES

Retainages are usually 5% of the contract amount. On some occasions, they can be as much as 10%, depending on the scope of the work and the language in the contract. These retainages protect you from problems that may crop up in the first thirty days after completion. If everything is all right after thirty days, you must pay the contractor in full. There is no special form for retainages; they should be covered in your contract. You will need a certificate of completion, indicating the date all work was completed, to establish the thirty-day waiting period.

CERTIFICATE OF COMPLETION

Certificates of Completion document the conclusion dates of all work performed. Chapter 18 gives an example of a completion notice. This form is important in determining your warranty and retainage periods. Contractors normally offer one-year warranties on their work, and the manufacturer's warranty applies to individual products. These warranties should start with the date on the completion certificate. These simple forms take the guesswork out of warranty claims and retainage disputes. They clearly establish the date all work was completed, inspected, and approved. These little pieces of paper can make a big difference if you have a major malfunction or problem.

ELIMINATE MISUNDERSTANDING

Many of the problems in remodeling are not caused by intentional deceit, they are caused by confusion. You are thinking one thing, and the contractor is thinking something else. You both have good intentions, but the conflict can get out of hand. Neither of you will want to give ground in the dispute when money is involved. With oral agreements, there is no way to determine who is right. Written agreements eliminate the source of confusion. Each party knows exactly what he is expected to do and what he will be getting from the contractual relationship.

Working with close friends can be the worst experience of your life. Business is business, and it can become a true threat to relationships. Friends don't want to insult each other; consequently, they avoid written contracts. Trust is not a factor, and the lack of a good contract can ruin your friendship. Money is a powerful thing and can cause people to forget about friendship. Financial disputes can turn into all-out battles. The friend you play golf with every week can become your worst enemy over a simple misunderstanding. Written contracts protect you *and* your friends.

Finally, it is over. The job is done and you are happy. There were no problems you couldn't handle, and everything went smoothly. You can attribute this to having everything in writing. Believe me, if you had left the job to chance, you would be a frustrated homeowner. By removing the risk of confusion, you coordinated a successful job. The vast majority of remodeling jobs that end in despair are the product of poor preparation and planning. The odds indicate contractors will try to gain control of a job and turn adversity into their advantage. Congratulations, you beat the odds!

People have two opinions about remodeling. The first is based on the misconception that remodeling is easy. This group of people think remodeling is something *anyone* can handle. Actually, remodeling is a challenging activity. Successful jobs look easy, because proper procedures are implemented and specialized professionals are used. The second group believes remodeling is the worst burden they could be asked to bear. They have heard wild accounts of every remodeling problem you can imagine. This view is wrong too. Remodeling isn't easy, but it is not a wicked curse either. It requires attention to details and planning, which means homeowners can run their own projects with the right preparation. A good general contractor will make the job look very simple. It's all a matter of how the job is executed. Look ahead, get everything in writing, and enjoy a job well done.

OUTLINE OF WORK TO BE DONE
BATHROOM REMODELING

_____ Obtain various product information.
_____ Review requirements of space: linen closet, door sizes, windows, additional electrical outlets (GFCI), fans, etc.
_____ Draw a rough draft of bathroom plans.
_____ Make a list of required materials for the job.
_____ Price materials.
_____ Make a list of subcontractors or general contractors for selection.
_____ Contact contractors for price quotes.
_____ Evaluate budget and affordability of bathroom remodeling.
_____ Make financing arrangements.
_____ Make a final decision on the plans for the bathroom.
_____ Obtain blueprints, if necessary.
_____ Apply for the necessary permits.
_____ Choose contractors and check their references.
_____ Meet with attorney to draft contracts and other documents.
_____ Schedule work.
_____ Schedule material deliveries.
_____ Schedule contractors.
_____ Start work.
_____ Inspect work.
_____ Obtain copies of all code enforcement inspections.
_____ Make payments as scheduled in the contracts and obtain signed lien waivers from contractors and suppliers.
_____ Inspect completed job.
_____ Make punch-list, if necessary.
_____ Make absolute final inspection and approval.
_____ Make final payments, except for retainages.
_____ Make retainage payments.

CATEGORIES OF WORK TO BE DONE

☐ Plans
☐ Specifications
☐ Permits
☐ Trash container
☐ Demolition
☐ Dump fees
☐ Plumbing
☐ Fixture installation
☐ Electrical
☐ Heating/ac
☐ Subfloor
☐ Insulation
☐ Drywall
☐ Ceramic tile
☐ Linen closet

☐ Trim
☐ Windows
☐ Doors
☐ Paint/wallpaper
☐ Underlayment
☐ Finish floor covering
☐ Hardware
☐ Wall cabinets
☐ Base cabinets
☐ Countertops
☐ Shower enclosure
☐ Bath accessories
☐ Cleanup
☐ Window treatments
☐ Personal touches

OUTLINE OF WORK TO BE DONE
KITCHEN REMODELING

_____ Review requirements of space: additional windows or appliances, eat-in area, built-in seating or storage, lighting, etc.

_____ Draw a rough draft of kitchen plans.

_____ Make a list of required materials for the job.

_____ Price materials.

_____ Make a list of subcontractors or general contractors for selection.

_____ Contact contractors for price quotes.

_____ Evaluate budget and affordability of kitchen project.

_____ Make financing arrangments.

_____ Make a final decision on the plans for the kitchen.

_____ Obtain blueprints, if necessary.

_____ Apply for the necessary permits.

_____ Choose contractors and check their references.

_____ Meet with attorney to draft contracts and other documents.

_____ Schedule work.

_____ Schedule material deliveries.

_____ Schedule contractors.

_____ Start work.

_____ Inspect work.

_____ Obtain copies of all code enforcement inspections.

_____ Make payments as scheduled in contracts and obtain signed lien waivers from contractors and suppliers.

_____ Inspect completed job.

_____ Make punch-list, if necessary.

_____ Make absolute final inspection and approval.

_____ Make final payments, except for retainages.

_____ Make retainage payments.

CATEGORIES OF WORK TO BE DONE

☐ Plans
☐ Specifications
☐ Permits
☐ Trash container
☐ Demolition
☐ Dump fees
☐ Plumbing
☐ Electrical
☐ Heating/ac
☐ Subfloor
☐ Insulation
☐ Drywall
☐ Trim
☐ Windows

☐ Doors
☐ Paint/wallpaper
☐ Underlayment
☐ Finish floor covering
☐ Hardware
☐ Wall cabinets
☐ Base cabinets
☐ Countertops
☐ Appliances
☐ Kitchen accessories
☐ Cleanup
☐ Window treatments
☐ Personal touches

OUTLINE OF WORK TO BE DONE
GARAGE CONSTRUCTION

_____ Choose style of garage to be built.
_____ Draw a rough draft of garage plans or obtain pre-drawn plans.
_____ Make or obtain a list of required materials for the job.
_____ Price materials.
_____ Make list of subcontractors or general contractors.
_____ Contact contractors for price quotes.
_____ Evaluate budget and affordability of garage.
_____ Make financing arrangements.
_____ Make a final decision on plans for the garage.
_____ Obtain blueprints.
_____ Apply for the necessary permits.
_____ Choose contractors and check their references.
_____ Meet with attorney to draft contracts and other documents.
_____ Schedule work.
_____ Schedule material deliveries.
_____ Schedule contractors.
_____ Start work.
_____ Inspect work.
_____ Obtain copies of all code enforcement inspections.
_____ Make payments as scheduled in the contract and obtain signed lien waivers from contractors and suppliers.
_____ Inspect completed job.
_____ Make punch-list, if necessary.
_____ Make absolute final inspection and approval.
_____ Make final payments, except for retainages.
_____ Make retainage payments.

CATEGORIES OF WORK TO BE DONE

- [ ] Survey
- [ ] Plans
- [ ] Permits
- [ ] Site preparation
- [ ] Footings
- [ ] Pest control
- [ ] Slab floor
- [ ] Framing
- [ ] Siding
- [ ] Roofing
- [ ] Trim
- [ ] Windows
- [ ] Small door
- [ ] Garage doors
- [ ] Garage door openers
- [ ] Electrical
- [ ] Insulation
- [ ] Drywall
- [ ] Paint
- [ ] Trash container
- [ ] Dump fees
- [ ] Hardware
- [ ] Landscaping
- [ ] Cleanup
- [ ] Personal touches
- [ ] Options:
- [ ]   Heating/ac
- [ ]   Plumbing
- [ ]   Interior trim
- [ ]   Floor sealant
- [ ]   Apron
- [ ]   Driveway repair or extension

OUTLINE OF WORK TO BE DONE
ATTIC CONVERSION

_____ Review requirements of space: stairs, built-in storage, closets, windows, new attic space ventilation, etc.
_____ Draw a rough draft of conversion plans.
_____ Make a list of required materials for the job.
_____ Price materials.
_____ Make list of subcontractors or general contractors for selection.
_____ Contact contractors for price quotes.
_____ Evaluate budget and affordability of the conversion.
_____ Make financing arrangements.
_____ Make a final decision on the plans for the conversion.
_____ Obtain blueprints, if necessary.
_____ Apply for the necessary permits.
_____ Choose contractors and check their references.
_____ Meet with attorney to draft contracts and other documents.
_____ Schedule work.
_____ Schedule material deliveries.
_____ Schedule contractors.
_____ Start work.
_____ Inspect work.
_____ Obtain copies of all code enforcement inspections.
_____ Make payments as scheduled in the contracts and obtain signed lien waivers from contractors and suppliers.
_____ Inspect completed job.
_____ Make punch-list, if necessary.
_____ Make absolute final inspection and approval.
_____ Make final payments, except for retainages.
_____ Make retainage payments.

CATEGORIES OF WORK TO BE DONE

☐ Plans
☐ Specifications
☐ Permits
☐ Demolition
☐ Repairs to existing ceiling
☐ Framing
☐ Stairs
☐ Dormer work, if required
☐ Plumbing
☐ Heating/ac
☐ Electrical
☐ Insulation
☐ Drywall

☐ Paint
☐ Interior doors & hardware
☐ Interior trim
☐ Underlayment
☐ Finish floor covering
☐ Wall cabinets
☐ Base cabinets
☐ Countertops
☐ Window treatments
☐ Trash container
☐ Dump fees
☐ Cleanup
☐ Personal touches

OUTLINE OF WORK TO BE DONE
ADDITION CONSTRUCTION

_____ Choose style of addition to be built.

_____ Review requirements of space: closets, additional baths, windows, door sizes, etc.

_____ Draw a rough draft of addition plans.

_____ Make list of required materials for the job.

_____ Price materials.

_____ Make list of subcontractors or general contractors for selection.

_____ Contact contractors for price quotes.

_____ Evaluate budget and affordability of the addition.

_____ Make financing arrangements.

_____ Make a final decision on the plans for the addition.

_____ Obtain blueprints.

_____ Apply for the necessary permits.

_____ Choose contractors and check their references.

_____ Meet with attorney to draft contracts and other documents.

_____ Schedule work.

_____ Schedule material deliveries.

_____ Schedule contractors.

_____ Start work.

_____ Inspect work.

_____ Obtain copies of all code enforcement inspections.

_____ Make payments as scheduled in the contracts and obtain signed lien waivers from contractors and suppliers.

_____ Inspect completed job.

_____ Make punch-lists, as necessary.

_____ Make absolute final inspection and approval.

_____ Make final payments, except for retainages.

_____ Make retainage payments.

CATEGORIES OF WORK TO BE DONE

- ☐ Survey
- ☐ Plans
- ☐ Specifications
- ☐ Permits
- ☐ Site preparation
- ☐ Footings
- ☐ Foundation
- ☐ Pest control treatment
- ☐ Backfill labor, if applicable
- ☐ Demolition
- ☐ Repairs to existing wall
- ☐ Framing
- ☐ Siding
- ☐ Roofing
- ☐ Exterior trim
- ☐ Exterior hardware
- ☐ Windows
- ☐ Doors
- ☐ Plumbing
- ☐ Heating/ac

- ☐ Electrical
- ☐ Insulation
- ☐ Drywall
- ☐ Paint
- ☐ Interior doors
- ☐ Interior hardware
- ☐ Interior trim
- ☐ Finish floor covering
- ☐ Wall cabinets
- ☐ Base cabinets
- ☐ Countertops
- ☐ Window treatments
- ☐ Landscaping
- ☐ Trash container
- ☐ Dump fees
- ☐ Cleanup
- ☐ Personal touches
- ☐ Gutters
- ☐ Decks

CONTRACTOR SELECTION FORM

Type of Service	Vendor Name	Phone Number	Date Scheduled
Site work			
Footings			
Concrete			
Foundation			
Waterproofing			
Masonry			
Framing			
Roofing			
Siding			
Exterior trim			
Gutters			
Pest control			
Plumbing/R-I			
HVAC/R-I			
Electrical/R-I			
Central vacuum			
Insulation			
Drywall			
Painter			
Wallpaper			
Tile			
Cabinets			
Countertops			
Interior trim			
Floor covering			
Plumbing/Final			
HVAC/Final			
Electrical/Final			
Cleaning			
Paving			
Landscaping			

NOTES/CHANGES

PROFESSIONAL SERVICES DIRECTORY

Type of Service	Vendor Name	Phone Number	Date Scheduled
Survey			
Attorney			
Financing			
Blueprints			
Accounting			
Appraisal			
Insurance			

QUERY FORM LETTER

Dear Sir:

I am soliciting bids for the work listed below, and would like to offer you the opportunity to participate in the bidding. If you are interested in giving quoted prices for the LABOR/ MATERIAL for this job, please let me hear from you, at the above address. The job will be started _____. Financing has been arranged and the job will be started on schedule. Your quote, if you choose to enter one, must be received no later than _____.

The proposed work is as follows:

Thank you for your time and consideration in this request.

Sincerely,

QUERY LETTER EXAMPLE

JASON P. PRICESHOPPER
937 GOFER STREET
CAMERON, MI 01987

April 3, 1991

Dear Sir:

I am soliciting bids for the work listed below, and would like to offer you the opportunity to participate in the bidding. If you are interested in giving quoted prices for the material for this job, please let me hear from you, at the above address. The job will be started in four weeks. Financing has been arranged and the job will be started on schedule. Your quote, if you choose to enter one, must be received no later than April 24, 1991.

The proposed work is as follows:

A new addition approximately 16' X 20', and two stories in height. It will include a family room, a bedroom, and a bathroom. Plans and specifications for the work are available upon request.

Thank you for your time and consideration in this request.

Sincerely,

Jason P. Priceshopper

CONTRACTOR QUESTIONNAIRE

PLEASE ANSWER ALL THE FOLLOWING QUESTIONS
AND EXPLAIN ANY "NO" ANSWERS.

Company name _____

Physical company address _____

Company mailing address _____

Company phone number _____

After hours phone number _____

Company President/Owner _____

President/Owner address _____

President/Owner phone number _____

How long has company been in business? _____

Name of insurance company _____

Insurance company phone number _____

Does company have liability insurance? _____

Amount of liability insurance coverage _____

Does company have worker's comp. insurance? _____

Type of work company is licensed to do _____

List business or other license numbers _____

Where are licenses held? _____

If applicable, are all workmen licensed?_____

Are there any lawsuits pending against the company? _____

Has the company ever been sued? _____

Does the company use subcontractors? _____

Is the company bonded? _____

Who is the company bonded with? _____

Has the company ever had complaints filed against it? _____

Are there any judgments against the company? _____

Please list 5 references of work similar to ours:

1. _____
2. _____
3. _____
4. _____
5. _____

Please list 3 credit references:

1. _____
2. _____
3. _____

Please list 3 trade references:

1. _____
2. _____
3. _____

Please note any information you feel will influence our decision:

_____

_____

ALL OF THE ABOVE INFORMATION IS TRUE AND ACCURATE AS OF THIS DATE.

DATE: _____

COMPANY NAME: _____

BY: _____

TITLE: _____

CHANGE ORDER

This change order is an integral part of the contract dated _____, between the customer, _____ _____, and the contractor, _____, for the work to be performed _____. The residence and job location is located at _____, in the city of _____, state of _____. The following changes are the only changes to be made. These changes shall now become a part of the original contract and may not be altered again without written authorization from all parties.

Changes To Be As Follows:

These changes will *increase/decrease* the original contract amount. Payment for these changes will be made as follows: _____.
The amount of change in the contract price will be _____ ($_____). If applicable, the new total contract price shall be _____ ($_____).

The undersigned parties hereby agree that these are the only changes to be made to the original contract. No verbal agreements will be valid. No further alterations will be allowed without additional written authorization, signed by all parties. This change order constitutes the entire agreement between the parties to alter the original contract.

_____
Owner

_____
Contractor

_____
Date

_____
Date

_____
Owner

_____
Date

SAMPLE CHANGE ORDER

This change order is an integral part of the contract dated _August 15, 1991_, between the customer, _Mr. & Mrs. J. P. Homeowner_, and the contractor, _Any Contractor Company_, for the work to be performed on _Mr. & Mrs. J. P. Homeowner's_ residence. The residence and job location is located at _135 Hometown Street_, in the city of _Moneytown_, state of _Ohio_. The following changes are the only changes to be made. These changes shall now become a part of the original contract and may not be altered again without written authorization from all parties.

Changes To Be As Follows:

1) The originally specified interior doors will be substituted with raised panel interior doors. These doors will be from the ROX company, model number 1370, product number 53. The doors will have six raised panels and will be of hollow core construction.

2) The originally specified kitchen sink will be substituted with an enameled, cast iron sink. This sink will be a product of the ABCDE company, model number 490, in Almond, color number 16.

3) The originally specified kitchen sink faucet will be substituted with an RDC, model # 956, chrome, two handle faucet.

These changes will increase the original contract amount. Payment for these changes will be made as follows: _Payment in full to be added to the final contract payment_. The amount of change in the contract price will be _an added cost of four hundred dollars ($400.00)_. If applicable, the new total contract price shall be _fourteen thousand, five hundred dollars ($14,500.00)_.

The undersigned parties hereby agree that these are the only changes to be made to the original contract. No verbal agreements will be valid. No further alterations will be allowed without additional written authorization, signed by all parties. This change order constitutes the entire agreement between the parties to alter the original contract.

_____
Mr. J.P. Homewner

_____
Date

_____
Mrs. J.P. Homeowner

_____
Date

_____
Any Contractor Co.

_____
Date

Financing

12

Home remodeling can be very expensive. Depending upon the scope of work, a project can cost more than a year's salary. This can be an alarming realization. How will you pay for the work? Often, there is no choice except financing. Sometimes financing isn't necessary, but it is the best option. In this chapter, we will look at the pros and cons of financing. We will also examine the many different methods of obtaining financing. The options available may surprise you. Financing can overshadow the excitement of remodeling, but this chapter will help you eliminate the dark clouds associated with home improvement loans.

Do you need to finance your project? Should you finance the job? Can you afford to finance the new improvements? Where should you apply for a loan? How long should the term of the loan be? These questions are raised when the thought of financing is entertained. Financing is a complex process with numerous variables. Even if you have the cash, you could gain tax advantages by financing the work. These tax advantages can increase the strength of your remodeling dollar. Before you pay cash, examine your tax consequences with a professional tax advisor.

REVIEW THE FINANCING AVAILABLE

If you decide to finance your project, running down to the local bank for a loan might be a mistake. First, step back and review all the financing plans available. Loans are not all the same; there can be extreme differences. Pay attention to detail and sift through the paperwork slowly. Treat loan officers as you would any other subcontractor. Shop

their deals, and compare the loan packages carefully. Making a loan commitment is a serious step. A quick decision on financing can mean financial ruin, so be cautious and talk with several lenders. Explore the different types of programs available. Home improvement loans are available in many shapes and sizes.

A loan with a balloon payment at the end of the term could cost you your house. The financial stress of having one large payment, due in five years, could put you into default and out on the street. A fixed rate loan may require higher monthly payments than you can afford. Adjustable rate mortgages can get expensive fast, if interest rates increase in future years. Should you commit to a loan for five or fifteen years? The answer depends on your long-range financial and ownership plans. Spend some time learning about home improvement loans before accepting one. It is a good ideas to be sure you are acquiring a loan that meets all of your needs.

SHOULD YOU SEEK FINANCING?

Do you have to finance your project? This question is easy to answer. If you don't have the money, you must seek financing. Should you finance your job? This is a more difficult question to answer. If you have the option of paying cash or obtaining financing, you have more to think about. The variables involved are based on individual opinions and financial planning. Do you want to spend all of your cash on the improvements? This is an individual decision only you can make. I believe in having cash quickly accessible in the bank and would prefer to finance work, to keep cash available upon demand.

If you invest all of your cash in the job, you may have trouble getting the cash back when you need it. When you secure a loan, you have monthly payments to make and interest charges to pay. Interest charges add to the overall cost of your job, but may be a tax advantage if a home equity loan is used to finance the job. These advantages could amount to savings on the income taxes you pay. When you offset the tax savings against the interest cost, you might find the results interesting. The added cost of the interest might be reduced by tax savings. Financing can increase your profit on a remodeling project.

Profiting from Financing

You may be wondering, why finance the job and pay interest when you don't have to? Maybe your cost will be higher, even after the tax savings. How does this make sense? On the surface it doesn't, but look a little deeper. By financing the job, you can invest your cash elsewhere. Depending on the investment, the cash can earn a higher rate than the interest you are paying on your loan. As an example, your home improvement loan is being charged interest at a rate of 10%, but your tax advantages reduce this cost by 30%. Therefore, the net cost of your loan is only 7%. Now, take the cash you would have spent on the project, and invest it in a safe investment. Using a conservative rate of return, say 8%, you earn a 1% profit on your money. Investing in a higher risk venture could yield a rate of return of 15% or more. This can produce profits in excess of 7%.

The result of this example is a profit. You are making money by borrowing money. Taxes must be paid on the interest you earn, but in many cases, these can be deferred. By the time you pay the taxes, you could be in a lower tax bracket. Through financing, your cash can be invested in a way that allows it to be liquidated quickly. If you invest all the money in your home, you could have to sell the house to get your money back.

Don't Lock Up Your Cash

Financial difficulties can force you to reclaim the money you invest in the home improvements. At these times, you aren't likely to be approved for an equity loan. Now your cash is locked up in the equity of your home. If you finance the job and invest your cash, you have ready access to the money. This is very comforting, since the loss of your job or a lengthy illness will not force you to sell your home.

Tax and investment professionals will be able to advise you intelligently on your personal benefits and risks.

Consider an equity line of credit to keep your cash available. With this option, the lender allows you to have a line of credit, secured by your home's equity. You invest your own money in the improvements and avoid interest charges. There are no monthly payments to be made, and you have access to your money when you need it. Once a line of credit is issued, you can borrow money when you need it, without further approval. When you arrange this credit line, you are guaranteed access to your invested money. This protects your cash reserve, in the event of an emergency.

CAN YOU AFFORD TO FINANCE?

Can you afford to finance your project? This question should be answered by you first and the lender second. Loan officers use ratios to determine the amount of monthly payments you are qualified to afford. If you don't fall into the right ratios, you won't be granted the loan. When this happens, you have to look to another lender or lower the amount you are attempting to borrow. You may be forced to adjust your budget and change the scope of work to be done. This is frustrating, but a more dangerous situation arises when a lender indicates you qualify for more than you need.

Banks are in the business of loaning money to make money. A lender's ratios deal with fixed, long-term debts. These include credit card, car loan, and mortgage expenses. Banks don't allow for car insurance, vacations, unexpected medical costs, or other miscellaneous expenses. Sometimes the bank ratios indicate you can afford payments that will actually be a burden, in the long run. The money you spend on groceries, hobbies, movies, or kid's toys is not considered, producing false ratio results.

ESTIMATE LOAN EXPENSES

You can use the same process to estimate loan expenses that you used to project your job cost. Talk to several different loan officers. Ask what loan amount you qualify for and what the payments will be. Ask how long it will take to pay the loan off. Then go home and do your own assessment of your loan qualifications. You can use the Loan Qualification Work Sheet at the end of this chapter to assemble the information.

List your fixed expenses. Fill in the regular monthly expenses you incur for food, gasoline, insurance, and other similar expenses. Allow a monthly figure for vacation, holiday expenses, and medical care. Put in a monthly expense amount for clothes, auto repairs, and anything else you anticipate a need for. Total the column with these monthly expenses, and add 10% for items you have forgotten. This is the amount of money you need to have every month.

Once you have established this figure, subtract the amount from your monthly net income. The amount left is what you can afford to pay as a monthly loan payment. This number will probably be less than what the loan officer indicated you could afford. Make your own decision, but don't leverage yourself into a loan that will adversely affect your daily life. Being strapped with heavy monthly loan payments can disrupt your lifestyle and induce stress.

WHERE TO APPLY FOR A LOAN

Where is the best place to apply for a loan? This is a question with a lot of good answers. Banks are the first place most people think of for a loan. Banks make home improvement loans and can offer competitive rates and terms. All banks have different loan programs, and it will be necessary to interview several to find the best deal. Start with the bank where your house is financed. If your home is paid for, go to the bank where you have your checking, savings, or C.D. account. You already have a relationship with this bank. You should have an advantage dealing with a banker who knows you.

Prepare a Loan Request Package

Prepare a loan request package before sitting down with loan officers. There is a blank form for this at the end of the chapter. The Loan Request Example located with the blank form contains the proposed use of the loan proceeds. It also details your intentions and the information you are requesting from the bank. The form has blanks to be filled in at the bank, such as the particulars of each loan available. Items such as interest rate, term, loan type, prepayment penalties, and other factors are included. When this form is completed, it will make it easy to compare the loans offered by different banks.

A comprehensive loan package will make your loan request more attractive to a lender. The more information you provide, the better your chances are of getting the loan. The bank will want to see your plans and specifications before rendering a decision. If you already have a certified appraisal, include a copy with your plans. The appraisal will show the lender what your project will be worth when completed. This makes the banker's job — giving an opinion on your loan request — easier. Show her your survey, the quotes for the job, and anything else you have collected. All this information will put the loan officer at ease, because the package reflects research and builds confidence in your abilities. All of these factors will make loan acquisition easier.

Most bank loan officers play strictly by the book. They will be looking for specific values and descriptions of the work to be done. Loan officers will respond favorably to a well-prepared loan request package. Having substantial equity in your home doesn't hurt either. Lenders will jump at the chance to make a safe loan. Banks make their money by making loans, and a high percentage of strong loans reflects well on the loan officer. If you convince the loan officer of the viability of your deal, you will get the loan.

Loan Officers

Loan officers come in two basic groups. Members of the first group are simply employees of the bank. These will be the hardest to persuade. They have a comfortable desk job and don't want to lose it. If they make too many bad loans, they will be terminated. These loan officers receive the same paycheck whether they make you a loan or not. There is little motivation for these employees to take a risk. Loan officers of this kind will only accept your loan proposal if it is golden. They won't take any chances on risky or mediocre loans, because they don't have to. Try to find banks with the second type of loan officer.

This second group receives a commission on every loan they make. These are the people you want to deal with. They will work with you to make a package fly, because their income is directly related to your successfully obtaining a loan. The terms of the loan can be the same as any other bank. The difference is in the loan officer's motivation. The approval of your loan means more money in the loan originator's paycheck. Although he must still follow basic banking rules, this motivation makes the officer more liberal. Commissioned loan officers will abide by the rules but are more likely to bend them than their salaried counterparts.

Your loan means money to these loan officers, and financial advancement is a strong motivator. As with the salaried originators, writing too many bad loans means risking their jobs. I'm not suggesting commissioned lenders will break the rules for a commission, but they will be much more lenient in their interpretation of your goals and qualifications. Commissioned originators will put forth extra effort to get your loan approved, because they are compensated for this effort. To find these loan officers, you need to visit several banks. The time invested interviewing loan officers will be well spent. When you find the right one, your financing will be a cinch.

CREDIT UNIONS

Another good source for home improvement loans is your credit union. Credit unions that offer home improvement loans often have lower interest rates than banks. Since credit unions operate differently from commercial banks, the loan can come together more easily. If you are a member of a credit union, talk with the loan officer there before committing to a bank. Credit unions are an excellent source of loans. Typically, you are working for the company that owns the credit union. They already know your work and wage history, as well as projections for your continued employment. This is a big advantage in that their risk is lower than that of a commercial bank. If you have good job security and credit, you will get the loan. Who could know better about your ability to repay a loan than your employer? Investigate this option before making your final financing decision.

LOAN SPECIALISTS

Some loan companies specialize in home equity loans. You will find them advertising in the newspaper and phone book. These loans differ from the equity credit lines discussed earlier in this chapter, and loan companies are often questionable. Be careful with any lender, but be especially cautious with loan companies. The interest rates offered from most loan companies will be higher than those of the bank, and they might require a second mortgage on your home. This requirement isn't particularly unusual, as any lender is going to want security for the loan.

If the amount of the loan is reasonably large, *all* lenders will want a mortgage on your home. The difference can be in the default terms. Most commercial banks share similar business practices when dealing with payment default and grace periods. Loan companies have a bad reputation when it comes to nonpayment. There are horror stories about losing your home one minute after midnight, when a payment is missed. When you sift through the exaggerations, there is some truth to reports. Don't get me wrong, not all loan companies are wolves in sheep's clothing. There are legitimate loan companies that offer competitive rates while providing quality service.

Loan companies offer some advantages over banks and can be a viable solution to your financing needs. Do not eliminate them from your comparisons. Treat their paperwork as you would any other contract. Review it and ask questions. Be certain you understand the language. Have the loan documents reviewed by your attorney before signing them, and confirm all terms and conditions. If your attorney approves the documents, the loan company could be the right choice for you.

For people with damaged credit, reputable loan companies can mean the difference in obtaining a loan. They will consider credit risks, which would be flatly denied by a commercial bank. If you had credit problems in the past, loan companies can be your best alternative. They consider loans from people with slow paying credit histories, and some will even loan to bankrupt individuals. Loan companies can make these high risk loans, because they don't have to sell the loans on the secondary market. Many times, the money they lend is supplied by individual investors. This gives a loan company more latitude in qualification guidelines. For homeowners with poor credit, loan companies are a viable alternative to commercial banks. Before signing any documents, remember to have them approved by your attorney. Your attorney can prevent you and your home from being gobbled up by unscrupulous loan sharks.

When you look in the classified section of your newspaper, you will see a variety of ads offering loans. Classified ads can mean trouble; be very cautious if you pursue the promises from these lenders. The loans offered here are privately funded and take on many shapes and configurations. Usually, these loans are geared to home improvement financing for people with poor credit. The interest rates will be high, and so will the risks you take. Some of these ads are aimed at people unable to get credit anywhere else. The idea is to appeal to people with poor credit, who have no other options. Banks will be prejudiced against these people, disregarding them as bad credit risks. If these people want a loan, they must deal with the private sector. These vulnerable waters are where the sharks swim, so be very careful.

It is possible to find a good loan from these ads, but you could get in deep trouble fast. Most of the groups offering money to lend are uncontrolled and play by their own rules. The ads are placed by individuals, loan companies, mortgage brokers, and an occasional bank. We have already discussed banks and loan companies, but what are mortgage brokers?

MORTGAGE BROKERS

Mortgage brokers make their living selling money. They act as the middleman, putting borrowers and lenders together. You can compare their role to that of a real estate broker. They bring together two parties wanting to do business. In return for these services, the broker receives a commission or percentage of the loan amount. The amount of the fee varies. A big factor in determining the fee is the amount of the loan. With a small loan, mortgage brokers customarily receive a set fee. With larger loans, they will accept a percentage of the loan amount.

Mortgage brokers offer advantages to the busy investor. A broker saves the investor time and allows him to go about his business — making deals. Mortgage brokers are familiar players in big money deals, but are not common in loans under $100,000. With smaller loans, the cost of a broker is often prohibitive. Minimum fees for a good broker will start around $500 and go up. Brokers receive this kind of money because of their knowledge and connections. For a simple home improvement loan, their expertise is not used to its full extent.

Some brokers are willing to work on smaller loans, and may organize your financing for as little as $250. If you decide to use a broker, ask pertinent questions before signing anything. If the mortgage broker requires a retainer or payment in advance, you could be paying for nothing. If the broker does not guarantee you a loan, you could lose the money you give him. If you are guaranteed a loan, watch

out. Most brokers do not have the ability or authority to approve your loan. This makes it almost impossible for them to guarantee you will receive a loan. Paying a fee up-front is bad business. Make your brokerage agreements contingent on production. Agree to pay a percentage of the loan amount *when you actually close on the loan*. With this type of agreement, you have nothing to lose and everything to gain.

Brokers may not be willing to accept these terms on a small home improvement loan. They may insist on a minimum fee to compensate them for the time they spend searching for prospective lenders. While this is understandable, it could be a waste of your money. If you are determined to agree to these conditions, make some requests of your own. Structure your deal around a contract. In your contract with the broker, require evidence of the efforts made to secure your loan. Copies of denial notices could be an acceptable form of documentation. Set a minimum number of lenders to be contacted, and require proof of your loan application to these lenders. Your attorney can help you with other ways to protect your money.

If a mortgage broker finds your financing, have the funding documents reviewed by your attorney. Mortgage brokers deal will all types of lenders. They could place your loan with a bank, an insurance company, an individual, or anyone else with money to invest. These lenders will have their own loan documents, which must be thoroughly scrutinized. If the loan is acceptable, the broker will have earned his money. You will have saved time and, in some cases, secured the only form of financing available. The project will be financed, and everybody will be happy. This is the way it should work, but don't expect too much success from a broker on the average home improvement loan. Mortgage brokers are really meant for larger commercial loans.

PRIVATE INVESTORS

Borrowing remodeling funds from an individual is another option. There are independent investors willing to loan money to homeowners for secured loans with a high yield. Private investors offer the advantage of providing financing tailored to suit your individual needs. The loans will probably be slanted to the advantage of the investor. This is to be expected, as they must have motivation to risk their money. It is up to you to protect yourself, so involve your lawyer in the deal. Seek professional advice on the terms and conditions of the loan and any second mortgages or liens required. Proceed cautiously and be alert.

Private investors are valuable to people with damaged credit. If there were valid reasons for your credit problems, the private investor may overlook them. The amount of equity in your home can also vanquish bad credit dilemmas. If the investor feels secure with your equity, you will get the loan. Private money is easier to obtain because of a lack of restrictions and rules. Private investors don't have to adhere to any set ratios or bank policies. If you have a strong game plan, they can make the loan. Under special conditions, the private sector can be the place to go for your financing. As always, have all documents approved by your lawyer before acceptance.

"IN-HOME" FINANCING

There is one other common source of home improvement financing worth detailing. This is referred to as "in-home" financing. You can apply for this type of loan, right in your home, through a general contractor. The general contractor acts as a dealer for a financing company specializing in home improvement loans. The interest rates on the loans will be slightly higher than bank rates, but in-home financing offers several advantages. There are differences between the financing companies offering these programs. I will give you some examples, based on a company I recently dealt with.

Application fees are not required, which can save you a few hundred dollars. The loan does not require an appraisal of your home, unless the loan is in excess of $7,500. Another big advantage is the lack of a second mortgage on your home. For loans under $7,500, no second mortgage is required. Instead, a statement is placed on file at the Registry of Deeds, to acknowledge publicly the money you borrow. This is called a Uniform Commercial Credit Statement (abbreviated as UCC). Loan approval can be granted in as little as twenty-four hours, and there are no closing costs.

Compare these procedures to bank requirements, and the savings begin to build up. Not having to pay for an appraisal saves you around $250. With no loan application fees, you save another couple of hundred dollars. The absence of closing costs can save you thousands of dollars. Then there is the time saved in credit approval; most loan requests can be answered in twenty-four hours. Some banks take weeks to approve or deny a loan. Finally, there are no prepayment penalties, and the term of the loan is determined by the loan amount.

This fast in-home financing is an attractive option. One of the most favorable aspects of this type of deal is the lack of up-front money. You are not required to pay a down payment or progress payment during the remodeling process. None of your money is at risk. You don't have to pay one-third to begin the work, one-third after the rough-in phase, and one-third upon completion. Instead, the contractors don't get paid anything until the job is completed and accepted by you.

Furthermore, the lender requires written notification of your satisfaction before paying the contractor. There are no verbal disputes, and the contractor cannot claim payment without your written authorization. All the companies I have dealt with have been reputable. I have never had a customer dissatisfied with this type of financing. This speaks highly for in-home financing programs. Undoubtedly, there are some disreputable companies involved in this type of financing. Again, be aware of what you are signing, and consult your attorney.

WEIGHING THE DEBT AGAINST THE BENEFITS

This covers most of the financing associated with home improvements. Committing to long-term debt requires much thought. You may be sacrificing some of your current freedom and flexibility. The luxury of a day off can disappear, if every dollar is needed to meet your monthly obligations. The new car may have to wait, and your fantasy vacation could remain nothing more than a dream. When you decide to put your home on the line, you may have to give up some of your extra perks.

Consider all of the relevant financial and personal disadvantages before signing any loan documents. Now you know why we spent so much time evaluating your home improvement, back in Chapter 4. Your remodeling project may not be worth the resulting limitations on your discretionary income. Once you sign the loan documents, it's a done deal. You will have to live with the loan and by its rules. For some homeowners, this isn't an acceptable option.

Evaluate your needs and shop for the best loan. Remember to take your loan request package with you on the interviews; it really can be an asset in securing a loan. Don't neglect to have all documents reviewed by a professional before signing. Your home could be at risk, so be certain your signature doesn't cost you your house.

Financing offers a variety of options for your project. It can allow you to do more work than you have available cash to pay for. Strategic financing can help you establish a profitable investment portfolio. Funding your remodeling project is an area that will require input from professionals. Armed with thorough information, you will be able to weed through the various financing programs. Carefully comparing the plans will enable you to discover the financing option best suited to your individual needs and resources. Consider all the angles, and consult with professionals before making your final decision. Meticulous financing preparation and investigation will save you considerable money in this phase of the remodeling process.

LOAN QUALIFICATION WORK SHEET

GROSS MONTHLY INCOME _____ X 25% = $_____

Most banks will allow you a maximum house payment equal to 25% of your gross monthly income. When you determine your allotted monthly payment, deduct your present house payment. The money left over is the maximum you can add in monthly payments to your present house payment. Compare this monthly amount with a loan amortization chart; it will tell you how much you can borrow from the average bank. This is the first method banks use to qualify loan applicants. The second one, below, deals with your additional long term debt. Add up all your long term, installment, monthly payments.

Car payments $_____
Boat payments $_____
Credit card payments $_____
Department store credit accounts $_____
Court-ordered alimony $_____
Court-ordered child support $_____
Bank loans (NOT YOUR HOUSE) $_____
Other long-term debt $_____

TOTAL MONTHLY PAYMENTS (DEBT) $_____

Now, multiply your gross monthly income by 33%. Subtract the total monthly payments listed above from this amount.

GROSS INCOME _____ x 33% = _____ - DEBT _____ = _____*

   * The figure you get is the amount of house payment you can afford using this qualification method.

Whichever of the methods produces the lower amount is the figure the bank will allow for your house payment. You must qualify both ways. Many times, the second qualification method disqualifies borrowers. Their car payments or credit card debt eliminate their ability to get the loan.

Different lenders will use different criteria in making their final decision. This method is not the final word. Even if you don't qualify here, talk to different lenders. If you own your own home and have equity in it, you have an excellent chance of getting the loan.

LOAN REQUEST FORM

The following will serve as a summary of information for the financing you offer:

CUSTOMER NAME: _____

CUSTOMER ADDRESS: _____

CUSTOMER CITY/STATE/ZIP: _____

CUSTOMER PHONE NUMBER: _____

JOB LOCATION: _____

PLANS & SPECIFICATIONS ATTACHED: Yes/No

PLANS & SPECIFICATIONS DATED: _____

LOAN REQUESTED FROM: _____

ADDRESS: _____

CONTACT PERSON: _____

DATE: _____

TYPE OF WORK: _____

TYPE OF LOAN REQUESTED: _____

TYPE OF INTEREST RATE: _____

NUMBER OF DISCOUNT POINTS TO BE PAID: _____

INTEREST RATE: _____

SECURITY FOR LOAN: _____

COST OF WORK TO BE DONE: _____

AMOUNT OF DOWN PAYMENT: _____

AMOUNT OF LOAN REQUEST: _____

AMOUNT OF EXISTING EQUITY: _____

EXPECTED VALUE OF IMPROVEMENTS: _____

TERM OF LOAN REQUESTED: _____

CERTIFIED APPRAISAL AVAILABLE _____

ESTIMATED TIME TO COMPLETE PROJECT: _____

TYPE OF IMPROVEMENT: _____

SURVEY COMPLETED: _____

LENDER CREDIT APPLICATION: _____

COMMENTS:

_____

_____

_____

_____

Thank you for your prompt response to my loan application. If you need any further information, please feel free to contact me at the address above. I look forward to doing business with you in the near future.

Sincerely,

LOAN REQUEST EXAMPLE

The following will serve as a summary of information for the financing you offer:

CUSTOMER NAME: _Mr. & Mrs. J. P. Homeowner_

CUSTOMER ADDRESS: _192 Hometown Street_

CUSTOMER CITY/STATE/ZIP: _Wahoo, ID 87906_

CUSTOMER PHONE NUMBER: _(000) 555-1000_

JOB LOCATION: _Same_

PLANS & SPECIFICATIONS ATTACHED: _Yes._

PLANS & SPECIFICATIONS DATED: _June 10, 1991_

LOAN REQUESTED FROM: _First S & L_

SUPPLIER ADDRESS: _2342 Bank Street_

CONTACT PERSON: _Larry Loan Officer_

DATE: _July 25, 1991_

TYPE OF WORK: _Remodeling_

TYPE OF LOAN REQUESTED: _Home improvement_

TYPE OF INTEREST RATE: _Fixed_

NUMBER OF DISCOUNT POINTS TO BE PAID: _2_

INTEREST RATE: _10.5%_

SECURITY FOR LOAN: _Second mortgage on subject property_

COST OF WORK TO BE DONE: _$20,000.00_

AMOUNT OF DOWN PAYMENT: _$4,000.00_

AMOUNT OF LOAN REQUEST: _$16,000.00_

AMOUNT OF EXISTING EQUITY: _$40,000.00_

EXPECTED VALUE OF IMPROVEMENTS: _$24,000.00_

TERM OF LOAN REQUESTED: _10 years, no balloon payment_

CERTIFIED APPRAISAL AVAILABLE: _Yes._

ESTIMATED TIME TO COMPLETE PROJECT: _90 days_

TYPE OF IMPROVEMENT: _Master bedroom and bathroom addition_

SURVEY COMPLETED: _Yes._

LENDER CREDIT APPLICATION: _Completed and included in package._

COMMENTS

_____

_____

_____

_____

Thank you for your prompt response to my loan application. If you need any further information, please feel free to contract me at the address above. I look forward to doing business with you in the near future.

Sincerely,

J. R. Homeowner

J. P. Homeowner

Making Deposit and Installment Payments

13

Knowing when to advance payments to contractors requires a very delicate balance of authority and acceptance. If you pay too soon, you have no control over the contractor. If you pay too slowly, the contractors will not continue to work for you. Your choice of financing, and agreements with various contractors and suppliers, will govern when payments will be made. The schedule of payments should be described in your contract. Payment terms need to be very specific and should include provisions for your inspection of all material and work before money is advanced.

SETTING UP A PAYMENT PLAN

Different contractors will want payment at different times. There are no set rules on when to pay; this is something negotiated between you and the contractor. Don't allow a contractor to pressure you into a so-called standard payment plan. There is no such thing. The payment plan you and the contractor agree to becomes the acceptable practice. Typical proposals will request a deposit when the contract is signed, usually one-third of the total contract price. The next payment is scheduled for the mid-point or rough-in phase of the job. This amount is also one-third of the total contract price. Finally, the last third of the agreed price is due in full upon completion.

Almost any proposal you receive from a contractor will have a payment request similar to this example. For many contractors, this is considered the standard payment schedule. If your job is small, it may be reasonable to break the payments into thirds. A reasonable deposit, with the balance due upon completion, would be a better approach from your point of view. Some proposals you receive will request a 50% deposit. This is ludicrous, even for a small project.

Never consider giving away half of the job cost in the form of a deposit. You leave yourself wide open for abuse under these conditions. Try to avoid deposits whenever possible. If they must be given, keep the deposit at 25% of the contract price or less. Some contractors will emphasize the importance of a cash deposit to make the contract binding. Money doesn't have to change hands to make a legal contract. None of the states I have worked in require cash to create a legal agreement.

Most laws only require a "promise for a promise" to establish a binding legal contract. All this means is that the contractor pledges to do the work, and you agree to pay for it. Promises of this kind are referred to as Valuable Consideration. "Good and valuable consideration" is the standard clause for most legal contracts. Keep as much of your money as possible, for as long as possible.

How You Can Lose Money

Many homeowners are willing to accept a contractor's terms without question. The majority don't realize they can request a different payment schedule. Since most consumers agree to the routine payment schedule, it can be hard to convince a contractor to consider alternative arrangements. It will be in your best interest to try for different terms. There are several objections to the so-called standard payment schedule. The most important objection is the potential loss of your hard-earned money.

When you hand over your deposit, you may never see it again. The contractor could skip town with your money before you knew anything was wrong. This example assumes the worst, but it can and does happen. A less cynical consideration is the risk of the contractor losing his business to pursuing creditors. Relentless collection demands could take your money from the contractor before your job is completed. Then the contractor would not have the money necessary to pay for your job's labor and materials. If the contractor is in trouble, your money is at risk.

What if the business has not paid its taxes? The company will be hit with a tax lien against all its assets, and your deposit money could be considered an asset. This is a serious problem. When a tax lien is applied to the assets of the business, your money is tied up. What assurances do you have of your money being safe? You are vulnerable when giving a deposit. Remember Dodge's most important rule: protect yourself at all times.

Another risk is one of misappropriated funds. Remodelers, plagued with debt, often resort to finance juggling. The contractor may take your deposit and use it to pay for another job's material. Even strong companies will limit their operating capital needs by spreading deposit money over several jobs. This is wrong, but it's done all the time. Normally, everything works out. It's when plans *don't* work out that you lose. Of course, you could sue the contractor to recover your deposit, but lawsuits are time-consuming and expensive. If the company is in financial trouble, what will you collect when you finally win the lawsuit? Maybe little or nothing. If a contractor files bankruptcy, there is almost nothing you can do to recover your money. You will have to take a place in line with all the other homeowners and creditors. Your options are extremely limited by the bankruptcy courts.

Keep Deposits Low

Bankruptcy circumstances are the exception rather than the rule. However, there are enough business failures to warrant caution. Keep any deposits given at a minimal amount to reduce your exposure. The deposit should not exceed 25% of the contract amount. This is still a fair deposit for the contractor, and you have lowered your risk. Do not give a deposit at the time you sign the contract. Authorize the deposit to be paid when materials are delivered and work is started. This approach re-duces the amount of time your money is at high risk. If a contractor can't afford to buy materials without your money, he should not be doing your job.

Established contractors deal with suppliers on a thirty-day account basis. When they buy materials, they have thirty days to pay for them. Requiring contractors to put materials on the job to initiate the payment schedule is not unreasonable. If they won't comply with this request, look for another contractor. Again, I must stress the importance of staying in control of your money and your project. You could easily get hurt financially by doing business with contractors who demand large deposits at the signing of the contract.

REQUIRE LIEN WAIVERS

When making any cash advances, require the recipient to sign a lien waiver. *Lien waivers should be required for every service rendered and all materials supplied*. There are examples of two different types of lien waiver at the end of this chapter. The first type is called a Short Form lien waiver. These are used individually for each cash disbursement to each contractor or supplier. The second style is referred to as a Long Form lien waiver. This form combines materials and services and has a place for several signatures. All vendors providing labor or materials sign on the same form. The long form is the one preferred by many attorneys, and it reduces paperwork. You many find the short form equally, if not more, effective, especially if your schedule requires payments to different people at different times.

Essentially, these forms state that the vendor receiving your money is releasing your property from the threat of a lien. I cannot stress enough the importance of obtaining these releases. Without lien waivers, you are at the mercy of contractors and suppliers, because any disagreement over payment can result in a lien on your property. There is no minimum requirement for a lien, even the company supplying one door for your job has lien rights. Liens are used to secure an unpaid contractor's or supplier's position until the courts render a decision. Liens are costly to remove, they cloud the title to your property, and selling a house with a recorded lien against it is *very* difficult.

Removing a Lien

Removing the lien will require payment of the

disputed amount or a court decision. The contractor can lien the house for any of the work he has done and for which he has not been paid. To win in court, you will have to prove you should not have to pay the amount in question. Lien waivers are your best defense. Once the contractor signs the lien waiver, he has no lien rights on the work described in the waiver. Lien waivers become a part of your arsenal of written documentation. If you show evidence of having everything in writing, the contractor's verbal claims will lose credibility. Maintain good records from the start of the job.

Going to court will get expensive fast. Even with a bogus claim, you will have to defend yourself. Your equity and home are at stake — you can't ignore a lien. An aggressive contractor will follow this lien with a lawsuit, to perfect the lien. Even if you have paid the contractor, you may have to appear in court to prove it. If you engage attorneys to represent you, they will charge you for all the time they spend on the case. These charges will involve more than actual time in court. The expenses include courtroom preparation and the time spent investigating your claims.

Attorneys' rates can easily be $125 per hour. Add this to the lost time and money on the job, and any savings you had to this point are rapidly depleted. It doesn't seem fair, but it is a fact. Often, liens are filed as the result of a misunderstanding. The contractor believes he is to be paid a certain amount, at a specific time, and the homeowner disagrees. The homeowner may feel it is necessary to withhold payment until problems with the workmanship are corrected. If you do not cover this possibility in your contract and neglect to get lien waivers signed for partial payments, you can lose in court. With the proper paperwork, you can avoid courtroom conflicts. Insist on having lien waivers signed by everyone you pay.

THE PROBLEM OF THE SECOND ADVANCE

Another problem with the three-part payment schedule is the second advance. When you give the contractor one-third as a deposit, he is always working with your money. When you pay the second third of the contract price, the contractor is way ahead financially. Most of the remodeler's profit is gained from the first and second payment. His expenses are covered, and when you make the second payment, he has most of the job's profit in hand. The last payment covers the actual cost of the remaining work but does not include much profit.

You have already put the contractor's profit in his pocket with the first two payments. Anytime the contractor has received more money than has been earned, you are asking for trouble. You have relinquished your power position, and the contractor can come to think he is in total control. It is unlikely you have the remodeling knowledge to anticipate every possible problem or recognize every probable conflict. Everyone gets a fair deal when you establish the rules up-front and in writing.

Paying in thirds can be a problem with any trade, but mechanical trades are historically the worst offenders. The three-part payment schedule caters to plumbers, electricians, and heating contractors. It is much easier for these mechanical trades to make their profits *before* completion of a job.

Losing Your Leverage

To illustrate this point, let's look at a very realistic scenario. You live in an upper middle class community. Your remodeling plans call for adding two new bathrooms and a master bedroom. Since the surrounding homes support large, impressive bathrooms, you want to invest in quality fixtures to get the best return for your dollar. You've also worked hard for this addition and want it to be both enjoyable and profitable. One of the bathrooms will adjoin the new master bedroom, and the other will serve your guests.

When you draw up your plumbing contract, you attach a detailed specification sheet. You do everything by the book. All your bases are covered, and nothing is left to chance. The plumbing contractor looks over your spec sheet and is impressed with your fixture selection. The plumber says he can do the job for $18,000 but will need a deposit when you sign the contract. The deposit request is for $6,000, one-third of the total contract price, which the plumber explains is the standard amount. He insists everyone requires three payments — it is an established business practice.

Many subcontractors have requested three-part payments, so you sign the plumber's contract and give him the $6,000 deposit. The plumber says he can start the work in about two weeks. This is acceptable, and you agree to the anticipated start date. The plumber leaves with your deposit, and you are excited about your new bathrooms. Four or five days later, after your check has cleared, the plumber calls. He says you need to meet with him about some of your fixtures. When you ask if there is a problem, the plumber says it is nothing to worry about, he just needs to go over a few items.

The plumbing contractor arrives, with your specifications sheet in hand. He explains that many of the fixtures you selected are special order items, requiring payment before the supplier will order them. This isn't too unusual, as special orders often require full or partial payment in advance. The designer fixtures are expensive, and the contractor tells you the prepayment amount needed is $3,200. After assuring you the fixtures will be delivered in about three weeks, the contractor leaves, check in hand.

Time has passed and you are ready to have your rough plumbing installed. You call to schedule the contractor, and suddenly, the ever-present plumber doesn't return your phone calls. Even worse, you can't find the contractor anywhere. You have given this guy $9,200, and you have nothing but a signed contract. The address on the contract is a post office box, and you have no idea what to do. At the worst, you have lost $9,200; at best, you have tied up $9,200 in a court battle. If this sounds like a worst case scenario, we will look at another outcome.

You call the plumber to do the rough-in, and he shows up as promised. By the end of the week, all your plumbing is roughed-in. The plumber explains he will come back and set your special order whirlpool tub as soon as it is delivered. The codes enforcement officer inspects and approves the work. Now the rough-in payment is due. The amount is one-third of the contract amount, or $6,000. The plumber explains you already paid $1,800 of this amount by prepaying for the whirlpool. This reduces the rough-in payment to $4,200. You make the payment and get your lien waiver signed. The plumber says he will be back as soon as the whirlpool comes in.

Time passes, and the plumber doesn't come back. Certainly, the whirlpool must have been delivered by now. You start calling, but the phone is always answered by a machine. No one returns your calls. Now let's do a little accounting. You paid the plumber a deposit of $6,000. Then you paid $3,200 for the special order fixtures. Now you have paid the rough-in amount of $4,200. The total contract amount is $18,000. So far, you have paid $13,400 to

the plumber. What do you have? You have about $1,000 worth of pipe and fittings installed, and four days labor for the plumber. You don't have any fixtures. At the most, the work completed is worth $2,200. This means the plumber has recovered his cost and is enjoying the use of $11,200 of your money.

Maybe there is no intent to defraud you, or maybe there is. If a contractor sets up enough of these deals quickly, he could leave the state with a tidy sum. Sound far-fetched? Some people are professionals at making a living by taking other people's money. Even if your contractor has every intention of fulfilling his contract, he has no reason to rush back to your job. When the contractor resumes work, he will have to spend the money you advanced and get your fixtures. His profit might amount to $3,600 when the job is complete. Right now, he has the use of over $11,000 of your money. Why should he hurry back? The plumber is able to call all the shots now. You are basically helpless. This is a position you don't want to be in. *Never* allow the contractor to gain control. You must set the pace.

STAY IN CONTROL OF THE MONEY

Whoever has the money has the control. You can get in real trouble with a so-called standard payment schedule. The potential for problems exists with any trade, but the risks are greatest with the mechanical groups. Carpenters are on the job most of the time and are easier to keep track of. The mechanical trades can complete their rough-in work within a few days. Then they are gone until the job is nearly complete. When they are holding your money, too many problems can happen. The contractor could misappropriate the money, go out of business, or file for bankruptcy. When several different subcontractors are involved on your project, it is critical to manage your disbursements wisely.

PROTECTING YOURSELF

How can you protect yourself from this type of problem? Obviously, you must maintain financial control, but this is easier said than done. A payment schedule will have to be negotiated with every subcontractor when you act as your own general contractor. Hiring a general contractor requires only one negotiation, and he has to dicker with the subs.

If you convince the general to play by your rules, you have it made. Another way to reduce payment problems is to use a general contractor with "In-Home" financing. Most of these plans don't deplete any of your existing cash with down payments or loan fees. Better yet, the contractors get one lump-sum payment, when the job is finished to your satisfaction. This eliminates the three-part payment risk altogether.

Whatever means you use, try to break the typical payment schedule. If a contractor wants the work enough, he will work with you on the terms. Perhaps he will accept a 15% deposit, and this is a compromise for both of you. The contractor gets a deposit, as a show of good faith on your part, and your position is stronger than it would be with a larger deposit. Many contractors feel the need for a deposit to secure your job in their schedule. If they schedule materials and workers, only to have you postpone or cancel the job, the contractors will lose money. They view the deposit as leverage to make sure you hold up your end of the agreement.

Be honest with your contractors, but express your concerns in a way that won't offend them. A seasoned contractor will understand your concern but may not be willing to alter his payment schedule. Established contractors will have been stuck for money more than once. This is the proverbial Mexican stand-off. The contractor doesn't trust the homeowner, and the homeowner doesn't trust the contractor. The difference is the contractor has the built-in protection of mechanic's liens. You have no protection. Work with your contractor to develop a satisfactory payment schedule. With a reasonable contractor, you should be able to come to acceptable terms.

OTHER FACTORS AFFECTING PAYMENTS

With a payment schedule agreed to, what are the other factors affecting the disbursements of payments? The most obvious is the completion of the prescribed work. Just as important is the *quality* of the work. You should inspect all work closely before agreeing to release funds. In most cases, common sense and attention to detail are all you need to approve the quality of a job. Are the fixtures secure? Do doors open and close properly? Are there any unsightly lumps in the carpet or finished walls? These are the kinds of punch-list items to check.

Many people assume the code enforcement officer will not approve the job unless everything is satisfactory. The code inspector's job is to ensure code compliance. He is not responsible for seeing the job is done to *your* satisfaction. In some areas, these inspectors do an outstanding job, but unfortunately, this isn't always the case.

Don't Expect the Inspector to Do Your Job

Many times, small towns with limited budgets can't afford expert inspectors for each trade. They use one inspector for several trades. This can create problems. You can't expect a master electrician to know everything about the plumbing code. Neither can an expert carpenter be fully versed in heating systems. When you require a single inspector to be responsible for multiple trades, the potential for oversights increases.

High population areas have codes officers for each trade, but they have to cover a larger number of inspections each day. Codes officers may not have the time, or the ability, to check for more than basic compliance. This means you need to verify the quality of the work yourself. If you aren't sure what to look for, consider hiring a construction management consultant.

CONSTRUCTION MANAGEMENT CONSULTANTS

Construction management consultants can be architects, independent consultants, or individual masters of each trade. Their services will not be cheap, but they can save you money in the long run. Their evaluation of the completed work will be unbiased and professional. These professional inspections can save you future frustration and problems. The expense should be between $35 and $100 per inspection — a small price to pay for peace of mind. A construction management consultant will go over the workmanship with you, allowing you to question whether items should be accepted. When the work has been inspected and meets with your approval, advance the required payments. Remember to have lien waivers signed with each payment for services and materials.

WHAT TO DO ABOUT CODE VIOLATIONS

There will be times when the work is not in compliance with the required codes. When this happens, notify the contractor, in writing, to correct the code violations. This can be done with a Code Violation Notification Form. Require the contractor to sign the form, acknowledging the work to be corrected. If you mail the form, do so by certified, return receipt mail. It is vital to maintain a record of your notification, and of the contractor's acceptance, regarding the code violations. This eliminates the contractor's ability to lien your property legitimately, for nonpayment of the scheduled installment payment.

Keep accurate records and document all correspondence with your contractors. If you are forced into court, these records can win the case. Do not pay the contractor until all code violations are corrected. These violations can bring the progress of your job to a standstill. As we have discussed, each trade relies on another. When the plumber has to wait for the heating contractor to comply with a code violation, everyone, including you, loses time and money. For this reason, it is wise to have your contract stipulate a retainage on each payment.

RETAINAGES

Retainages are a safeguard against unknown problems and normally amount to 5 or 10% of the payment amount due. Retainages are surrendered when the contractor complies with certain criteria. Final retainages should be withheld from each of your subcontractors for thirty days after completion of their work. This allows for hidden or unforeseen problems to crop up. You cannot arbitrarily hold money due to the contractor, so include provisions in the contract allowing you to hold a retainage.

Keep tight reins on the contractors. Be fair, but don't put yourself in quicksand. Maintain strong financial leverage throughout the job. Money is a major motivator, and all contractors will respond to monetary motivation. A contract is good, but nothing is better for getting what you want than money. Trying to enforce a contract is expensive and time consuming. If you must prevail upon the courts to settle a dispute, even if you win the dispute, you lose. You lose time, money, and happiness. Good contracts and the right payment procedures keep you out of the judicial system.

CONFLICTS ABOUT MONEY

Money accounts for most of the conflicts in remodeling. The initial argument may be started over material, but ultimately it is about money. Let's assume you don't like the doors supplied by a contractor. There is more involved than your preference — you don't feel you should have to pay a premium price for unacceptable merchandise. Returning the doors will require someone's time and transportation. The contractor will be charged a restocking fee if he returns the doors. These problems cost the contractor money. Prices may have increased, and the replacement doors may be more expensive. The remodeler never planned on spending time or money changing doors. Everything involved in the change will cost the contractor money.

A dispute about doors is really about money. The doors are the focus of the problem, but money is basis of the problem. If you are willing to pay extra, the contractor would be glad to satisfy your requests. If not, this argument can grow into a serious conflict. You refuse to pay the contractor until you get the doors you want. The contractor refuses to work until he is paid for the work already completed. Something has to give. The contractor might file a lien and a lawsuit; you might try to sue the contractor. All of this will cost both of you more than the expense of changing the doors. By this time, the doors aren't the issue. Now you are both angry and defending your positions to the end.

This need to prevail hurts both of you. The contractor isn't getting paid, and your job isn't being completed. A weak contract probably caused the problem in the first place. Perhaps the doors weren't clearly specified. The next perpetrator was a vague payment clause. It called for payment in full when the doors were installed, and was not contingent on your inspection and approval before disbursement. Now you have lost your leverage and are stuck with doors you don't want. By the letter of the contract and payment clause, the contractor is entitled to his money. You have a real problem, and little chance of defending your position in court. The moral of the story: insist on thorough, clear, written agreements. Make sure there is no room for error or questions in your contract and payment clauses.

SHORT FORM LIEN WAIVER

CUSTOMER NAME: Mr. & Mrs. J. P. Homeowner
CUSTOMER ADDRESS: 192 Hometown Street
CUSTOMER CITY/STATE/ZIP: Wisetown, OH 00690
CUSTOMER PHONE NUMBER: (101) 555-4567
JOB LOCATION: Same
DATE: July 25, 1991
TYPE OF WORK: Remodeling
CONTRACTOR: Plumbing Is Us
CONTRACTOR ADDRESS: 432 Pipe Place, Plumb City, OH 00690

DESCRIPTION OF WORK COMPLETED BY CONTRACTOR TO DATE:
Underground plumbing, rough-in plumbing, installation of shower, installation of water service and sewer.

PAYMENT RECEIVED TO DATE BY CONTRACTOR FROM CUSTOMER:
Eight hundred dollars ($800.00).

PAYMENT RECEIVED BY CONTRACTOR FROM CUSTOMER ON THIS DATE:
Two thousand, five hundred dollars ($2,500.00).

TOTAL AMOUNT PAID TO CONTRACTOR INCLUDING THIS PAYMENT:
Three thousand, three hundred dollars ($3,300.00).

The contractor acknowledges receipt of all payments stated above. These payments are in compliance with the written contract between the parties above. The contractor hereby states payment for all work done, to this date, has been paid in full.

The contractor releases and relinquishes any and all rights available to said contractor, to place a mechanic's or materialman's lien against the subject property for the above described work. Both parties agree, all work performed to date has been paid for, in full and in compliance with their written contract.

The undersigned contractor releases the customer and the customer's property from any liability for non-payment of material or services, extended through this date. The undersigned contractor has read this entire agreement and understands the agreement.

_____   _____
Your Plumber   Date

CODE VIOLATION NOTIFICATION

CUSTOMER NAME: Mr. & Mrs. J. P. Homeowner
CUSTOMER ADDRESS: 192 Hometown Street
CUSTOMER CITY/STATE/ZIP: Ourtown, MO 00580
CUSTOMER PHONE NUMBER: (000) 555-1212
JOB LOCATION: Same
DATE: July 25, 1991
TYPE OF WORK: Electrical
CONTRACTOR: Flashy Electrical Service
ADDRESS: 689 Walnut Ridge, Boltz, MO 00580

OFFICIAL NOTIFICATION OF CODE VIOLATIONS

On July 24, 1991, I was notified by the local electrical code enforcement officer of code violations in the work performed by your company. The violations must be corrected within two business days, as per our contract dated July 1, 1991. Please contact the codes officer for a detailed explanation of the violations and required corrections. If the violations are not corrected within the allotted time, you may be penalized, as per our contract, for your actions, delaying the completion of this project. Thank you for your prompt attention to this matter.

_____
J. P. Homeowner

_____
Date

Keep Your Contractor Honest

14

Contractors have mixed reputations. They are like any other profession, there are good ones and bad ones. As a consumer, you have to try to find the good ones. The process for finding contractors was explained earlier. Now we are going to examine ways to make sure these contractors give you what you want. The two most important elements in controlling a contractor are money and a firm contract. Some of the ways to maintain control have already been touched on. Here, we are going to expand on the methods for commanding respect and maintaining control.

ESTABLISH CONTROL EARLY

Control is established during your initial negotiations with contractors and suppliers. A comprehensive contract, which you supply, will cement your dominant position. Proposals supplied by contractors will not be slanted to benefit you. There are two sample contracts at the end of this chapter, which will give you an idea of how to prepare your contract. One of the contracts is for use with general contractors, and the other is for subcontractors. Show these examples to your attorney. Explain the scope of work required, and have the attorney draft a solid, legally binding contract for your job. The cost will be well worth the price. A good contract is critical to the success of any remodeling job.

Subcontractor agreements will differ with the various trades. The basic language will remain the same, but some clauses will change. These clauses will be directly related to the type of work the subcontractor is supplying. The language required in a foundation contract will differ dramatically from that in a roofing proposal. The contracts provided in the back of the chapter are only samples. Although they are based on actual contracts, they may not be legal in your state. When your contracts are prepared by a local attorney, you know they are legal and enforceable. A good contract must contain both of these elements. There is a big difference between *legal* and *enforceable*.

CREATE A WRITTEN CONTRACT

When you talk to a contractor, you may be creating a legal contract. Contracts don't have to be in writing to be lawful; verbal contracts are perfectly legal. The problem is implementing a verbal contract. If you only have an oral agreement, how will you enforce it? There will be nothing in writing to substantiate your claims. When a dispute occurs, it is your word against the contractor's. This can be an impossible situation to settle fairly. This is the difference between *legal* and *enforceable*. Talk to your attorney, and get the proper documents for the job. It is difficult for a contractor to argue with the terms of a written contract, which he signed.

The various components of a contract can be complex or simple. The main objective is to have every aspect of the job covered in writing. You don't need fancy legal terms; you only need a clear, concise description of the agreed-upon work and terms. Take a look at the examples at the end of the chapter. You will get a good idea of what you should include in your contract. Require the main elements and be specific; your attorney will advise you on the legal details. Don't settle for a vague or simplified form contract. Personalize the contract to meet the needs of your particular job.

Information from the Contractor

One of the first sections of your contract should focus on the contractor's information. These details should include the company name, the principals of the company, a physical address, and all available phone numbers. Don't accept a post office box as an address. Insist on a physical location for the business. This will be beneficial if you have to serve the company with legal papers. Get as many phone numbers as you can, so try for home phones and home addresses, too. A contractor may not want you to bother him at home, but if you can obtain this information, you are ahead of the game.

In this phase of the remodeling adventure, the more information you have, the better your chances are of obtaining what you want. Contractors with bad intentions will not be cooperative in giving extensive information. They don't want you to be able to find them. They will try to hide behind answering machines and post office boxes, to reduce your ability to make personal contact. Requesting extensive information will reduce the chances of a bad experience.

Describing the Job Location

The next important element is an accurate description of the job location. You should use the street or legal address of your job in the contract. A street address is sufficient, but a legal description removes any doubt. Legal descriptions include your lot number, block number, and the tax map section of the property. In some areas, a legal description will be the same as your deed description. Deeds frequently summarize property in the metes and bounds format. Regardless of the language, your attorney will know what type of legal description to use. A detailed location for the work to be completed is extremely important.

There have been times when work was performed on the wrong house. One such instance involved the resurfacing of a gravel driveway. A customer called a stone company and requested several loads of stone be added to their existing driveway. The company agreed to bill the customer for the work and asked for the delivery address. The customer gave his address and directions. The work was scheduled for later in the week. The home-

owner said he wouldn't be home, but the driver could drop off the stone and leave the bill in the front door. This was acceptable to the company and the work was scheduled.

The day for the delivery arrived. When the customer returned from work, he was surprised not to find any stone in his driveway. It was late, and the stone company had already closed for the day, so the customer called the company the next morning. When the customer asked the owner of the company why his stone had not been delivered, the owner insisted it had been delivered. He checked his driver's tickets from the previous day, and confirmed the delivery had been made. Obviously, this was confusing for both parties. The owner of the company agreed to investigate the situation and call the customer back.

The owner then received another phone call, from a friend. His friend said a mistake had been made. He went on to explain that he had come home and found new gravel in his driveway. There was also a delivery ticket in his front door, but the ticket was made out to a customer in another part of town. The street number on the ticket was correct, but the street name was wrong. The delivery had been made to South Street but was intended for South Circle.

One simple word was responsible for a potentially large problem. The friend who received the stone had not ordered it, and it would be nearly impossible to remove the gravel without damaging the existing driveway. Consequently, the company had to give the delivered gravel to the unintended address. They also had to make good on the original delivery request to the South Circle customer. This was embarrassing and costly.

The problem had occurred because of a faulty street address. The agreements had been made by phone, and the mistake was easy to make. The dispatcher had not asked for a color or description of the house for the delivery. If she had, maybe the mistake would have been noticed before the stone was unloaded. In this particular case, everything worked out. The original customer received his stone delivery one day late, and the friend agreed to pay for the stone, even though he hadn't ordered it. The company gave him the gravel at a discount, and everybody ended up happy.

This story is based on actual events. and the friend who received the unintentional delivery was my father. This was my first exposure to the need for clear, concise, written agreements. I was only a child, but the memory stuck with me. I'm sure this experience has saved me thousands of dollars over the years. I learned firsthand about the importance of good property descriptions. This case involved less than a thousand dollars and the surface of a driveway. It could have involved much more. Imagine my father's reaction if he had found all his roof shingles removed, or half of the house repainted! How can you keep a job on schedule when workmen or materials are going to the wrong property? Don't underestimate the need for clear, legal property descriptions in your contract.

SCOPE OF THE WORK

The next element of the contract is the scope of the work. The information in this section will vary from trade to trade. This is where you describe the material to be supplied and the work to be done. Be specific, including model numbers, brands, lumber grades, colors, and any other pertinent information. Leave nothing to the imagination. This is the body of the contract. Turn it all loose here and name every item to be installed. Don't take anything for granted, and do refer to a set of attached plans and specifications.

Elaborate on any areas or items that seem vague or confusing. Spend enough time on this section to be totally satisfied with your job description. If you aren't thorough here, the contractor can run rampant. This is where you can assure quality products and service. To keep your job running smoothly and on budget, you must ensure against misunderstandings and human error. Without the proper wording, your job can slide downhill fast. It is not enough to say you want the contractor to supply and install a white shower. You need to reference the location of the shower, as shown on your plans. The type and model number, as listed on your specifications, should also be detailed. You spent considerable time preparing your plans and specs, and this is where your efforts will pay off.

In the scope of work section, you can simply require all work to be done in compliance with the attached plans and specifications. If the plans and specs are done correctly, this is all you have to say. Mention in the contract that the attached plans and specs will be signed by all parties. Have the contractor review and sign the plans and specs before you release the contract. This removes any doubts about which plans and specs go with the contract. If you are dealing with several subcontractors, make sure each contract has a legible set of plans and specs attached. Many homeowners will reproduce their blueprints on a copying machine, to save money on drafted duplicates. This only saves you money if the copies are complete and easy to understand. I have seen many copied plans that were too light to read or had vital information blurred or blanked out. Another drawback to photocopied plans is distortion; these copied plans cannot be used to make scale measurements.

CONTRACT CHANGES

The next clause will deal with contract changes. This section should clearly state your position on deviations from the contract. Oral agreements should not be valid, so require all changes to be in writing. Protect yourself from surprise billings with extravagant extras by stating your right to dishonor any claims unsubstantiated in writing. If you get these bills, you won't have to pay them, unless a change order was issued and signed. This one clause can save you hundreds or even thousands of dollars. Don't omit it. It protects you from unauthorized additional expenses.

Written change orders protect the contractors too. They know that if they are asked to do additional work, it will be detailed in the change order. The terms of payment will also be specified in the change order. The contractors know they are assured of getting paid the correct amount when the terms are in writing. All too often a customer will request additional work, then deny authorization for payment. These are usually small changes the customer assumed would be done as part of the original price. This problem won't exist when change orders are used.

Written change orders provide you with a simple way to control your budget and job progress. If a change must be made, find out how it will affect other trades. In this way, you eliminate the risk of agreeing to a change only to discover it will throw the entire project off schedule. You can also negotiate alteration costs in advance, and weigh the change's effect on your budget in advance. Change orders provide you with a checks and balances system, to keep job costs from getting out of control. (At the end of Chapter 11, you will find both a Sample Change Order and a blank Change Order Form.)

EXCLUSIONS TO THE CONTRACT

Contractors will want exclusions in the contract and may attempt to include extensive latitudes in a contract you provide. I have included an example of a contract, from Anytime Contracting, at the end of the chapter, for your inspection. When you read the contract, you will see the exclusions. It is not unreasonable to allow some of these clauses. Contractors have to protect themselves from homeowners and guard against unknown conditions. You can count on resistance to your contract if you don't allow *some* exclusions. Try to get the contract signed without exclusions. If you can't, agree to include an addendum for the exclusions. There is a sample addendum at the back of the chapter.

What are exclusions? Exclusions protect the contractor from certain circumstances. They deal with existing conditions and unknown conditions. Carpenters want exclusions dealing with your existing structure. If a carpenter finds rotted structural members, he wants to be protected from having to replace them. The exclusions may address your existing second floor joists or your unseen exterior wall structure. Since these are items that cannot be seen, they can't be planned for. You will have to be reasonable on these exclusions. You can't expect a carpenter to venture blindly into a termite-ridden house and make it structurally sound without additional charges.

For a plumber, the exclusions will deal with your existing plumbing system. The plumber has no way of knowing if your sewer is filled with tree roots. He will not guarantee the installation to work properly if existing conditions prevent proper drainage. This is a legitimate exclusion. The same is true of water pressure. If your house has undersized water pipe, the plumber's new installation can't work to its full potential.

There have to be limits to exclusions. If the exclusion can be removed by a site inspection, don't allow the clause. As an example, an electrician might try to exclude responsibility for the adequacy of your existing electrical service. This is ridiculous. With a site inspection, a competent electrician can evaluate your electrical service and determine if the service is adequate to support the proposed changes. Don't let contractors walk all over you when it comes to exclusions.

A carpenter who is too lazy to crawl under your house and examine existing conditions is not entitled to an exclusion. When an exclusion concerns the existing floor structure, it should only be allowed for areas inaccessible to inspection. A good carpenter can tell a lot about your home from visible signs. He can judge the depth of your exterior walls by probing around electrical outlets and measuring windows. This gives him much of the information he needs for structural planning. It is easy to estimate the size of floor joists with a few simple measurements, and a good remodeler can make very educated guesses. More often than not, these guesses will be correct. The point is, don't be too free to allow exclusions. You are contracting professional remodelers; make sure they have confidence in themselves. If they doubt their own ability, how can you have confidence in them?

PRICE AND PAYMENT SCHEDULE

When you get to the price and payment schedule, take your best shot. Make the contract tight, and don't give in on any points unless you have to. Be prepared to compromise, but don't volunteer paying for services yet to be rendered. Initially, tell the contractor he will receive payment upon completion. Make the contractor rebut this clause. The less you offer in the beginning, the more you have to bargain with later. Try to avoid giving deposits until after material is delivered and work is started. Strive to pay as little as possible with each phase. Appear confident that other contractors will accept your terms, and play your hand to the end. If you really want a particular contractor, give only what you have to in order to retain his services.

TIME FRAME FOR COMPLETION

Include a time frame for the work to be completed. If you don't know exactly when the job will start, give the contractor a specified period of time to begin. For example, you could require the contractor to start the work within four days of your notification. On the day the contractor begins the job, ask him to sign a contract addendum listing the commencement date. The time frame you establish in the contract for his phase of the job will begin with this date. Refer to the time of completion clause in the sample contract at the end of the chapter. These clauses must contain the words, "Time is of the Essence."

These five simple words carry a lot of weight. They cement the importance of complying with a required time frame. Without the time is of the essence clause, your time requirements don't have as much meaning. You must regulate the individual production components to keep your entire project on schedule. Even if you use a general contractor, be certain to include time parameters and a completion clause. An attorney can explain further the importance of such language in your contract.

Penalty Clauses

If the ability to make money is a strong motivator, then the threat of losing money is even more powerful. Including a daily cash penalty clause, for each day your completion agreement is not met, will enforce your production requirements. The amount of the penalties is up to you and the contractor to decide. For subcontractors, I use $100 per day. For a general contractor, I would suggest a minimum charge of $250 per day. This clause will almost guarantee an expedient job, but you must be fair in the time allowed for completion. This can be accomplished by asking the contractor how long the work will take. Adding one week to the time given by the contractor will establish a reasonable time for completion. Be prepared to hit resistance to this clause.

Even after contractors tell you how long the job will take, they will squirm when you include a penalty clause. Don't eliminate the clause. Extend it if you must, but don't remove it. A competent contractor will be willing to commit to a reasonable completion schedule. If the contractor refuses to allow any penalty clause, look for another contractor. This one obviously doesn't have faith in his abilities. Any good contractor will know approximately how long his job will take. The only reasons for refusing a penalty clause are incompetence or bad intentions. This clause prevents your project from dragging on for months. If the job does run late, at least you are financially compensated for the inconvenience.

State in the contract that these penalty charges will be deducted from monies owed to the contractor. Without this stipulation, you will have to pay the contractor in full for the contract amount, then pursue the contractor for payment of the penalty. Getting a contractor to pay *you* is tough, so this is a losing proposition. Make arrangements to deduct penalties from the money owed; it's much easier to collect.

If the contractor protests that unforeseen problems will affect his completion projections, take the objection away. Explain to the contractor that your change order clause requires written agreement of the time and costs to perform any additional work. This means if he runs into legitimate problems, the completion date will be extended by the time frame specified in the change order. He is protected from the unknown, and your time is of the essence and penalty clauses protect you from costly delays. Creating an amicable contract, for all parties concerned, will keep your contractors honest and your job on schedule.

Your money is the best tool you have for controlling a contractor. Never let the contractors have the upper hand, and keep them leveraged into the job until the end. If the contractor has money invested, he will work to get it returned. If the remodeler is holding your money, he has little reason to work. This power is won or lost in the contract. Maintaining control is critical to your job, and money is critical to maintaining control. The contract will be your vehicle of control, but without the proper clauses you won't be able to maintain dominance. Spend enough time on the contract to avoid a regrettable job.

READY TO START THE WORK

Once you have signed contracts in hand, you are ready to start the work. If you have a general contractor, all you have left to do is authorize the starting date. You can go about your daily life and leave the details of the job to the general contractor. You don't have to do much, except inspect the work and write checks. Your penalty and production clauses will force the general contractor to expedite subcontractors and materials. He will be responsible for keeping the job on track. If subcontractors don't show up, the general will have to deal with the problems. When the wrong material is shipped, the general will take care of it. Your part in the job is minimal during the remodeling or construction process. Usually, the less you do, the quicker and better the job will go.

STICK TO CHECKING THE WORK

Homeowners can get in the way and slow production down. If you are using a general contractor, let him earn his money. Leave the daily worries and work to the contractor, but look everything over at the end of the day. The workers will be gone and you won't be in the way. You can be of the greatest assistance by making notes of any problems or questions you might have. Go over these notes with the general contractor — you may have discovered flaws he didn't know about. You are paying the general contractor to handle the job, so let him do it.

There is no shame in hiring a professional. Remodeling is a tough business, and some of the people in the business are rough characters. It can be very intimidating to walk up to a 320-pound bricklayer and tell him his work isn't satisfactory. General contracting is not a job for everyone. You have to be firm and most of all, you have to maintain control over the job. You can't allow vendors to get the better of you. At some point, they are going to try to break you down into ignoring the rules of remodeling. If you allow this to happen, you are going to lose the contest. Stick to the rules and stay on top of the job.

IF YOU ARE THE
GENERAL CONTRACTOR . . .

If you are going to act as your own general contractor, your responsibilities will be ongoing. After all your contracts are negotiated, you have to obtain your permits and order material. You must have the right material available when the subcontractors need it. Scheduling subcontractors will start out easy, but will certainly become complicated before the job is done. You will base your schedule on the intended completion dates given for each phase of the work. This will look good on the calendar, but you will inevitably have to change your schedule often.

Something can happen to disrupt even the best schedule. A material delivery will be wrong or delayed. If you wait too long to place an order, work will have to stop. A subcontractor will run into unexpected problems with existing conditions and be slowed down. You will have to reschedule the other subs and material deliveries. Weather can ruin your production schedule quickly. The construction of additions and garages can be put on hold by inclement weather. Every day of production you lose is a day you have to call the subs. Damp, humid conditions can prevent your drywall mud from drying. The drywall process is time-consuming in any case. When complicated by the effects of damp weather, it can feel like it takes an eternity. These are unavoidable delays.

Maintaining the Production Schedule

It is your job, as the general, to maintain a smooth production schedule. I believe this is the hardest part of being a general contractor. The general has very little personal control over the events affecting a job schedule. All a good general can do is react quickly and effectively. With some foresight and effective planning, some of the delays can be avoided. Weather is uncontrollable, so all the general can do is develop a contingency plan. If weather will affect a trade, such as roofing, allow for weather in the contract. Adding a little heat in the room will help the drywall mud to dry. Tarps may make it possible for trades, such as carpenters or siding subs, to work in the rain.

PLAN TO PREVENT PROBLEMS

At this point, you may be wondering why your contract should include so many protection clauses. Knowing there will be obstacles beyond your control, you must guard against situations you can control. Even with the best contract in the world, you have no guarantees problems will not develop. What you do have is protection from unnecessary delays and contractor deceptions. Contracts will bridle unfair practices, and contingency plans will allow you to deal with the unexpected.

In Chapter 10, you were encouraged to deal with parties amicably, when negotiating for your best deals. One of the by-products of polite negotiations is the large list of subcontractors and suppliers you develop. Having a wide selection of subcontractors available helps to reduce the effects of undependable workers. If a subcontractor leaves you high and dry in the middle of a job, you can approach the next best contractor on your list. You may have to accept a less-than-ideal agreement with the new sub, but you avoid having the job come to a standstill. Knowing where alternate materials can be purchased defuses some supplier-related problems.

Professional general contractors have the experience and contacts to overcome unexpected problems. Most homeowners don't have this advantage. Your best defense is a good offense. Plan everything well in advance. Order your materials early and check each shipment for accuracy. Plan for problems and have backup subcontractors for each phase of the work. Include a clause in your contract to allow you to use these alternate subs if the primary sub doesn't perform properly. Properly wording the clause can allow you to deduct any additional expenses you incur by using the replacement contractor from the original sub's bill. Follow the job closely and always be looking ahead. Your organizational skills will be your best weapon in the war against time.

If your project falls behind schedule, you will lose money. If contractors are able to hit you with extra charges, it will cost you money. A thorough contract, complemented by written agreements, will help protect against costly problems. Keeping your contractors honest isn't difficult. It is a simple matter of basic knowledge and written agreements. You can get all the knowledge you need from books, and written documentation will do the rest. You must exhibit strong confidence and conviction to your contractors. The way you present yourself will have a lot of bearing on who controls the job. Written agreements give you the basis for control, but it is up to you to exercise the control.

RICHARD & RHONDA SMART
180 HOMEOWNER LANE
WIZETOWN, OH 99897
(102) 555-6789

REMODELING CONTRACT

This agreement, made this 12th day of May, 1991, shall set forth the whole agreement, in its entirety, between Contractor and Homeowner Contractor: Generic General Contractors, referred to herein as Contractor. Owner: Richard and Rhonda Smart, referred to herein as Homeowner.

Job name: Smart Kitchen Remodel

Job location: 180 Homeowner Lane, Wizetown, OH

The Homeowner and Contractor agree to the following:

SCOPE OF WORK

Contractor shall perform all work as described below and provide all material to complete the work described below. All work is to be completed by Contractor in accordance with the attached plans and specifications. All material is to be supplied by Contractor in accordance with attached plans and specifications. Said attached plans and specifications have been acknowledged and signed by Homeowner and Contractor.

A brief outline of the work is as follows; this work is only part of the work, and all work referenced in the attached plans and specifications will be completed to the Homeowner's satisfaction. The following is only a basic outline of the overall work to be performed:

• REMOVE EXISTING KITCHEN CABINETS
• REMOVE EXISTING KITCHEN FLOOR COVERING AND UNDERLAYMENT
• REMOVE EXISTING KITCHEN SINK AND FAUCET
• REMOVE EXISTING COUNTERTOP
• REMOVE EXISTING ELECTRICAL FIXTURES, SWITCHES, AND OUTLETS
• REMOVE EXISTING KITCHEN WINDOW
• SUPPLY AND INSTALL NEW KITCHEN CABINETS
• SUPPLY AND INSTALL NEW KITCHEN SINK AND FAUCET
• SUPPLY AND INSTALL NEW KITCHEN UNDERLAYMENT AND FLOOR COVERING
• SUPPLY AND INSTALL NEW KITCHEN COUNTERTOP
• SUPPLY AND INSTALL NEW ELECTRICAL FIXTURES, SWITCHES, AND OUTLETS
• SUPPLY AND INSTALL NEW KITCHEN GREENHOUSE WINDOW
• PATCH, SAND, PRIME, AND PAINT WALLS, CEILING, AND TRIM
• COMPLETE ALL WORK IN STRICT COMPLIANCE WITH ATTACHED PLANS AND SPECIFICATIONS, ACKNOWLEDGED BY ALL PARTIES.

COMMENCEMENT AND COMPLETION SCHEDULE

The work described above shall be started within three days of verbal notice from Homeowner, the projected start date is 6/20/91. The Contractor shall complete the above work, in a professional and expedient manner, by no later than twenty days from the start date. Time is of the essence regarding this contract. No extension of time will be valid without the Homeowner's written consent. If Contractor does not complete the work in the time allowed, and if the lack of completion is not caused by the Homeowner, the Contractor will be charged one hundred dollars ($100.00) per day, for every day work is not finished, beyond the completion date. This charge will be deducted from any payments due to the Contractor for work performed.

CONTRACT SUM

The Homeowner shall pay the Contractor for the performance of completed work, subject to additions and deductions, as authorized by this agreement or attached addendum. The Contract Sum is Ten thousand three hundred dollars ($10,300.00).

PROGRESS PAYMENTS

The Homeowner shall pay the Contractor installments as detailed below, once an acceptable insurance certificate has been filed by the Contractor, with the Homeowner:

Homeowner will pay Contractor a deposit of one thousand five hundred dollars ($1,500.00), when demolition work is started.

Homeowner will then pay two thousand dollars ($2,000.00), when all demolition and rough-in work is complete.

Homeowner will pay three thousand dollars ($3.000.00), when walls have been painted, and cabinets, countertops, and flooring have been installed.

Homeowner will pay three thousand, two hundred dollars ($3,200.00) when all work is complete.

Homeowner will pay the final five hundred fifty dollars ($550.00) within thirty days of completion, if no problems occur and are left uncorrected.

All payments are subject to a site inspection and approval of work by the Homeowner. Before final payment, the Contractor, if required, shall submit satisfactory evidence to the Homeowner that all expenses related to this work have been paid and no lien risk exists on the subject property.

WORKING CONDITIONS

Working hours will be 8:00 a.m. through 4:30 p.m., Monday through Friday. Contractor is required to clean their work debris from the job site on a daily basis, and leave the site in a clean and neat condition. Contractor shall be responsible for removal and disposal of all debris related to their job description.

CONTRACT ASSIGNMENT

Contractor shall not assign this contract or further subcontract the whole of this subcontract without the written consent of the Homeowner.

LAWS, PERMITS, FEES, AND NOTICES

Contractor is responsible for all required laws, permits, fees, or notices required to perform the work stated herein.

WORK OF OTHERS

Contractor shall be responsible for any damage caused to existing conditions. This shall include work performed on the project by other contractors. If the Contractor damages existing conditions or work performed by other contractors, said Contractor shall be responsible for the repair of said damages. These repairs may be made by the Contractor responsible for the damages or another contractor, at the sole discretion of Homeowner.

The damaging Contractor shall have the opportunity to quote a price for the repairs. The Homeowner is under no obligation to engage the damaging Contractor to make the repairs.

If a different contractor repairs the damage, the Contractor causing the damage may be back-charged for the cost of the repairs. These charges may be deducted from any monies owed to the damaging Contractor by the Homeowner.

If no money is owed to the damaging Contractor, said Contractor shall pay the invoiced amount, from the Homeowner, within seven business days. If prompt payment is not made, the Homeowner may exercise all legal means to collect the requested monies.

The damaging Contractor shall have no rights to lien the Homeowner's property for money retained to cover the repair of damages caused by the Contractor. The Homeowner may have the repairs made to their satisfaction.

WARRANTY

Contractor warrants to the Homeowner all work and materials for one year from the final day of work performed.

INDEMNIFICATION

To the fullest extent allowed by law, the Contractor shall indemnify and hold harmless the Homeowner and all of their agents and employees from and against all claims, damages, losses, and expenses.
This Agreement entered into on May 12, 1991 shall constitute the whole agreement between Homeowner and Contractor

_____   _____

Homeowner   Contractor

Remodeling Rip-offs

15

The title of this chapter says it all. This is a compilation of schemes to take your money. All of the accounts represent circumstances that could happen to you. People think disasters only happen to the other guy. The purpose of this chapter is to illustrate how effectively professional con men can take advantage of you. When you enter the realm of remodeling, you need to have your eyes and ears open. This is a field tainted by bad operators. Some of the people posing as remodeling contractors are blatant frauds. Your money and your house are at stake. Don't allow room for errors, there will be plenty of mistakes made without even trying.

The people you will be dealing with are professionals. Using the proper screening procedures, the professionals will be quality remodelers. Without caution, the professionals may be rip-off artists. Your knowledge and judgment will be tested to determine what kind of professional you are dealing with. After seventeen years in the business, I have seen and heard the majority of the horror stories.

Here are some examples of these stories and documented events. I am going to relate these stories in a first person style. Many of the stories are based on true events, and some of them are taken from personal experience. The true scenarios are mixed with hypothetical situations, to protect the parties involved. The first one starts like this:

TOO MUCH SUCCESS IS BAD FOR BUSINESS

I was hired to work for an established remodeling contractor, to increase the company's volume of business. My position involved many tasks, but sales were my primary objective. When I was offered the position, the owner showed me the company's gross sales for the previous year. This business was a small one, owned and operated by an individual. The company had only grossed about $125,000 in the last year. The owner's goal was to reach a quarter of a million dollars in sales for the coming year.

The position fitted my personality. I could come and go as I pleased. The only requirements were producing sales. This was easy for me; I had been selling remodeling jobs for years. I designed a marketing plan for my new employer. It was based on direct mail, television, radio, telemarketing, and door-to-door campaigns. Our goal was to convey an image of success, through extensive advertising.

Previously, the company had relied on yellow page ads, an occasional ad in the newspaper, and word-of-mouth referrals. The owner was on most of the jobs, they ran smoothly, and the quality of the work was good. I was impressed with the quality control and felt this could be a career with a bright future. Selling for a respected contractor would be easy. I had plenty of happy customers to give as references, and the company enjoyed a good business rating, with no complaints. This was a salesman's dream come true.

The public knew and respected this remodeler. He was well established, and enjoyed an excellent reputation in the best neighborhoods. He worked from his home to keep his overhead low. The contractor enjoyed being on the job and talking with the homeowner. This is a real confidence builder. When homeowners can talk with the owner of the company, they feel secure. My job couldn't have been easier. My sales leads were provided to me, and I went out and sold the jobs.

The combination of the company's good reputation and my well-honed skills produced a high volume of sales. I was closing between 50 and 65% of all the estimate requests I went on. I was collecting large deposits with every job sold, and this cash injection fueled the growth of the company. The owner added new employees, new trucks, and rented a commercial space for the office and warehouse. He hired a full-time secretary and increased my advertising budget.

The additional advertising brought in more estimate requests. I arranged for the company to be an authorized dealer of on-the-spot financing. With the addition of easy financing, the sales figures ballooned. The company had more work than it could do, and cash flow was flooding in. Based on the sales after only six months, the company would gross over $500,000 by the end of the year.

The owner had only hoped for $250,000; now it looked like we could easily double that figure. I was a hero — my efforts had catapulted the business into the major leagues. At this point, you are probably wondering how this success story has any effect on homeowners looking out for fraudulent contractors. You are about to see an example of the importance of looking below the surface of a company.

From outside appearances, this contractor was reaching the pinnacle of quality. He had been in business for years and was growing. There were many jobs in progress, and the company showed signs of thriving. This successful appearance made customers comfortable and confident in the company. Unfortunately, there were several changes happening to the company, but the public only knew what they could see.

Rapid growth had forced the owner to hire new employees, and there wasn't time to screen them. To meet production schedules, the company needed workers on the jobs immediately. These workers were not capable of producing the quality of work the company was known for. The inexperience of the new help showed in the work, and jobs in progress were starting to suffer. The owner had his hands full scheduling work and paying bills. The lack of his presence at the jobs encouraged lower quality in the work being done. Homeowners were frustrated, because they could no longer talk with the owner. He didn't return their phone calls and

only went to the jobs to collect money.

All the new company acquisitions were financed or paid for from the general operating account. The overhead of the company rose rapidly, and the company's growing pains were transferred to the customers. This rapid expansion was gaining momentum, and the owner no longer had a clear concept of the requirements of each job. On the surface, potential customers were still impressed with the company, and sales were still on the rise.

Then two changes took place, which would be the beginning of the end for the contractor. First, the owner started to believe he was going to be rich. The company bank account was larger than ever before. He could not recognize this was the result of large deposits, collected for jobs that had not yet started. With this newfound artificial wealth, the owner stumbled. Then he became involved with drugs and worsened the whole situation. He lost his perspective and his interest in the customers and their jobs. His only focus was on the customer's money. I could see the company was in deep trouble, and spent hours trying to reason with the owner. My suggestions were ignored, and the problems continued to build.

Roofs were leaking, jobs were not being finished, and customer complaints were growing. The owner spent most of his time trying to find ways to avoid customers and bill collectors. He began to insist on excessive deposits for every job. Deposits were being spent on everything except the people's jobs. The company's credit had been cancelled with many suppliers, due to late payments. When the time came to buy material for a job, there was no money. The owner got caught up in the thrill of success, but was unwilling to take the necessary steps to ensure continued success. When the owner insisted I sell more jobs than our schedule could accommodate, I resigned.

The customers were hurt in many ways. Some jobs were never finished. Many jobs never got started, even after deposits were taken. The quality of the work was below industry standards, and eventually there was no company left to maintain warranty work. This was a disaster; everyone lost. There was very little warning to the customers, and the business went down fast. How can you protect yourself from such whirlwind destruction of a seemingly reputable contractor?

Regardless of how successful a company appears, stick to the rules of remodeling. First, do your homework. Require current references, and check them out personally. Get everything in writing. Avoid giving large deposits, and don't advance money until work is completed to your satisfaction. Inspect all work closely. Require lien waivers to be signed with every cash disbursement, and never assume anything. You may still become involved in an unfortunate incident, but you will be prepared and better protected if you follow the rules.

THE ESCAPING CONTRACTOR

The next story was told to me by a homeowner. This homeowner called me for an estimate on a new sunroom. The homeowner really grilled me, asking more questions and requesting more verifications than you can imagine. I thought it was unusual that she knew to ask such pertinent questions, and asked her why she was requiring this dissertation. Her answer was simple. She had just been defrauded by a so-called contractor and had learned from experience. This experience was costly but left an impression she wouldn't soon forget.

In her case, the woman called a contractor from a classified ad in the newspaper. She wanted to save money and thought the contractors in the paper would be less expensive. The contractor came out and gave her a quote on the work. He then said he could do the job for less if she supplied the material. The contractor explained that his cost would be less if he didn't have to supply the material. He gave several reasons to justify the price reduction, and the homeowner thought she had made a good deal.

The contractor took out a form contract and filled in the appropriate information. It was a very simple, one-page proposal, covering all the normal items. After all, the homeowner was supplying the material, and the proposal was for labor only. The customer signed the proposal and gave the contractor a $2,000 deposit. They agreed the work would start on the following Monday, to allow time for the homeowner to have the material delivered.

Monday morning found the material and the contractor on the job. It looked like everything was going according to plan. The contractor had a cup of coffee and discussed the job with the customer. The customer had to go to work, and the contractor walked out with her to inspect the material. All the material was stacked in the front yard. There were high quality sliding glass doors, expensive casement windows, and framing lumber. The homeowner

drove away, and the contractor got busy sorting material.

When the customer returned home, she was pleasantly surprised to see how much of the material had been used. Since the room was being built in the rear of the house, the material had to be moved behind the house. Excited to see how much work was done, she dashed around the house. Turning the corner, she was shocked. The job hadn't been started, but the material was gone. It took some time for the reality of the situation to sink in; she was a victim of fraud.

The so-called contractor had taken a $2,000 deposit when she signed the proposal and had maneuvered her into supplying more than $6,000 worth of material. Now she was out $8,000 and had no idea how to find the rip-off artist. The phone number she had called was an answering service, and the address on the proposal turned out to be bogus. She didn't even have a clear recollection of the truck he was driving. It could have been rented under a false name anyway. This type of dilemma isn't common, but it can happen. What did she do wrong?

She made a snap decision to sign the proposal. The deposit was too large a sum, especially for a labor-only contract. References were neither requested nor checked. Placing all the material on the job at one time increased her risk. She didn't verify the contractor's state or local license. To sum it up, she simply didn't follow Dodge's remodeling rules.

SMALL-SCALE RIP-OFFS

Not all remodeling rip-offs are on such a grandiose scale. Most remodeling fraud is done in much smaller measures. It is harder to detect, and the guilty contractor can continue to operate in the same location, despite adverse business practices. If the contractor's actions are exposed, restitution is usually made without a lot of publicity. Some contractors may not even consider their actions wrong. There are other types of activities that also affect the consumer. While not direct fraud, they are deviations from verbal commitments. Such unprofessional acts continue to hurt the image of remodeling contractors. A classic example is known as job juggling.

Job Juggling

Job juggling is a frequent complaint of homeowners involved with contractors. It may be hard to believe, but general contractors are also constant victims of job juggling from subcontractors. When a general contractor is subjected to job juggling from a sub, the homeowner feels the effect. A general contractor is only as good as the subcontractors working under his supervision. The promises made to you by a general are based on commitments made to him by the subcontractors.

Job juggling is difficult to avoid. Contractors want to stay busy and, to do so, will take several jobs within the same time frame. When these jobs get out of sync, or cash flow problems occur, job juggling results. When bills come due, a contractor has to generate cash. This is especially true of companies without a cash reserve from which to operate. The quickest way for a remodeler to generate cash is by job juggling. The consumer suffers because the job is prolonged, completion dates aren't met, and inconveniences are created.

Job juggling is the art of moving from job to job, doing as little as is necessary to generate cash. This can mean contracting new jobs to obtain deposit money or doing just enough work on a project to receive a draw. Sometimes job juggling is used as a facade, to make the customer happy by seeing workers on the job. The problem is, these workers are only there to make an appearance. They may leave after an hour or two, but the contractor can honestly say he had workers on the job.

Some contracts require the contractor to work on the job every day, and job juggling meets the criteria of this clause. They may not get much work done, but they are there every day. The intent behind this clause is to expedite the job, but it falls short due to creative job juggling. This problem can be solved with clauses requiring a definite date of completion and penalties for delays. A sample Completion Clause is provided at the end of the chapter. Job juggling loses its effectiveness in the face of clauses such as these.

The most common reason for job juggling is cash flow. Contractors send in crews to do just enough to be eligible for a cash advance. For example, if your contract authorizes a payment when drywall is hung, that's all the contractor has to do. The drywall doesn't have to be taped, and he doesn't have to apply the first coat of joint compound. All he has to do is hang it and collect the cash. You have to pay for this minimal effort, because the contract says you will.

Logic dictates doing as much as possible in every trip to a job as the most cost effective approach. After all, money is lost in travel time and loading and unloading tools. Why would a contractor only hang the drywall and leave, when he could tape and coat it in the same day? The need to generate cash often overpowers logic. The contractor can spend half the day on your job and half a day on another job, and get two checks instead of one.

This type of scheduling is expensive for the contractor and inconvenient for the customer. The contractor knows money is being lost by working in this manner. He also knows the customer will not stay happy for long when subjected to these work habits. Even with this knowledge, contractors still perform the "Now you see them, now you don't" game. You can eliminate job juggling with a strong completion clause in your contract.

The clause will include a start date and a completion date. It will allow you to charge the contractor a penalty fee for every day the completion date is exceeded. The clause should allow you to deduct these penalty fees from the money you owe the contractor. You should also include the option of bringing in another contractor to complete the work if the production schedule is not met. With proper wording, you can deduct the new subcontractor's charges from money owed to the original sub. The threat of losing the job to someone else, and of having to pay that person to take his work, will effectively deter a contractor from job juggling.

The Low Bidder

Another unfair business practice involves the manipulation of a homeowner. This is performed by contractors who will give you a very good price just to get your job. They appear to be the best value of all the contractors bidding the work. You award the job to the contractor and commend yourself for the money you are saving. This can be a short-lived, false sense of satisfaction.

This group of cutthroat contractors is expert at going in as the low bidder and walking away with the most profit. How can that be possible? They do this by substituting material and charging extra for work you assumed was included in the original price. They can maneuver you into a position of either accepting their terms or spending several months in litigation to resolve the conflict.

In the beginning, everything will appear normal. The contractor will give you his contract to sign and tell you how happy you will be with the job. These

REMODELING RIP-OFFS ▪ 165

manipulators will usually emphasize the amount of money you will be saving by using them. They are authentic contractors, and appear as reputable as any of the others you have interviewed. When you sign their contract, you lose control. They are telling you what you will get. The terms will be ambiguous and many of the promises will only be verbal. Several problems accompany these contractors.

You review the contract and question the inclusion of a clause about substituting materials. If your plans and specifications are incorporated into the contract, why does the agreement include a substitution clause? The contractor may try to characterize this clause as a safeguard to protect against job delays. He will verbally explain that substitutions will only be made if the original items aren't readily available when needed.

Of course, the clause doesn't specify what the replacements will be. It only says the material may be substituted with a similar product. While a toilet is a toilet, the quality, size, and price can range dramatically. A basic builder-grade toilet can be purchased for less than $50. The one you specified may sell for as much as $300. They are both toilets — both have a tank, a seat, and a bowl — but that is where the similarities end. If the contractor installed the builder-grade toilet, would you consider this substitution fair?

Of course not. You would demand the toilet you specified. The contractor would then remind you of the substitution clause and refuse to change the toilet. To settle this dispute, you would have to go to court. In the meantime, the contractor would lien your house, for lack of payment. This gets expensive fast. The contractor knows your easiest alternative will be to accept the toilet. He has held you hostage with threats of a costly court battle and time delays. Now it becomes clear why the other contractors' prices were higher. The contractor with the low bid never intended to use the more expensive toilet.

This problem can be avoided with proper wording in your contract. Substitution clauses are normal and often necessary. The deciding factor is how they deal with the substitutions. Detail what the acceptable alternate choices will be, if the original product is not available. Include make, model number, color, and any other descriptive language you can. Insist on a written change order, authorizing necessary substitutions. Leave nothing open for interpretation or negotiation. Only allow substitu-

tion if the product is unavailable from at least three major suppliers. This wording will protect you from this type of bait-and-switch scam.

Paying a Premium for Extras

Another game low-ball contractors play is adding up the extras. Once they have the job, they will start to take advantage of you. When you signed the contract, you questioned the light fixture allowance of $200. It didn't seem like enough. You were assured it would be sufficient, because you would be saving money by buying from the contractor's supplier. This made the contractor seem like a nice guy, saving you money by letting you get the fixtures at his builder cost. The contractor also said you could upgrade the fixtures later if you wanted to. You entered into the contract and planned your budget based on the contract amount.

When you went to select your light fixtures, you were appalled by the prices. Your $200 allowance would easily be exhausted by the purchase of one chandelier. After an exhaustive inspection of the supplier's selection, you realized you would have to spend more than the allotted amount. You picked out what you wanted and the price was $500. Sure, the contractor allowed you to upgrade, but it cost you an extra $300. Now, here is the real clincher. You thought getting the fixtures from the contractor's supplier meant you would get them at his cost. Wrong. He never said you would benefit from a price reduction, only that you could get the fixtures from his supplier. With the markup built into the light fixtures, the contractor picked up a nice profit from the extra cost.

This move wasn't illegal, and it didn't leave you much of a choice. You were in a bind. You needed lighting, but didn't want to cheapen your new space with cheap, plastic light fixtures. These contractors know how to play the game. This one tactic kept the original bid price $300 lower than the contractor's competitors. The agreement was all in writing, so what could you have done differently? You could have specified the light fixtures in advance. This would have removed the need for an allowance. Then what you got would have been what you wanted. The cost would have still been $500, but you would have known the cost before starting the job.

There are many other areas where extras can be added up. When you contracted the job, you expected door knobs to be included with the doors.

You didn't specify them in the contract, because you assumed handles must come with the doors. The contract stipulated: the contractor shall supply and install three hollow core, interior doors and two bi-fold closet doors. It didn't say anything about door knobs or hardware. When this question comes up, what will the contractor say?

He will point out you didn't specify these items, and that you never questioned the contract. The contractor will try to convince you he thought you were supplying the items. He may even complain that you are now trying to take advantage of him. This isn't a big expense, so you pay extra for the items. When this continues with other items, the extras add up. You can spend hundreds of dollars on small extras.

These unexpected costs will blow your budget out of the water. Now it is easier to see how your original bid was so low. These extras can be avoided with detailed specifications. The specifications should be made an integral part of your contract. Require written change orders for any deviation from the contract, including substitutions. These safeguards will lower your risks and keep your job on budget.

Being aware of potential risks is half the battle of avoiding them. Remodeling isn't destined to be a bad experience; the key is educating yourself and following the rules. There are some fraudulent contractors out there, but they are far outnumbered by reputable contractors. Your odds of getting involved with a bad contractor will be minimized if you use the information you learn from this book.

Remodeling can be a fabulous experience. With the right contractors, you can enjoy seeing your dreams come to life. It's hard not to get excited about revamping your house. You can make all the changes you want and can afford. You won't have to put up with outdated features any longer. Coming home from work every day will be an adventure, as you get to see how much of the remodeling work got done. All this excitement can cloud your judgment. Getting excited is part of the joy of remodeling, but it is important to keep your excitement under control. Corrupt contractors will play on your emotions and use them to take your money any way they can. Don't get sloppy in the middle of the job. Use the principles and knowledge you have taken the time to learn. In order to assure a pleasant job, take the time to follow Dodge's remodeling rules. You can protect yourself by anticipating deception, and you can disarm unethical efforts with comprehensive written agreements.

SAMPLE COMPLETION CLAUSE

COMMENCEMENT AND COMPLETION SCHEDULE

The work described above shall be started within 3 days of verbal notice from the customer, the projected start date is 10/2/91. The Contractor shall complete the above work in a professional and expedient manner by no later than twenty (20) days from the start date. Time is of the essence in this subcontract. No extension of time will be valid without the customer's written consent. If contractor does not complete the work in the time allowed and if the lack of completion is not caused by the customer, the contractor will be charged one hundred dollars ($100.00) for every day after the completion date. This charge will be deducted from any payments due to the contractor for work performed.

The Decision

16

By now, you know more about remodeling than some contractors. You have learned all the basic elements required to enjoy a successful job. The expenses of remodeling have been discussed and you know how to get the most for your money. The only hurdle standing between you and your remodeling dreams is the final decision. Now you must resolve to do the project and decide how to get the job done. For some, this will still be difficult. Your project may require a sizable investment. You have read the horror stories and are not convinced the benefits outweigh the risks. In cases such as this, I recommend you list the pros and cons of your project. Categorizing the information in black and white may surprise you. Reviewing the advantages and financial gains of your remodeling plans may eradicate your fears.

CONSIDER YOUR QUALIFICATIONS

The best place to start is the beginning. Reconsider your qualifications to be your own general contractor. Now that you know what is required to run the job, do you feel competent to manage the entire project? Take the time to consider this decision thoroughly. Try to determine how qualified you are to run your own job. Organizational ability is the first quality to analyze. Are you confident you can coordinate the whole job? How does your regular job compare with the skills needed to be a general contractor? Is your profession centered around personnel management?

This can be a big advantage when you tackle your remodeling project. If your daily job includes managing people, you have at least one of the needed qualities of a good general contractor. Managing and manipulating subcontractors will be similar to overseeing your employees. Subcontractors may present a bigger challenge, because they can be very independent and a little rough around the edges. Most of them can't be compared to the people you might manage in a dress shop or bank. Examine your overall aptitude to regulate and supervise other people's activities. The ability to organize and manage people and events is one of the most important traits of a good general contractor.

Dealing with Problems

Do you deal well with problems that catch you unprepared? Does your job require you to be a problem solver? To do a good job contracting your own work, you will have to solve problems. Some predicaments might require a decision in a matter of minutes. Can you perform well under pressure? Do you tend to stress out easily, lose your temper, or become confused under pressure? If so, contracting your own job will be a mistake. Having the ability to stay calm and in control is needed for the job. Everyone gets angry when problems arise, the difference is in the way you react to that anger. Think about the stress factor. It will become a part of your job as a general contractor.

Assembling Information

In your job, are you required to work with or assimilate intricate information? Remodeling depends on detailed paperwork. If you work in the medical or legal field, you could be a prime candidate for the general contractor position. Take an unbiased look at your personality. Do you take notes during your business phone calls? If you request information from another department at work, do you write down the name of the person from whom you requested it? At home, do you keep your deposit slips to reconcile with your bank statement? For your receipts, which do you use: an organized filing system, the shoe box method, or the trash can approach? If executing methodical plans and maintaining detailed documents don't suit your nature, hire a professional to manage your job.

Negotiating Prices

Review your abilities to be a prudent shopper and resourceful negotiator. Are you the kind of person who carefully shops for the best prices? This self-control and patience will benefit you as a general contractor. Will you dicker over prices at a craft fair, or do you simply not buy items that exceed your price range? A successful general must be able to seek out the most advantageous arrangements possible. During your last job interview, did you negotiate for the salary and benefits you wanted, or accept what the boss offered? Do you emphasize your exemplary performance during a pay review, or just welcome any raise you get? Saving money is the difference between a gratifying remodeling project and just having some changes made to your house. If you are capable of effectively negotiating good prices for work and materials, you will put money in your pocket.

Understanding the Job

In general, how much do you know about remodeling and construction? Your full-time job probably won't be of much help in this category, unless you are employed in the trades. The average occupation will not provide you with the knowledge needed for the technical aspects of remodeling. This is not a critical issue. You don't have to be able to lay a brick foundation or solder pipes to manage a remodeling project. You only have to learn enough to keep the contractors in line. If you are willing to commit time to studying, you can pass the remodeling knowledge test.

Deciding on Financing

Financing is one of the easier decisions to make. After reading Chapter 12, you know your options. Be cautious in the documents you sign and do

what suits you best. There is no big mystery to financing. If you need it, attempt to get it. If you don't need it, you have a choice. You can pay cash or finance the job to conserve your cash. The details of arranging for financing will be handled by your lender. You only need to know how much you can afford and how long you are willing to make loan payments. After that, you will simply compile and compare information from the many financing sources available. Once you find the program that best suits your needs, the lenders will handle the rest of the financing details for you.

The financial aspects of contracting can be handled by the average homeowner. There is no need for highly specialized knowledge here. You will need to determine preliminary cost parameters, which will be refined as you receive quotes on the project. Accurate expense projections must include both hard and soft costs. Amounts for everything from permits to carpet must be incorporated into your calculations. After you establish your finished budget, it will be crucial to stick to it. How are you at handling money? Will you be able to account for expenses and keep track of costs throughout your job's progression? Regardless of whether you use a general contractor or coordinate the work yourself, you must be able to keep your job on budget.

Allowing for Time

These are the main qualities needed for a successful remodeling job. The only other essential factor is time. Will you have enough time to run the job? Plan on a few hours each day. Some days will require more time than others, depending on the size of the job, the trades involved, and your organizational skills. If you can handle the responsibilities of general contractor, you will enjoy a handsome savings on the cost of your job. If you have any doubts at this point, call in a professional to manage the job. The extra cost will be worth it, so you can enjoy a job well done. Don't be discouraged, you have already learned plenty of ways to save money in other areas of the project.

DETERMINING THE SCOPE OF THE WORK

Now you can put the question of managing the job to bed. The only thing left is to determine, once and for all, the scope of the work to be done. Take this opportunity to review your design ideas. Are you sure you're happy with your designs? Once you are into the job, making changes will be costly and inconvenient. If it's been awhile since you looked at the design, you may take one look and have several new ideas. Since you came up with your original design, you have investigated a lot of new products. Maybe you will want to incorporate these products into your design.

Double-check the design for accuracy — don't build yourself into a money pit. Make the best use of your time and money by making any needed changes now. Don't wait until the final plans are drawn or the job is started. Your design decision is one you will live with for a long time. It will affect the resale value of your home, so don't make a hasty decision on the design. Study it carefully and be sure it is what you want. If the design doesn't excite you, it probably needs a few changes. But don't be blinded by excitement to the extent of investing in an undesirable improvement.

EVALUATE YOUR PROJECT

Draw on the evaluation techniques you learned in Chapter 5 to be certain your project will benefit your bank account, as well as your family. Approaching remodeling with a casual attitude will result in disappointment. Altering your home is serious business and major money can be made or lost. If it's done right, you will enjoy a healthy equity gain for your efforts. When you sell, this translates into profit. Remodeling is an excellent way to increase your family's nest egg.

Can you think of a better way to make money than improving your living conditions? With the right improvements, the profits will stagger your imagination. You can have new space to enjoy and increase the value of your largest investment. If you act as your own general contractor, the profits go off the charts. Remodeling is one of the safest investments you can make, and most projects add value to your home.

The financial benefits of a strong improvement will figure prominently in your final decision. It can be like having someone match your investments with free money. You invest $10,000 and get an equity gain of $12,500. This means you make $2,500 for improving your home, and you don't pay taxes on the profits until you sell the house. Even then, a good accountant can show you how to defer your tax consequences. Remodeling offers profits beyond your wildest dreams. When you add value to your home today, it should increase in all the future years of your homeownership.

Perhaps an example will make your decision easier to make. Assume you are considering an addition with a market value of $25,000, and you are the general contractor. Your immediate equity gain, as the general, can amount to 20% of the value, or $5,000. To calculate your total profit ten years from now, you need to estimate the percentage amount by which property values in your area will increase. We will assume the annual appreciation rate for your location is 7%. To determine your long-term gains, start to multiply each year's value by 7%.

At the end of ten years, your $25,000 addition is worth more than $49,000. Your instant equity was worth $5,000, and now you can add more than $24,000 to that figure. Your total profit from the job is in excess of $29,000. This is a lot of money to earn for only a few months of part-time work. Moreover, all the time your investment was growing, you were enjoying the benefits of the new addition. This is an unbeatable deal.

All you have to do is make the best use of your abilities. It's no different from jockeying for a promotion at work. The people who make their move, and are qualified, receive the financial rewards. If you choose the right remodeling project, you can hit the jackpot. Bringing the job to a successful conclusion will result in a plentiful profit for a part-time effort. The key to remodeling riches is choosing the improvements that cost the least and add the most value.

REMEMBER SALES AND VALUE TECHNIQUES

A profitable project will follow the principles of appraising. Base your ultimate decision on the comparable sales and value techniques you learned in Chapter 7. Comparing your house to closed sales will indicate if your project will withstand the test. Assume finishing off your basement will cost $8,000. Using the cost approach, an appraiser could assign a value of $8,000 to the job. However, before deciding on a final value, the appraiser will evaluate the improvement using a market evaluation. In this approach, the appraiser may find a finished basement is only worth $6,500 to the buying public. For you, this could mean investing $1,500 more than the appraisal would support.

An improvement like this is only feasible if it is something you really want. It is not a good business decision if the expense is more than the equity gain. You spend $8,000 to realize a $6,500 gain and lose $1,500. You should not decide to go with this kind of remodeling job unless the improvement is absolutely worth it to you. The chances of recovering your investment are very poor. If you are remodeling for profit, decide on projects that add more value than they cost. Your investment of $8,000 could be worth over $10,000, with the right project. Look over the projects listed in Chapter 7. These are the real money makers. If you are considering one of these, you're on the road to rewards.

New additions are especially suited to the part-time general contractor. They don't cause as much disruption to the basic operation of your household. You have the latitude to schedule and coordinate the job as time allows. Bathrooms and kitchens require an expeditious completion. You can't afford to have these areas out of service for an extended time. Additions are different. An addition can take sixty days or six months to complete. It won't have a negative effect on your home life during the construction. These projects offer the highest profits to the part-time contractor. You can save even more money by doing some of the construction and completion work yourself.

PREPARING PLANS AND SPECS

When you are satisfied with the feasibility of the project, concentrate on how to get it done. You will need finalized plans and specs. Do you want to pay an architect to develop them for you? The final decision on the use of an architect is a big one. If you can get what you want without using an architect, you will save a significant amount of money.

For most projects, the free plans offered by your material supplier will suffice. Talk with your potential supplier and verify his ability to provide your plans and specs. Confirm that the plans are, in fact, free of charge. It is usually at the commitment stage that you will uncover any hidden charges for this service. Nobody gives you something for nothing — the price for the plans and specifications may be hidden in your material costs. Evaluate all the costs, and be sure the plans are worth the overall expenses. If the plans are truly available for free, give them a lot of consideration. The money saved here will go a long way with your project.

The chances are good you can use the blueprints from a material supplier. They won't have as many details as architectural plans, but for simple projects, they will get the job done. I don't like the specifications that accompany these free plans. They don't go into enough detail. Free plans and specs can't be beat for price, and many contractors use these same plans and specifications. There is nothing wrong with what you get, the problem lies in what you don't get. You cannot rely on the specifications provided with free plans. Vague plans and specifications can ruin your project. They can cause your cost estimates to be well below actual cost. Don't save on your plans at the expense of your entire job.

Plan on writing your own specifications if you don't engage an architect. We discussed ways to develop detailed specifications in Chapter 3, and in most cases, you will be able to prepare your own specs. Large projects, involving engineered changes, can require professional specifications. Before deciding against an architect, weigh the advantages to your individual situation.

Drafting companies are the other alternative we discussed. These companies can provide you with quality prints to work from. They will include as much detail as you request. You will be charged for their services, but the expense should be much less than that of an architect. You will still be faced with the lack of custom specifications. The bottom line is, you are going to have to allow time to create your specifications. Even with architects, you will have to tell them what to include.

Evaluate your job and what you are willing to pay for the design phase of the project. If the job is really basic, you may be able to use your own line drawings. If the project is moderately simple, go with free plans. For jobs requiring extensive structural work, get good blueprints from either an architect or a drafting firm. If your time is very valuable, architects may be the best solution. Be prepared to wait for professionally prepared plans.

Architects can have heavy backlogs of work and getting architectural plans can take months. Drafting companies will probably produce your plans in just a few weeks. The lumber yards may be able to complete their plans in a week or less. These time factors will have some influence on your decision. Explore all the facets of this important aspect, and do what you feel is best.

If you decide to try to use your preliminary line drawings, be sure to have the contractor review and approve them in writing. An experienced remodeler will know what work and code requirements are needed for most projects. Talk with your contractors and the codes enforcement office. See if you really need elaborate blueprints for your project. If your job can be done from your own drawings, you will save even more time and money. If you decide to work from your line drawing, be sure it's accurate. Poorly drawn plans produce disappointments later.

DECIDING ON CONTRACTORS

Congratulations! At this point you are able to make the final decision on precisely what work to do and how to pay for it. The only step left is to determine exactly who to use in performing the work. When you are ready to put your job out to bids, follow the steps in Chapter 9. Prices will tell you a lot, but don't be blinded by low bids. Make sure the low bids aren't too low. The contractor with extremely low bids isn't always the best value. Remember the story about the woman who lost her sunroom deposit and materials to the cheapest guy in town. The bid process isn't too complicated, but it is time consuming. Choosing your suppliers will be simplified with the procedures recommended in Chapter 9. Selecting your contractors will be a little more difficult.

You will have to meet with several people, and much of your time will be spent on the phone. Some of these calls will have to be done during normal working hours. Do you have the flexibility to make personal calls from work? If you don't have the time, hire a professional to handle the day-to-day complexities of remodeling.

Whether you are seeking a general contractor or a subcontractor, the principles are the same. Chapter 8 dealt with this process. Pay attention to these suggestions and be on the lookout for con-artist contractors and professional sales techniques. Choosing your contractors is one of the hardest decisions you will have to make. You have to look at more than just prices. You need to match the right contractors to the right jobs.

Look for Experienced Remodelers

Concentrate on the Do's and Do Not's of hiring tradesmen. Don't hire a framing specialist to install your intricate trim. Don't engage a commercial plumber for your residential remodeling job. You want to find contractors with extensive experience in the kind of work you want done. In heavily populated areas, there will be specialists. In some cities, plumbers specialize in bath and kitchen remodeling. They don't do repair work, install new construction, or do commercial jobs. They work with bath and kitchen remodeling every day, and that is all they do. If you want to remodel your home's plumbing, these are the experts you want.

These specialized plumbers know their business. By doing the same thing every day, they have extensive experience in all phases of their work. Their counterparts do different types of plumbing. While a new construction plumber may know the basics of kitchen and bath remodeling, he may or may not be expert at it. When something goes wrong, he may not know how to correct the problem. This lack of experience in remodeling will cause difficulties the experts wouldn't have. A general plumber may overcompensate for his lack of remodeling experience in the price he gives you. In this case, the price will be much too high. If the job is underestimated, the plumber will have to try to cut corners to avoid losing money. You will be ahead of the game financially if you engage experts whenever possible.

In rural areas, there isn't enough work to allow heavy specialization. Tradesmen must be able to do a wide variety of work. Your carpenter may have built a tool shed last week, flower boxes the week before, and a garage just last month. Rural plumbing can include everything from stopped-up drains to installing hog watering devices. When a contractor tells you he has built garages before, ask him how many, when, and where? If the answer is one, last year, for his uncle, you may need to get additional bids.

All contractors will have personal preferences on the type of work they like. Ask what kind of work they enjoy before you begin to describe the work you need. Make the closest match you can. By asking what they do best before describing your job, you will get more honest answers. Once I overheard a new construction carpenter complaining about interior remodeling. He didn't appreciate having to take off his work boots to go into a customer's home. When I rejected his bid to finish an attic, he couldn't understand why. I told him I only use professionals who understand the importance of a clean job, as well as clean carpets. The moral of the story is, try to use experienced professionals who prefer the kind of work you have to offer. You will get a better price and better quality from these contractors.

Think long and hard before committing to the contractors. Be sure all your paperwork is in order. Don't make the contractor decision until you are convinced you have found the right people. Interview as many contractors as you can, and avoid making on-the-spot commitments. Check out the contractors and their work carefully. Use the Contractor Comparison sheet below during your final evaluation. Review what you have learned, and follow Dodge's rules. You can never be sure of your decision until the job is done. The best you can do is avoid the common problems and be prepared to deal with the unknown ones.

The purpose of this chapter is to help you prepare for your final decisions. Up to this point, all the work has been administrative. Now the actual remodeling work can start. You are about to enter the working world of remodeling. This is where your extensive preparation and planning will pay off. Finally, you will be able to see the design and specifications you worked so hard on become a reality. The paper profit figures you generated, based on careful negotiations and thrifty shopping, are about to become concrete equity gains. Enjoy having made wise, profitable remodeling decisions. Chances are, you will have to make some on-the-spot decisions before the job is over. Until the unexpected happens, you can sit back and watch your project take shape.

CONTRACTOR COMPARISON SHEET

	CONTRACTOR 1	CONTRACTOR 2	CONTRACTOR 3
CONTRACTOR NAME			
RETURNS CALLS			
LICENSED			
INSURED			
BONDED			
REFERENCES			
PRICE			
EXPERIENCE			
YEARS IN BUSINESS			
WORK QUALITY			
AVAILABILITY			
DEPOSIT REQUIRED			
DETAILED QUOTE			
PERSONALITY			
PUNCTUAL			
GUT REACTION			

NOTES

On-the-Spot Decisions

17

Remodeling involves working with unknown conditions. When you open up a wall, you never know what you will find. I have discovered old money, wild animals, snakes, termite damage, and a host of other surprises. Existing conditions can wreak havoc with the best-laid remodeling plans. These unexpected complications dictate a change of strategy. Some of these problems will require fast decisions, either to save time or to rectify an emergency. Remodeling crews are expensive — you can't afford for them to stand around very long. In most cases, you can protect against problems before they occur with a strong contract. If the unimaginable happens, the ability to reason through situations will enable you to make rational decisions.

HANDLING UNKNOWN STRUCTURAL DAMAGE

The homeowner will be responsible for most on-the-spot decisions. It will be up to you to decide what should be done about the bats living in your attic. When the carpenters tell you about a problem, they expect an immediate resolution. When the subfloor in a bathroom is removed, many problems may be found. What will you do with rotted floor joists? If your old toilet leaked, the water may have caused structural damage. Also, bad grouting around ceramic tile can allow water to run down walls and ruin wall and floor structures.

Your initial plans — to replace the vinyl floor and plumbing fixtures — can turn into a full-blown remodeling job. What started as a $2,000 job is now going to cost $5,000. This figure can go much higher

if the bathroom is on the second floor. In this case, additional repairs would have to be done. If not, the damaged structure would give away at some point. Your bathtub could wind up under the house, or the toilet could drop through the ceiling into the kitchen. The repairs must be made, and you have to decide what to do. What would you do?

This example is not unusual. Bathrooms hold a lot of moisture, and structural damage can go unnoticed for years. Something as simple as replacing the toilet can turn into a nightmare. When the toilet is removed, the plumber may discover rotted floor joists. Typically, it is only the subfloor that has been heavily damaged. If this is the case, consider yourself lucky. The cost to replace the subfloor and your vinyl floor covering will be around $1,000. You were expecting a bill for $185 to replace your toilet. You wind up with an estimate for $1,185 because of existing problems. This scenario happens time and time again. Should you accept the facts and authorize the repairs? You know they have to be done, and the plumber is pressuring you for an answer. Wait, don't authorize anything yet.

Determine the Details of the Work

What are the details of the work? The contractor says you will have to replace your entire subfloor, underlayment, and vinyl floor covering. He has also points out the expense of removing the debris from your property. To do the job right, the plumber indicates he will have to remove your vanity until the new floor is installed. Then he will have to come back to reset the toilet and vanity. The carpenter tells you about the need to replace your baseboard trim. When the trim is replaced, it will need to be painted. The workmen estimate the combined total cost at $1,185 but won't guarantee the price. You are told there could be more damage, so they can't commit to a quoted price.

At this point, thank the contractors, and tell them you will get back to them with your decision. Get them out of the house, get away from the pressure, and think about the predicament. The urgency of the situation may make you feel you have no choice but to have the contractor make the necessary repairs. Slow down, and go back over the techniques and rules you learned in putting your job out to bids. Would you accept the first bid you got, without making any comparisons? No, the first order of business is to get other quotes. Call other contractors, and ask what they will charge to make these repairs to your bathroom. Don't tell them what the first contractors said needed to be fixed. Let the new contractors tell you what work is required. I'm willing to bet you will get several different answers.

Get Comparison Quotes

Some remodelers will see this call as an opportunity to try to sell you on remodeling the whole bathroom. They will look at the subfloor and vinyl, and tell you this is the perfect time to remodel. Since you are faced with extensive disruptive repairs, why not go ahead and do a complete remodel job? If you are planning to update the room in the future, this option may be worth considering. If remodeling the room is what you want to do, fine, but don't be talked into doing more than you want or need to do. If you don't want to do a complete remodel job, ask the contractor simply to quote the work you called for.

You may find a few contractors who suggest doing as little as possible. They will advise putting shims under the toilet to keep it from rocking. These are the face-lift contractors, who will give you ideas like caulking around the base of the toilet and tub to reduce the moisture. The list of band-aid repairs will go on and on. Avoid these guys. You will be paying them now, only to pay a good contractor again in the future.

One of the contractors should offer you the right option. When you find an experienced contractor, he will be able to give you a viable choice. When toilets leak, the subfloor starts to rot around the toilet. The water is absorbed into the floor and

spreads. If this condition continues, eventually the floor joists will be damaged. The majority of toilet problems are noticed before severe structural damage occurs. Most typical flooring repairs are very simple.

The contractor should be able to cut out the bad section of subfloor and replace it with plywood. The repair doesn't have to involve removing your entire floor. The vinyl flooring will need to be replaced, but all the other major expenses can be avoided. You won't need new baseboard trim or painting. The vanity will not need to be removed. There won't be extensive debris to haul away. The amount of labor involved is greatly reduced, and the total cost of the repairs should be less than $500. This is a lot better than the $1,000 you thought you would have to spend. The result is a solid subfloor and a new vinyl floor covering. The effect is the same as the $1,000 repair. The only appreciable difference is the money you saved.

PLANNING FOR PROBLEMS

Proper planning eliminates most on-the-spot decisions. Many of the problems that catch you off guard are the result of not thinking. Think your project through completely before starting the work. Ask the contractors what type of problems might happen. Experienced remodelers have a good idea of what to expect from a job. They can be of great help to you in the planning stage. If you address potential problems before they happen, you will lower your stress level during the job. Even with the best planning, unplanned incidents occur. Knowing how to deal with these problems is important. Quick decisions can turn into mistakes and disappointments. There will be very few problems that require an immediate answer. Avoid deciding on a solution without reflecting on the problem.

Don't Let the Contractor Call the Shots

Contractors will want you to decide quickly. They don't want to pay their workers to stand around waiting for your answer. Remember, these contractors are working for you. Maintain your power position, and don't let them tell you what to do. Allow the contractors to make suggestions, but don't automatically accept their recommendations. The decision to accept their ideas without thought can be very expensive. If you are paying for it, contractors will take the path of least resistance, regardless of cost. Don't hesitate to get additional opinions on decisions requiring major investment. You could become a victim of a greedy contractor. Stay in control. It's your house and your money, so make your own informed decisions.

What type of snap decisions are you likely to face? Anything you can think of, and some things you can't imagine are possible. There are some problems that come up frequently. These are the ones we are going to concentrate on. Plan to encounter some obstacles during the course of your job. The following problems are examples of the most common occurrences. They will give you an idea of what to expect.

UNKEPT PROMISES

The most common problem in remodeling is unkept promises. These can be promises made by contractors or suppliers. When you have work scheduled and it doesn't go according to plan, you have several problems. Remodeling is a business that revolves around accurate scheduling. An unkept commitment affects everybody. What happens when your electrician doesn't show up to rough-in your electrical work? The first consequence is not having your electrical work done. The ripple effect is your need to reschedule all the other subcontractors. You will have to notify the insulation contractor of the delay. The drywall contractor will have to be postponed, and the painter will have to be rescheduled. The list continues to grow. One subcontractor can ruin your entire job schedule.

Subcontractors

A strong contract will help to alleviate this problem. The subcontractor may still stiff you, but you will have recourse. You should have the ability to penalize him financially if your contract is worded properly. This threat will keep the job rolling. If it doesn't, exercise your contractual right to bring in a replacement subcontractor. Going over this information with each sub, before the job begins, will impress your intentions upon all of them. Let them know time is critical, and you can't afford down time. Be cordial but be firm and don't give on this issue.

Suppliers

Suppliers are harder to control. They can be undependable and can bring your job to a dead stop.

The hardest working contractor can't operate without materials. Many times you will be promised delivery dates, which come and go with no material. This is a constant problem. When your remodeling crews can't work, they will go to another job where they can. They have to feed their families and must work to make money. You can't expect them to wait indefinitely for missing material. Once they leave your job, getting them back can be difficult.

You have to retain control over suppliers, the same way you do with contractors. When you place a material order, get the name of the individual taking the order; write it in a material log. There is a Material Order Log form at the end of this chapter for your use. Record the date and time you ordered the material and the delivery date you were promised. Then call back the next day, and ask the manager of the store to confirm your delivery date. Make written notes of this confirmation and get the manager's name. If delivery day comes and the material doesn't, go to see the manager. Go in person and take your log with you.

When you sit down with the manager, ask where your delivery is. Explain your need for the material to be delivered on schedule. Chances are, you will get a runaround at first. Suppliers have long lists of excuses and are professionals at blaming other people for their inadequacies. They will try to accuse the manufacturer, the freight company, a distributor, even the truck driver. When this happens, produce your log, and show the manager the history of your order. When the manager sees your log, the answers may change. Written dates, times, names, and confirmations are hard to argue with.

If the manager doesn't have your material in stock, ask her to check with other suppliers. She won't want to do this. Tell her if she doesn't, you will. Be prepared for a variety of reactions. The manager may give in and promise to have your order on site by the end of the day. On the other hand, the manager may tell you to take your order and stick it in your ear. After all, you are only giving the company one job's order. The manager may decide she can do without your business and your aggravation.

In this case, inform her of your intention to file a formal complaint against her business if the matter is not resolved. This is extreme action, but it will get results. The key to your strength is the log. Well-documented complaints receive attention. The manager will not want to be involved in a documented complaint — she could lose her job. After all, she confirmed your order and delivery date personally. This leverage should get your material on site fast.

Supplier-related problems cause the most trouble during remodeling. A special order that isn't placed could cost you six weeks in time. When completing your material order log, request order numbers. All special orders will have some type of order or reference number. When you are given these numbers, you have some proof the order was placed. It is important to have material delivered *before* you need it. This gives you time to check the order before it's required. If something is missing, you have time to react before the job is interrupted. Plan ahead, and check all orders closely. Compare the material order to the delivery ticket and check for back orders. If items are in boxes or crates, inspect them for damage. You don't want to wait until the plumber is ready to install your new tub to find out it is defective.

PROBLEMS WITH ANIMALS

On-the-job problems will happen. Any time you are working with existing conditions, problems can be present. Animals can cause some of the worst, and most unexpected, problems. Over the years, I've worked around animals many times. Your own pets are a potential problem you probably haven't considered. You will need to make arrangements to allow workers to come and go in your house freely. Do not think you can ask contractors to take on the added responsibility of keeping your pet in the house. By the same token, provide any necessary protection to the contractor, from your pet. Your lovable canine companion, who would never hurt a flea, may become confused or frightened by strange workmen invading its home. I have seen many a placid puppy become a raging ball of claws and teeth.

The presence of wild animals is always an unwelcome surprise. Right now, I'm working on a house inhabited by raccoons. Forest creatures can cause some interesting remodeling problems. Once, when I was working on a house in the mountains, strange events started happening. The job had progressed to the finished drywall stage. The drywall was hung and had been coated with the first coat of drywall compound.

The next day, there were holes in the walls. The first hole was around the water supply pipe to the toilet. We thought the plumber had made a mistake and enlarged the hole to correct a problem. When confronted, the plumber denied knowing anything about the saucer-sized hole. We found the next hole in the ceiling of a closet. Later that day, I was downstairs with the painter, when we heard a loud banging upstairs. Upon investigation, we were confronted by an angry Norway rat, the size of a rabbit. Our construction had disturbed its domicile, and the rats were claiming homestead rights in the customer's house. This problem required a professional exterminator.

It isn't too unusual to find wild creatures living in and around rural homes. I've run into rattlesnakes, bats, and skunks. Is there any way to prepare for these unwanted neighbors? Contractors may find signs of wild animals, if you require them to inspect your property before bidding the job. Bats are not difficult to detect, as they leave quite a mess. Some animals will burrow under or into your home, and these holes may be found during an inspection. I once came face to face with a skunk family while crawling under a house to check existing conditions. Some animals can be removed without harm, and others will require more serious measures. You have to deal with each case independently.

INSECT INFESTATION

When the insulating contractor comes out of your attic with bad news, sit down. Insulators can be the first people who have been in your attic for years. When they go up, they could come down with discouraging information. They may tell you about small piles of sawdust in your attic. These sawdust piles indicate wood-boring insects. These little creatures can do more damage than a beaver. These bugs are in the wood when the house is built and, under the right conditions, they become active. They eat through your rafters and ceiling joists, which weakens your roof structure and calls for prompt, serious action.

The removal of these wood-infesting insects can be very expensive. If you are a victim of these brutal bugs, contact pest control companies. Call several, and request damage reports and extermination estimates. Some wood eaters can be stopped by treating the wood; others require a total fumigation of the house. The difference in cost is extensive. Be sure of the type of creature you are dealing with. Don't allow yourself to be sold a tented fumigation you don't need. Spend the time to make rational decisions. Call in professional building contractors to evaluate the structural damage. Is there any way to avoid this problem? If the insulator had inspected the attic as part of his initial bid, he might have seen the problem then.

DAMAGE TO EXISTING CONDITIONS

If you are remodeling a room upstairs, you can be in for some unexpected revelations. Envision the remodeling work upstairs, requiring moving walls and installing new subfloor. You are sitting at your breakfast table, listening to the pounding and beating of the carpenters. You think how happy you are to be leaving for work in five minutes. When you come home, you go up to inspect the day's work. The carpenters made good progress, and everything looks acceptable.

You go downstairs to watch the evening news on television. When you sit back in your recliner, you notice spots on your family room ceiling. A closer look reveals exposed nail heads. There are entire lines of them speckling your ceiling. The demolition work upstairs pushed the nail heads through the ceiling. Then you discover small spots of white powder on your carpet, from the old drywall compound. What should you do now?

Call the carpentry contractor and explain what has happened. Ask when he is going to repair your ceiling. With the right language in your contract, this will be the contractor's problem. Your contract should include a clause regarding damage to existing conditions or other contractor's work. You can see an example of a Damage Clause at the end of this chapter. This clause specifies that damage done to your home, or to another contractor's work, is the responsibility of the contractor causing the damage. Including the right phrases in your contract will solve many problems before they happen.

HOW TO MAKE A QUICK DECISION

Quick decisions are dangerous. If you are at work, your mind isn't on remodeling. When your contractor calls you at work with a problem, you aren't in the best position to make a good decision. If the situation has to be dealt with immediately, consider the following options. Get all the information from the contractor, and agree to call back in fifteen minutes. Fifteen minutes isn't a lot of time,

but it will allow you the opportunity to think. Any remodeling problem can wait a few minutes for a solution. Take a coffee break, and review the circumstances. Decide if you should go home and see the problem. Many modest problems can be solved on short notice over the telephone.

If your recessed medicine cabinet requires moving an electrical wire, authorize the electrician to do it. This is a simple, inexpensive problem. For the more complex problems, take time to evaluate the alternatives. There could be a rudimentary solution the contractor has overlooked. Use your own judgment, but avoid immediate decisions whenever possible. When problems arise, don't panic. Allow enough time for your system to settle down before making a decision.

If the problem is expensive or complicated, wait until the next day to make your decision. When an inexperienced homeowner is confronted with pressing problems, he often doesn't know what to do. Usually, the first reaction is one of anger. You have to work through the anger before you can make a good decision. This could take a day or two. If the problem is big enough, allow yourself the necessary time to calm down.

Handling Truly Threatening Problems

Another common reaction is one of fear — some problems are threatening. A lot of this has to do with the way the contractor presents the problem. Some contractors try to sell work using scare tactics. They hope you will decide immediately to correct the deficiency, without shopping for prices. This approach is effective with many consumers. If the customer feels there is impending danger, he will act quickly. When he does, he usually doesn't act properly. This is why so many contractors rely on scare tactics for sales.

If you are presented with a problem involving possible danger, you should act quickly. You should call the local codes office, and request an emergency inspection. Before you actually call the codes office, apprise the contractor of your plans to do so. The urgency of the repair may dissipate quickly. If the contractor is exaggerating, he will probably change his opinion when he learns the code officer will be coming in response to his claim. If the contractor sticks to his story, you probably do have a real problem.

Wait for the code officer to arrive before making a decision. He will be able to advise you on the nature of the problem and extent of the repairs needed. Once you know what needs to be done, start getting some quotes on the work. You are not obligated to allow the existing contractor to have the work. Realistically, he should give you the best price, but he may try to take advantage of his working relationship with you. Get other bids before awarding an expensive, unplanned job to the existing contractor. He won your original job with good prices, and he is already working on the job. Unless he is trying to take advantage of you, his prices should be competitive. If his price is competitive, let him do the job. Even if his price is a little higher, give him the work. You already know something about him and his work. This is an advantage over dealing with unknown contractors.

FOUR RULES FOR DECISION-MAKING

Common sense will get you through most on-the-spot decisions. The first rule is, try to avoid making rash decisions. The second rule requires you to be fully informed. The third rule is to shop prices, if it is an expensive decision. The fourth rule is to get everything in writing. If the existing contractor will be doing the work, use a change order. If a new contractor will be doing the work, complete a contract for the work. Follow the rules and most of your decisions will be good ones.

Let's review the purpose of each rule. Avoiding rash decisions will protect you from mistakes made in haste. Any quick decision has the potential to be a bad decision. If you don't take the time to think, you are leaving yourself wide open. Full-time contractors develop an ability to make on-the-spot decisions, through years of experience and mistakes. Their judgment has been honed to a sharp edge, as a result of years in the business.

As a homeowner, you don't have the experience on which to base quick answers. This increases your risk of failure. Don't expect to be able to compete with the pros when it comes to quick decisions. Do the best you can. Take your time and make the best decision possible, using all the available information. The decision may cost you a little money, but you have already saved money by price shopping or running your own job. These are offsetting qualities. Don't worry about the small stuff; direct your attention to the job's success.

The second rule is critical to a good answer for on-the-spot decisions. Your decision will be based on the information you have available to evaluate. The more information you have, the better your decision will be. Request all available information. When you have compiled the information, study it. With enough thought, the answer to the question will come to you. Stick to your first decision. If you start second-guessing yourself, you will regret it. Go with your gut instincts — they prevail in most circumstances.

If you get surprised with existing problems, take the time to gather quotes. This rule can be worth more money than all your efforts to this point. Sometimes the repairs can cost more than the original job. You shopped for contractors to do your job and you should shop for contractors to do your big repairs. Use the same techniques used to find the first contractors. Follow all the same rules and don't treat large repairs lightly. This is one place a contractor can take you for the financial ride of your life. If you don't question the prices, you will never know if you paid too much.

The fourth rule is one of the most important. Getting everything in writing is the golden rule. Never abandon it. Even if the repair is only a few hundred dollars, get it in writing. Without a written agreement, you could easily be facing a mechanic's lien. Any work done on your house could result in a lien. There is no need for this. If you put everything in writing, you eliminate unnecessary risks. Use change orders and all the other forms I have discussed. Repairs can cause you more trouble than the primary job.

You are now well informed on how to handle emergency situations. You should be able to recognize the difference between an inconvenience, a problem, and an emergency. You know what to do and how to do it. This information is valuable in all conditions. If you are your own contractor, the information is crucial. If you employ a general contractor, the information will help you meet the challenges and reduce your stress level. Snap decisions are an often overlooked aspect of remodeling. Your newfound knowledge will protect you; it will shelter you from mistakes and save your bank account in an emergency. Now you can move ahead with your project with confidence.

MATERIAL ORDER LOG

SUPPLIER: _____

DATE ORDER WAS PLACED: _____

TIME ORDER WAS PLACED: _____

NAME OF PERSON TAKING ORDER: _____

PROMISED DELIVERY DATE: _____

ORDER NUMBER: _____

QUOTED PRICE:

DATE OF FOLLOW-UP CALL: _____

MANAGER'S NAME: _____

TIME OF CALL TO MANAGER: _____

MANAGER CONFIRMED DELIVERY DATE: _____

MANAGER CONFIRMED PRICE: _____

NOTES AND COMMENTS:

_____
_____
_____
_____
_____

DAMAGE CLAUSE

SAMPLE CLAUSE FOR CONTRACT

CONTRACTOR LIABILITY FOR DAMAGES TO EXISTING CONDITIONS

Contractor shall be responsible for any damage caused to existing conditions. This shall include work performed on the project by other contractors. If the contractor damages existing conditions or work performed by other contractors, said contractor shall be responsible for the repair of said damages. These repairs may be made by the contractor responsible for the damages or another contractor, at the discretion of the homeowner.

If a different contractor repairs the damage, the contractor causing the damage may be back-charged for the cost of the repairs. These charges may be deducted from any monies owed to the damaging contractor by the homeowner. The choice of a contractor to repair the damages shall be at the sole discretion of the homeowner.

If no money is owed to the damaging contractor, said contractor shall pay the invoiced amount, from the homeowner, within seven business days. If prompt payment is not made, the homeowner may exercise all legal means to collect the requested monies.

The damaging contractor shall have no rights to lien the homeowner's property, for money retained to cover the repair of damages caused by the contractor. The homeowner may have the repairs made to his satisfaction.

The damaging contractor shall have the opportunity to quote a price for the repairs. The homeowner is under no obligation to engage the damaging contractor to make the repairs.

Nearing the End

18

The end of the job is in sight. All that is left are minor adjustments and touchups. You have conquered the remodeling challenge and emerged victorious. The job has turned out wonderfully, and the small problems along the way are forgotten. Now you think all you have left to do is enjoy the new improvements. Wrong, there are still many details to cover, and events can still go awry. Don't ignore the final elements of your project. A common error is to get too lenient at the end of a project. Mistakes made at this point will cast a dark shadow on the entire job.

HANDLING LAST MINUTE PROBLEMS

Your contractors are anxious to finish their work, get paid, and get on to the next job. In the rush to finish, accidents can happen. This is the time most senseless problems occur. Toilets get broken, carpets get soiled, and walls get scraped by fixtures and appliances. The last few days of the job can be the most trying.

You've worked hard to get to this point. The vinyl flooring in your kitchen is perfect. The cabinets took weeks to get, but are finally installed. Tomorrow the plumber and the electrician are coming to finish their work. All of your new fixtures and appliances will be working by the time you get home from work. You are excited and can't wait to try everything out.

When you come home the next day, your heart sinks. The first thing you see is a big gouge in your new kitchen floor. The vinyl is torn and wrinkled. At this moment, nothing else matters; all you can

think about is the ruined designer flooring. After several weeks with no major mishaps, you thought you were out of the woods. Now, your floor is torn. It's ripped in front of the dishwasher, most likely torn when the dishwasher was pulled out to be connected. The question is, who's responsible for the repair or replacement of the floor?

You know it is either the plumber or the electrician, but you don't know which. They were the only trades in the house today. Both of them had connections to make to the dishwasher, and either one could have done the damage. After calling both contractors, neither will take the responsibility for the torn floor. What can you do? You can't blame both of them. Nobody was home to see which contractor tore the vinyl. You will probably have to absorb the cost of repairing the floor. How could this have been avoided?

Scheduling Subcontractors

There is no way for you to prevent a tear in the vinyl, these accidents happen. They shouldn't happen with experienced workers, but they can. Your mistake was in the way you scheduled your subcontractors. If the plumber had been working in the house alone, he would have to be the guilty party. You would have much more leverage under these conditions. It would be hard for the plumber to lie his way out of the situation, if he was the only trade in the house that day. Throughout the job, it is best to only have one trade on the job at a time.

This is especially important during the final phases. Sometimes, the contractor isn't even aware he caused the damage and will flatly deny it. You might think anyone with any semblance of intelligence would know if he had torn your floor or scraped your walls. Cramped quarters lend themselves to unintentional damage. Putting several tradesmen to work in a small area spells trouble. They will not be as productive, and accidents are more likely to happen. They may not realize that while passing one another in the hall, they scratched the wall with their tools. If you can't be on the job personally, careful scheduling is the best way to place proper blame for accidents.

Attention to Detail

Pay particular attention to detail near the end of the job. If something is damaged, you need to know *when* it was damaged. If a problem is overlooked, you could be blaming the wrong contractor for the damage. Never underestimate the possible problems that can occur during the last week of the job. The tendency to relax will cause you unnecessary grief. You've gone this far, follow the rules and stick it out to the end.

INSPECTING THE WORK

You will need to inspect all the finish work before giving final payment for the services rendered. This inspection should be done after all the contractors claim to be completely finished. As a result of a final inspection, you will develop a punch-list. This list will include all the items that still need attention. You should make separate punch-lists for each trade. An example of a Punch-List for a bathroom project is given at the end of this chapter. It should be used as a guide when making your final inspections, to help you know what to look for. It is crucial to get these punch-list deficiencies corrected before final payment is made.

USING PUNCH-LISTS

Punch-lists cover every aspect of the job. They deal with doors that don't shut properly and places where the paint needs to be touched up. Having the adhesive labels and product markings removed from your floor and fixtures should be included. Windows should open and lock easily, and any paint should be scraped from the glass. If you included landscaping, make sure the grass seed has started to grow. Check every phase carefully. It is much easier to have the contractor fix his mistakes before final payment is made.

INSPECT THE WORK TWICE

You should inspect the work twice before presenting the list to the contractor. Conduct your first inspection in natural light. Open the drapes, and go over the job under optimum daylight conditions. Then repeat the same inspection with artificial light, in the evening. The type and amount of light will affect the appearance of the completed work. Fixture colors will appear different in incandescent and fluorescent light. They look even more dissimilar in natural light. The same is true of paint colors.

Paint

Painters have been known to use less expensive paints of colors similar to the upgraded choices for which the customer was charged. Homeowners have been known to misjudge the appearance of colors they picked from small paint chips. Is there any way to verify that the painter used the correct paint? Yes, you could require him to leave any leftover paint. This is not unreasonable, since you paid for the paint and can use it for future touchups. If the product is in the original container, you can easily verify it is the correct paint. If the paint is in large, unmarked buckets, your only other option is to have a sample from the paint store. When you pick out the paint for your project, request samples of the colors on pieces of wall and trim board. Stain colors look different on various types of wood and should be applied to the type of trim you will use. These procedures should eliminate surprise results at the end of the job, and they will help to keep the contractor honest as well.

Flooring

Flooring choices are made from small samples. The actual carpet or vinyl can look very different once it is installed. Expect to find some minor differences in the installed products. If the differences are drastic, compare the product numbers on the contract with the products installed. Confirm you got what you paid for. If the wrong product was installed, you want to find out now. There is still time to have the problem resolved before final payment is issued. Although you may decide not to have the entire carpet torn out and replaced, you can certainly require restitution for accepting the wrong product. Check the carpet and vinyl installation for ripples and lumps. Seams should be invisible, and all necessary thresholds in place, before the flooring job is considered complete.

Drywall

Drywall work frequently finds itself on punchlists. Good drywall finishers are rare. If possible, try to look for drywall imperfections after the painter applies the first coat of paint. Catching a problem at this point will eliminate the need to repaint repaired areas later. It is especially important to inspect drywall under various lighting conditions. If you look at the job in natural light, it can look fine. You pay the contractor and he leaves. Incandescent light from your lamps will amplify a poor drywall job. When you look at the workmanship in the evening, you may find ripples and bad seams on your ceiling. If you signed a certificate of completion and satisfaction, you're stuck with the work. Don't be too fast to sign the completion certificate. Be sure everything is suitable before signing off on the job.

Fixtures and Appliances

Personally test all your new fixtures and appliances. Electricians can forget to wire fixtures. Your new dishwasher may not run. It looks nice, but it doesn't work. Are the circuits in your electrical box marked correctly? If the circuit breaker is labeled for the water heater, it should control the water heater. Suppose in the future you need to repair the water heater. If you throw an improperly labeled breaker, it will quite literally be a real shock. Electrical items are rarely checked, but they should be. If a new or additional heat source was installed, turn it on and make certain it works. Don't wait until temperatures drop below freezing to discover a faulty thermostat.

Test everything yourself. Go into your new bathroom and gently rock the toilet. Is it secured properly? Have the drop-in lavatory bowls and tub been caulked? Examine the water connections under bath and kitchen sinks, and at the toilet tank, for leaks. Fill your sinks and tubs with water; let the water out and make sure the drains work properly and do not leak. Don't assume everything is acceptable just because the contractor told you the work passed the final codes inspection.

ENSURING INSPECTIONS

Were all the required code enforcement inspections actually completed? Ask for copies of the approved inspections, and don't make final payment until you have copies of the inspection reports. Don't be surprised if many small items are turned down on the final inspection. Code officers usually give the job a comprehensive inspection before issuing a final approval. If the project is large, a certificate of occupancy is required before you can inhabit the new space. The certificate of occupancy will not be issued until all other inspections are completed and approved. Without the certificate of occupancy, the code officer can prohibit you from using your new space. Be sure to have this certificate before making any final payments.

Have you looked *under* your new addition? Is the crawl space insulated? Did the contractors leave scrap wood on the ground under your addition? Don't ignore what you can't easily see. Inspect every aspect of the work done. Crawl spaces aren't attractive places, but you need to inspect them. Scrap wood left on the ground can encourage termite infestation. The insulation may have been omitted from the crawl space, simply because a worker didn't think about it. As a consumer, you *have* to think about it. If you are paying for a vapor barrier, make sure it was installed. A quick crawl under the addition can reveal a lot. Contractors don't expect you to go into these areas. If they are intentionally going to let something slide, this is where they will do it.

CHECK EXISTING AREAS FOR DAMAGE

Check existing areas of your home, which may have been affected during the remodeling project. If workers were in your attic, make sure your insulation is undisturbed. Now is the time to check your ceilings, carpets, walls, and floors. Look closely for scratches, cracks, and cigarette burns. If your contract was worded correctly, you will not have to accept these damages. If repairs need to be made to existing sections of your home, list these on a punch-list as well.

USING YOUR PUNCH-LISTS

Using the sample punch-list as a guide, you will be able to conduct a good inspection. The sample will prompt you on the kind of items to inspect. When you are done, meet with the contractors and go over the punch-lists. Explain what you found and how you want it corrected. This shouldn't be a problem with a strong contract as your shield. A good remodeling contract will clearly deal with punch-lists. When the corrections have been made, inspect the work again. Check all the items just as thoroughly this time. Look for problems that may have been caused by correcting the items on your original punch-list. Use the same procedures. If everything is all right, you can sign off on the job.

CLEANUP AND MISCELLANEOUS ITEMS

Before making your final payments, there are few more chores to take care of. Has the job been cleaned up to your satisfaction? If not, get it done now. Once you sign off and give final payment, what you see is what you get. Request all the owner's manuals and warranty cards before making final disbursements. You might be surprised how often these items can't be produced. Contractors are notorious for trashing these documents, but don't let them get away with it. You need the owner's manual and warranty cards. If the contractor doesn't have them, make him get new ones.

If you don't have the contractor's warranty period included in your contract, get it in writing now. This should have been in your contract; it's easier to cover this in the beginning than in the end. Most remodelers warranty their work for one year. Product warranties vary, depending on the manufacturer. If you have questions about the warranties, get them answered before final payment.

FINAL PAYMENT

With all this behind you, the final payment is the next step. Smart contractors will want you to sign a certificate of completion and acceptance. There is an example of this form at the end of the chapter. The form basically states your acceptance of all work done and your satisfaction with the quality of the work. For such a small form, the consequences it harbors are great. *Don't sign this form until you are completely satisfied with every aspect of the work*. Once you verify your satisfaction with the work, the contractor is off the hook.

HOLDING A FINAL RETAINAGE

I recommend including a final retainage clause in your contract, to provide you with an additional protection period. These clauses allow you to retain an agreed-upon amount of money for thirty days. Many times, everything works fine on the final inspection. A week later, there may be minor leaks in the compression fittings of your plumbing, or a light may begin to flicker. This happens all the time. There is a break-in period, and as you use some items, they may need minor adjustments. Most contractors will come back to take care of these adjustments, but some can be very difficult about putting more time into your job. If you are holding a cash retainer, the odds of getting the contractor back improve dramatically.

Retainages are usually not more than 10% of the final payment. This isn't a lot, but it does offer some motivation for the contractor to return. You can't hold a retainage unless it was agreed to in your contract. Your written agreement with the contractor is the backbone of your job. It details everything and reduces confusion. When properly composed, it also gives you leverage and protection. If a contractor refuses to correct a problem, at least you have some money set aside to pay someone else to make the repairs. You can even pay yourself to fix the problem, if you are able to do the work. Seriously consider including a detailed retainage clause in your contract. This little stratagem can eliminate hours of frustration.

CALL-BACKS

With or without retainages, call-backs are a bother. No contractor is going to want to come back and fix something for nothing. They got paid for what they did, and call-backs are a fact of life. Warranties and retainages obligate contractors to fix the problem, but they still will not want to come back. Although contractors know, sooner or later, they will have to respond to your complaint, many will try to make it later rather than sooner. This can be extremely frustrating for you.

Call-backs are a part of warranty work. When something doesn't function properly, the contractor is called back to fix it. Nobody likes call-backs. The customer doesn't appreciate having to request repairs on recently installed work, and contractors don't like correcting their mistakes for free. It would be wonderful if there were no need for call-backs. Unfortunately, the need is there and call-backs are a part of remodeling. The best you can hope for is a cooperative contractor.

From the contractor's perspective, he hopes for a reasonable homeowner. It is impossible to guarantee there will be no problems with a remodeling project. All contractors are going to make mistakes. There will be circumstances beyond their control. Although using experienced tradesmen may reduce problems, it doesn't assure a lack of call-backs. The best remodelers available will still get an occasional call-back. Reputable contractors will respond to your request for call-back service promptly. Realistically, they should respond to call-backs quicker than new work. Your job is done and paid for. If you are having a problem, they should respond promptly. Unfortunately, this attitude is not universal.

A lot of contractors put call-backs at the bottom of their priority list. They go to new work first, because these jobs are generating fresh income. The contractor figures you can wait — he already has *your* money. This is the wrong attitude. You paid your final payment, and you are entitled to what you paid for. If you have a problem, *you* should be taken care of before a new project. Too many contractors are only interested in cash flow and ignore your request for warranty service.

When this is the case, you lose. Your call-back is not a paying job, so you no longer have any leverage. The contractor has your money and is in no hurry to rush back to your job. Is there anything you can do? You can try to stress the value of a favorable referral to the contractor. He should be concerned with customer relations, reputation, and good business practices. Whether he is or is not is a different story. When call-backs arise, retainages may have already been paid. What can you do if the contractor won't respond to your requests? Without your financial leverage, do you have any effective options? Good contractors will respond quickly. It's the marginal or bad ones you have to worry about.

WARRANTY WORK

If your original contract addressed warranty work, you have an advantage. You have a written instrument, signed by the contractor, guaranteeing warranty work. This contract can still be used as a threat. If the contractor won't respond to your call, play your contract card. Explain to the contractor that you only want what was promised in the contract. If he still balks, get mean!

Threaten to sue the contractor for breach of contract. Advise him of your intention to file formal complaints with every available agency controlling contractors' licenses. Some agencies to name are: the Code Enforcement Office, the Better Business Bureau, the Chamber of Commerce, the state and local licensing jurisdictions, home builder and trade associations, and any other applicable agency. Not all of these are licensing agencies, but they all affect the contractor's business. This may sound ruthless or extreme, but if the contractor is jerking you around, you have to regain some leverage. You shouldn't have to be subjected to this kind of treatment. You upheld your end of the contract; make the contractor uphold his part of your agreement.

INSURANCE

If everything went right, your house has a higher market value now. The replacement cost of the home has increased, which dictates a call to your insurance agent. It will be necessary to increase your insurance coverage. When you call your insurance agent, remember to allow for new furnishings. If you added space, you will most likely add personal belongings. These belongings should be added to your insurance policy. A new insurance inventory should be done; your old inventory will be outdated. Providing photos of your new improvements and furnishings will create a very accurate insurance inventory. This will make your life easier if you have to file a claim. When you give the insurance agent figures for the value of the improvements, use retail figures, not your cost. If a disaster requires you to replace the improvements, you may not want to do it yourself. Allow enough insurance coverage to hire professionals.

Fire Claims

Many big insurance claims involve fires or fallen trees. You did a good job contracting your addition, but if it is heavily damaged by fire, you are not the best person to contract the repairs. Fire jobs require highly specialized talent. They cannot be considered remodeling. Fire jobs are in a class by themselves, and fire-related work will test a remodeler's mettle. Estimating the repair costs is very difficult. There is a lot more to these jobs than meets the eye.

Fire jobs present nasty working conditions. They reek, from the smoke and water damage, and you don't always know how extensive the damage is. This is no place for a part-timer. If you are possibly contemplating contracting your own fire job, forget it. You must have extensive experience to be qualified to do the job. The average contractor isn't qualified either. If you are dealing with a fire job, find a specialist. Fire jobs are no place for novices.

THE JOB IS COMPLETE

The completion of the job should be a joyous day. You have successfully executed a complicated task. You saved money and still got everything you wanted. This provides a warm feeling of relief and happiness. You avoided the pitfalls and traps. You beat the odds. Now you can truly enjoy the results of your efforts. With the successful completion of your project, you deserve a reward. Whether you engaged a general contractor or ran the job yourself, the result is a completed, successful job.

When you approach the end of your project, you will be elated. There will be a strong sense of pride in your accomplishment. When you started planning your job, you had little to no experience. You mustered the courage to face intimidating odds, and everything has turned out fine. Now you can't understand why people make such a fuss over remodeling. Your personal experience has proved the horror stories wrong. This was a time-consuming project, but it wasn't too difficult.

Reaching a successful completion was a matter of education and self-discipline. You studied your options before beginning the process. This knowledge guided you to a successful end. Your self-discipline allowed you to stick to the remodeling rules. The rules helped you avoid the pitfalls and gave you a good template to follow. The money you saved was substantial. All in all, this was a rewarding and pleasurable experience. There were no miracles or magic needed to orchestrate the project. It only required a clear head and sensible decisions.

Where do all the bad stories come from? They are originated by uninformed consumers. These homeowners don't expend the same energy, or research their actions, the way you did. For the unprepared self-contractor, remodeling can be a less than desirable experience. You should be proud — you've almost made it to the finish line. You made the right decisions. You learned to make the most of your abilities. By taking an active interest in the job, you can appreciate the work that went into it. This was not an effortless responsibility. What will you do with the money you saved? You can put it in the bank or treat yourself to a celebration. A good plan is to do a little of both.

Don't take your work hat off yet. Invest some of your savings and treat yourself to some goodies for your efforts. Allow yourself some rewards for your hard work. In the next chapter, we are going to talk about interior decorating. This offers a valuable way to spend some of your savings. These expenditures will amplify the effects of your new space. Your choices in decorating will allow the opportunity to get the most from your remodeling project. The right moves with the interior choices will personalize your remodeling efforts.

This is where you get all the contractors out of your house and put your personality in. You are about to indulge in the world of serenity again. All the heavy work is done. The house is beginning to look more like a home and less like a construction site. You are done with the stress of managing the crews and suppliers. All that is left is the fun of adding your special accessories. This final stage of the remodeling process will be meaningful and enjoyable.

PUNCH-LIST

BATHROOM REMODELING PROJECT

ITEM/PHASE	O.K.	REPAIR	REPLACE	FINISH WORK
Demolition				
Rough plumbing				
Rough electrical				
Rough heating/ac				
Subfloor				
Insulation				
Drywall				
Ceramic tile				
Linen closet				
Baseboard trim				
Window trim				
Door trim				
Paint/wallpaper				
Underlayment				
Finish floor covering				
Linen closet shelves				
Linen closet door				
Closet door hardware				
Main door hardware				
Wall cabinets				
Base cabinets				
Countertops				
Plumbing fixtures				
Trim plumbing material				
Final plumbing				
Shower enclosure				
Light fixtures				
Trim electrical material				
Final electrical				
Trim heating/ac material				
Final heating/ac				
Bathroom accessories				
Cleanup				

NOTES

_____

_____

_____

_____

_____

CERTIFICATE OF COMPLETION AND ACCEPTANCE

CONTRACTOR: Willy's Drywall Service
CUSTOMER: David R. Erastus
JOB NAME: Erastus
JOB LOCATION: 134 Faye Lane, Beau, VA 29999
JOB DESCRIPTION: Supply and install drywall in new addition, as per plans and specifications, and as described in the contract dated 6/10/91, between the two parties. Hang, tape, sand, and prepare wall and ceiling surfaces for paint.
DATE OF COMPLETION: August 13, 1991
DATE OF FINAL INSPECTION BY CUSTOMER: August 13, 1991
DATE OF CODE COMPLIANCE INSPECTION & APPROVAL: August 13, 1991
ANY DEFICIENCIES FOUND BY CUSTOMER: None
NOTE ANY DEFECTS IN MATERIAL OR WORKMANSHIP: None

ACKNOWLEDGMENT

Customer acknowledges the completion of all contracted work and accepts all workmanship and materials as being satisfactory. Upon signing this certificate, the customer releases the contractor from any responsibility for additional work, except warranty work. Warranty work will be performed for a period of one year from August 13, 1991. Warranty work will include the repair of any material or workmanship defects occurring after this date. All existing workmanship and materials are acceptable to the customer and payment will be made, in full, according to the payment schedule in the contract, between the two parties.

_____   _____
Customer   Date   Contractor   Date

Reaping Your Rewards

19

The sawdust has settled, and the army of contractors is gone. Your china isn't shaking anymore, and you can actually hear the sound of your refrigerator running again. How long has it been since your house was quiet enough to hear the appliances humming? All you've heard recently was the buzz of saws and the pounding of hammers. This return to normal is almost abnormal. After weeks or months of destruction and construction, you have become accustomed to being displaced in your own home. Now it is quiet. You have regained the private use of your home and almost don't know how to act. It has been so long since you could truly relax, but now all is well.

After a day or two, you will become accustomed to the absence of the contractors. Late evening phone calls to workers have ceased. You can park in your driveway again. The plastic can come off the carpets now, and the plumber's torch won't be setting your smoke detector off anymore. This is proof; there is life after remodeling. Really, the whole process wasn't as bad as all the stories you had heard. Your job went well, and the results are fantastic. You made more right decisions than wrong ones, and it's time to start enjoying your new space. Where should you start? There are still a few small items to tend to, some finishing touches to be made. You want to do some decorating, but you aren't sure what you want. How should you proceed?

At first, you will feel strange at not having to deal with the remodeling process. Those urges to check out the job will subside after a short time. You won't keep waking up in the middle of the night, wondering what you forgot. By the end of the week, you should be adjusted to what had been a normal lifestyle before the remodeling process began. Take some time for yourself. Give your brain a rest. It has worked hard during the construction. Don't jump immediately into decorating and customizing your new improvements.

THE FINAL PHASE

When conditions have returned to normal and you've accepted them, you can begin the final phase. This part is fun. You get to personalize your recent improvements. The space was added or remodeled to your specifications, but now you have the opportunity to add your signature to the job. The odds are good that the job went well, and you have some money left over. This is the money saved by being an informed consumer. You earned it, and now you can spend it without feeling guilty. This is money you would not have, if you hadn't invested your time in the project. Unlike taking money from your paycheck, this is your reward money for a job well done.

Almost any type of home improvement will allow for your personal touch. Putting your signature on the job makes it complete. This is when the space becomes more than a nice job. It becomes *your* nice job. What you do with the space now can determine the overall effect of the completed project. The right furniture, decorations, and accessories can improve the best remodeling job. The wrong choices will depreciate all of your efforts.

Decorating is very important to the success of a remodeling effort.

EXTERIOR DECORATING

People usually associate decorating with interior work. While this is where the most garnishing is done, decorating the outside of your home is important too. The outside of the home is what people see first. A home's exterior appearance casts the mold for first impressions. People's opinions of the entire house will be prejudiced by a barren exterior. Landscaping is an often overlooked area of decorating.

Landscaping

When you add space to your home, landscaping is a primary element of the finish work. Some people neglect this work completely, while many homeowners plan to do the landscaping themselves. Frequently, landscaping is not even considered until the project is done. Other times, you find it is not calculated into the budget at all. This mistake will have a negative impact on your new addition. If you didn't budget for the work, you will be surprised how expensive landscaping can be. A trip to the nursery will empty your pockets quickly. Either through omission or procrastination, landscaping gets little priority.

New additions deserve landscaping. As your eye travels down the length of the existing house, existing shrubbery makes the impression complete. Then you get to the addition. It is bare and appears to have been glued to the side of the house. This is a bad contrast. Landscaping is an important part of your home's appearance. Spend the time and money to finish the exterior of the job. Make the first impression a positive one. Don't keep putting off the landscaping because you can't see it from within the home. Do it while you are involved in finishing the project, or it may never get done.

Gutters

The same situation can develop with gutters. If the rest of the house has gutters, the addition should also have gutters. You should strive to maintain continuity in the home's exterior. If the existing house has shutters on the windows, put shutters on the addition. The existing lawn may have taken a beating from material deliveries or excavation work. Don't neglect repairing it. Bald or brown spots in the lawn detract from your home's appearance. Before you can consider the job officially complete, this type of outside decorating is required.

Garages

Exterior decorating is often overlooked on garages. Like a room addition, the garage is an extension of your home. Whether it is attached or detached, a garage is one of the building blocks of your home. When you landscape a garage, make sure it complements the house. During the design stage, you concentrated on ways to tie the house and garage together, so continue this attention to detail. You made certain the roof would be the same color as the house. The siding and trim colors match the house. Now it's time to view the garage has a vehicle to complement your home. Install flower boxes, plant shrubs, or hang a flag. Once the exterior blends well, personalize the inside of the garage.

One of the primary functions of a garage is to provide storage. Now that you have all this space, allow the creative side of your personality to develop imaginative solutions to storage problems. Adding pegboard to the walls provides an easily accessible repository for tools and hoses. Installing straps to suspend bulky items from the ceiling requires minimal time and investment. In this way, cumbersome items such as tents, sleds, and skis are conveniently accessible, yet out of the way. If you are always tripping over bicycles, consider hanging them from the wall in the corner of the garage. Constructing a simple 2" x 4" frame will corral those wild trash cans, which inevitably end up in the middle of the garage floor. These are easy, inexpensive ways to personalize your garage while maximizing its potential.

MAKING DECORATING CHOICES

No matter how complete your specifications were, there will be enhancements to make. Planning is effective, but you can't visualize everything before it exists. Now you have a tangible space to work with. You know what it looks like and how you would like to customize it. The paint color is no longer on a 2-inch chip. It's right there in front of you, on the walls and ceilings. For weeks, you stared at that little color chip. You were tempted to run out and buy some accessories for the new room, but you resisted this urge. You knew the paint might

Custom cabinet knobs can have centers to match or complement wall covering or countertop material. Courtesy of Worthy Works.

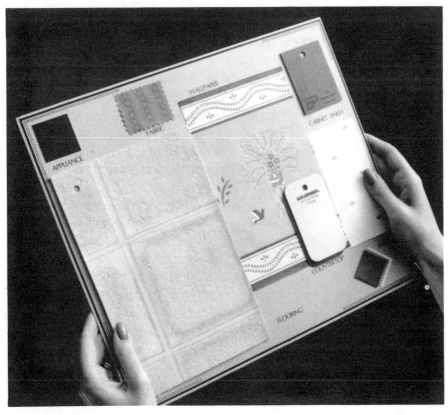

Many companies offer design services to aid you in making design and decorating choices. Shown is the Design Plus Decorating Board, which helps you coordinate appliances, fabrics, wall covering, cabinets, flooring, countertops, and paint. Courtesy of Aqualine.

look different when it was installed. Your decision to wait is paying off. There is no doubt now what the color looks like. You can match and buy your accessories without fear.

The wallpaper and carpet are installed, and you can see exactly how they look together. Until now, it was impossible to picture how they would actually appear. The choices complement each other well. Everything is real, nothing is clouded in speculation, and the job is almost perfect. With the addition of a few personal items, it will be exactly what you want. At the end of the remodeling project, assemble any leftover pieces of carpet and wallpaper. If you want to save money decorating, here is an economical way to harmonize a room.

USING LEFTOVER MATERIALS

Don't underestimate the importance of scrap carpet. Save these remnants to patch or repair damage to your carpet in the future. Dye lots differ slightly with each roll of carpet, so matching your carpet to repair a burn or stain can be impossible. If you have pieces of the original product, you are assured of an exact match. Trim a piece of scrap carpet, and you have an area rug or welcome mat. These small floor coverings tie your new and existing spaces together. What about the remaining wallpaper, how much do you need to keep? Set a small amount aside to fix an occasional rip, and use the rest for decorating. Excess wallpaper can really consolidate a room's appearance.

You can cover any size box with leftover wallpaper, and create coordinated storage for everything from jewelry to shoes. Accent a lamp shade with strips of patterned wallpaper. Use wallpaper as a decorative mat for pictures, and hang them throughout the house to create a feeling of continuity. Something as simple as covering drawer pulls or lining shelves with wallpaper will give the room a finished look. Simple scraps can become your most effective decorating resource.

Bedrooms

If you added bedrooms, what can you do to make them special? All the major elements were installed during the construction. What will you do to make the room warm and homey? Window treatments can set the pace for all your rooms. The statement made with curtains and draperies shapes the focus of the room. Think about it. When you look into a bedroom, can you tell what kind of person sleeps there? Even with the bed made and everything in drawers and closets, the personality of the occupant is apparent.

Your decisions on decorating will say a lot about you. Take the opportunity to accent the space with curtain patterns on pillows or bed ruffles. Accessories will allow you to express the personality you were forced to contain during the design stage of your job. Once you make a personal statement in a room, repeat it throughout the space.

The bedspread can be as informative as the curtains. The type and color of a bedspread can affect a room's entire appearance. A light-colored spread will make the room brighter. This helps to give the appearance of a larger space. A large comforter, and a pile of bed pillows, can demand immediate attention and become the decorating focus of a room. A handmade quilt accents country-style furnishings. Small touches really do mean a lot. The right bedspread can give an old bed a whole new appearance. A unique idea for children's rooms is a do-it-yourself bedspread. Make or purchase a bedspread consisting of black and white line drawings. Then, allow your child to color the spread with permanent magic markers. This is an excellent and cost-effective way for children to personalize their rooms. Proper decorating can personalize a room or maximize the visual effect of your space.

Think about the illusion you wish to create. Do you want the room to appear larger? Use light-colored window treatments to achieve this effect. Miniblinds are a good choice when used with sheer curtains. This combination provides a modern, functional solution to the problem. Your furniture should be petite. Don't opt for a massive headboard on the bed or a huge imposing mirror over the dresser. Tall furniture, such as wardrobes or hutches, will also shrink the appearance of a room. Avoid dark-colored woods, which create a heavy, closed-in feeling. Consider a modern approach with light-colored or white furniture.

Do not clutter a small room with a lot of unnecessary accents and accessories. Keep the space open, and use selective decorating to spotlight specific areas or features of the room. Think twice before placing items on your walls. Large pictures and wall hangings reduce the room's size in the mind's eye. Install mirrors instead, to give the impression of vast, open space. Mirrors can also be used to move your eye around a room, or to highlight areas you want to

Closet organizers you can install yourself can unclutter crowded storage space and increase storage volume. Courtesy of Clairson International.

Walk-in storage closets are equipped with all-wall storage units that maximize storage capacity and keep everything in view. Courtesy of Clairson International.

Closet Carousel is an electric push-button revolving storage system that saves space because it eliminates the aisles needed for walk-in closets. Courtesy White Home Products Inc.

For deep closets with wasted space, StorMate™ moveable built-ins install on track in front of hanging or shelf storage and slide side-to-side to gain access to hanging clothes behind. Courtesy of White Home Products.

draw attention to through the use of reflection.

CLOSETS

If you want to invest the money in a decorating technique that is both inexpensive and functional, put your money in your closets. Custom closet components will increase your home's marketability and its efficiency. Space-saving closet units eliminate clutter and provide organized storage for everything from shoes to toys. You can either construct these accessories yourself or purchase complete storage systems from any number of manufacturers. An effective organizational strategy provides racks for shoes, shelves for bulky items like sweaters, and an abundance of closet rod space. Many of the manufactured units have adjustable shelves and rods to conform to your family's changing needs. Many people consider closets as insignificant little storerooms and ignore their potential. Spending money to customize your closets will transform them from inconsequential catch-alls to valuable utility units.

BATHROOMS

The bathroom is usually the smallest room in the house, but these private chambers can have a tremendous effect on your home. When company comes to call, they will remember specific areas of your home. The average visitor may never see your bedroom or your basement. Only dinner guests are likely to see your kitchen or the formal dining room. The memories your visitors take home are formed around a few basic areas of your home. The foyer, the living room, the hallways, and the bathroom are the areas most guests see. These areas create the opinions of your friends and guests and should reflect your influence accordingly.

When it's time to add the finishing touches to your bathroom, you have lots of inexpensive options. Remodeled bathrooms have new walls, floors, ceilings, and fixtures. All of these items are expected. It's the simple accessories that turn a bathroom into an elegant showroom. Bathroom remodeling is expensive. You spend all that money, only to find the accessories can make or break the whole room. Your high fashion, lowboy toilet deserves more than a cheap, chrome paper holder hanging next to it on the wall. A designer paper holder will extend the feeling of a well-done room.

The rich oak vanity and Corian® top will lose their regal impression when surrounded by common accessories. The toothpaste-stained chrome toothbrush holder will be what guests remember. The antique porcelain lavatory faucets won't attract much attention when accented by a white enameled medicine cabinet. White enameled medicine cabinets with sliding mirrored doors should be avoided. Although they were customary years ago, now they tend to be associated with old houses. There are many options you can select beyond this old standby. Investing in a mirrored wall cabinet provides an attractive complement to the bathroom, as well as storage for miscellaneous toiletries.

Shower curtains do not command the same respect as glass enclosures. Curtains tend to mildew and cheapen your new bathroom. You can have a quality enclosure installed for less than $250, while a quality curtain can cost $50 or more. For the extra $200, you get the enhancing appearance and function of a glass enclosure. The glass doors will provide an appropriate finish to your newly installed shower, but curtains only hide your new investment. There is an abundance of effective spray cleaners that enable you to avoid the detergent buildup often associated with shower doors. With a shower enclosure, there will also be less chance of water escaping onto your new floor. This investment will be well worth it in the long run.

Towel holders should embellish your wall space, not detract from it. The towels themselves play a major role in the visual performance of your fashionable bathroom. Take some of your remodeling savings and buy towels to match your new environment. Window treatments also play an important role in your bathroom decor. They should be in keeping with the rest of the room. If you have a linen closet in the bathroom, install hardware that matches the hardware on the vanity. A small bowl of potpourri provides a pleasant fragrance and adds a touch of class. If you chose a subtle palette of white or bone for your fixtures and vanity, use wallpaper and towels to add splashes of color to the bathroom. Use your wallpaper scraps to create a coordinated panel on vanity doors or to line vanity drawers. These are the small details that can add grace to even the busiest bathroom.

Bathrooms must be functional as well as attractive. If the bath serves the entire household, allowances should be made for all members of the family. A grab bar on the tub is a good safety feature for adults and children alike. Consider adding

Your foyer should make a good first impression. This one features an insulated, weatherstripped steel entry door. Courtesy of Stanley Door Systems, Inc.

shelving in areas between fixtures or next to the vanity, to provide accessible storage for toiletries and children's toys. Install a second, lower-level towel rack for smaller children, or perhaps a magazine holder for the reader in the family. These little accessories don't cost much, but they can ensure your new bathroom remains neat and attractive.

THE FOYER

The foyer is the first area visitors see inside your home. The foyer and entry-way should be well appointed and functional. The actual furnishings will depend on the style and scheme of your home. Umbrella stands, coat racks, artwork, and antiques are some of the more popular foyer accents. Make these choices carefully. This is going to be the first interior space seen by guests and appraisers. Keep the area open and uncluttered, with room to remove bulky overcoats.

If the foyer serves as the main entry for your family, provide accommodations for smaller children. Avoid throw rugs, which may catapult kids into the next room. Provide coat hooks or pegs three feet off the floor. Even if the next owner does not have children, these make convenient hangers for umbrellas, keys, or fanny packs. Install a light fixture in the foyer that casts attractive shadows. This is where the first impression of your home's interior is made, making the foyer a focal point of the house.

LIVING ROOM

Living room decorating tips could fill an entire book. The basics center around the same principles as other areas discussed. Plan the whole decorating scheme before buying furniture, and work to achieve harmony with the accessories you use. Choose your theme and build around it. If you have a family room, the living room should be considered formal. Choose appropriate furnishings to indicate the purpose of the room. Formal living rooms are used for entertaining and should exude both a feeling of comfort and an air of dignity. Arrange the room to provide unobstructed movement, and position furniture groupings to encourage dialogue among guests. Properly arranged accessories will tie the entire space together. This is the place to display your treasured family portraits, antiques, books, and collectible items. These objects reflect your personal taste and serve as catalysts for stimulating conversation.

If you want to add a touch of grandeur to your formal living room, consider decorative wood trims. It's never too late to add ornate trim to windows, doors, and mantels. This can be the crowning touch that bestows the feeling of elegance upon the room. Using these same trims to embellish picture frames and mirrors will reflect the lavish facade throughout the room. Attaching half-round shelves to the living room walls will intensify the formal effect and provide additional space to exhibit distinctive accessories. Look for cost-effective ways to accentuate the atmosphere for each room you decorate.

If you are going formal, keep the whole room formal. Your windows should have draperies, not curtains. Consider using boxed valances at the top of each window and duplicate the drapery pattern on throw pillows. The lighting should be adequate but not overpowering. You can illuminate the space by adding some spark to the fireplace with brass and glass doors. For about $250, these doors increase energy savings and add beauty to your living room. If your budget did not allow for a fireplace, you may want to consider investing in an operational decorative fireplace. Many of these units are extremely attractive and provide the charm of a real fire. They have the advantage of not needing a chimney or flue. Some of these ornamental fireplaces operate on gelled alcohol fuel. Others give the appearance of a fire, by means of electricity. Best of all, your fireplace is completely portable. It can be relocated to another room or moved with you to your next house. Creative decorating can produce the illusion of opulence on a shoestring budget.

FAMILY ROOM

Family rooms offer unlimited decorating options. You can break some rules with family rooms; they are meant to be fun. A brick wall at one end of the room is fine. Herringbone, tongue and groove paneling is striking. Commercial-grade carpet is acceptable. Almost anything goes with the family room. Family rooms are usually the most lived-in room of the house. They should be comfortable and enjoyable, but this does not mean they have to be cluttered and disorderly. If your original design did not provide built-in storage, invest some of your savings in bookcases and chests. The casual atmosphere of a family room furnishes an excellent opportunity for bargain decorating. Visit secondhand stores and outlet warehouses, and purchase furnishings that will be functional, comfortable, and durable.

To save time and money, involve the whole family in the decorating process. Put your children to work sanding and repainting an old table, and get Dad to install shelves. Invest in items that will facilitate organized, enjoyable living conditions. Install petite bi-fold doors on bookcases to keep toys and games out of view. Pillows can prove to be your least expensive and most functional family room accessories. Scattering pillows of various sizes throughout the room supplies material for everything from sleeping quarters to a fluffy arsenal.

The family room furniture doesn't even have to match. You can put your favorite recliner in the family room. So what if the cat has scratched the arms to threads. It still works, and it's the most comfortable chair in the house. Your little girl's bean bag chair may not complement your wife's overstuffed love seat, but everyone needs a favorite place to sit. Family rooms are great. If you don't have one, you should add one. They are good investments and a lot of fun.

Look for ways to accommodate your family's needs, and feel free to do whatever you want with the family room. You are paying the mortgage, and you need a place to enjoy your life. If you can, follow the basic rules of good taste. If you can't, then make an effort to contain your indiscretions to areas you'll be able to hide later. If you want to plaster the walls with pictures, do so knowing you will have to patch the holes before you sell the house. You will also have to paint the walls. If you decide to apply fluorescent paint colors or team logos, be prepared to install wallpaper before you list your home for sale. Essentially, it is your house to decorate as you please now, but consider money spent on extreme personal expressions as water under the bridge.

Wood stoves may soot up ceilings and walls, but I can't think of a better place to install them than the family room. You will probably spend most of your time in this room, so it might as well be warm and cozy. This room is your haven — you can do what you want with it. The smell and feel of wood heat are unique. Depending on the design of your home, installing a wood stove is not outrageously expensive. When installed properly, your wood stove can easily be disconnected and moved with you to your next home. In a formal living room, tree bark and ashes would cause chaos; in the family room, they add character.

KITCHEN

You can be cavalier with some areas, but other locations require strict attention to the rules. While kitchens offer endless possibilities for decorating, keep in mind they have a tremendous influence on your home. You can arrange the room to follow any scheme, so long as you strive to maintain an organized, efficient work space. Many of the major decorating ideas can come from books and magazines that deal specifically with kitchens. The basic ingredients of a successful kitchen are universal. These elements are lighting, counter space, appliances, and cabinets. You covered most of these areas in your remodeling plans. Direct your decorating thoughts to small appliances and accessories.

Consider appliances that hang under your wall cabinets; they will keep the counter space open and uncluttered. If you don't have a built-in trash compactor, reserve your base cabinet space by placing the trash can in full view. This waste receptacle does not have to be unsightly simply because it holds trash. Placing the trash can in a large wicker basket is one way of concealing it. You can buy or build a decorative wooden shell to hide the can. View your trash can as an opportunity to design an attractive, functional kitchen accessory. Use some creativity in the kitchen.

The kitchen sees a lot of activity. Even if you dine in restaurants frequently, you will still make many trips to the refrigerator. Much of your home life is spent in and around the kitchen. Invest the time and money to make this time efficient and enjoyable. Free up additional cabinet space by installing decorative racks and hangers for pots and pans. You can never have too much cabinet space, and an investment of this kind is money well spent. Locating racks on the inside of cabinet doors will keep spices, sponges, and towels organized and out of sight. A well-designed and appointed kitchen is a pleasure to work in. If the kitchen is large enough, consider purchasing a small cafe table and chairs. You would be surprised how often this diminutive dining area will be used. Morning coffee, waiting for the oven timer to go off, organizing shopping lists, reading the mail, and late night snacks are all catered to with a simple table and chairs.

THE JOB IS DONE

When you have finished your decorating, the job is truly done. You have completed the entire project. Not only did you get exactly the finished job and personalized accessories you wanted, you saved money doing it. This is a magnificent feeling. All the time you invested in the beginning has been rewarded with a completed job and cash savings. The feeling of contentment is hard to describe. Knowing you did it yourself makes the whole project more rewarding. Even if you hired a general contractor, you deserve a lot of credit for the part you played.

Finding the right general contractor wasn't easy.

You spent your time and used your abilities to find just the right person for the job. This took effort and foresight. Many consumers would simply have asked for three or four estimates and chosen the contractor with the lowest price. You knew better. You followed Dodge's rules and won the game. Laying out the plans and specs required hours of your time. Even if professionals produced the final drafts, you developed the guide for them to work from. Without your research and input, your job might never have become a reality. Negotiating for the best prices required patience and skill. By getting your quotes in writing, you stayed within your budget, a goal not always met by professional contractors. This is a notable accomplishment.

Selecting the right products made the job come together. Each product and item now complements the others, and this can be attributed to your research and your dream book. The dream book allowed you to choose from all the products on the market, and shop for the best prices available. This compilation of products was a direct result of your efforts. Perhaps your best efforts were in avoiding the professional rip-off artists. All the contractors involved in your job were reputable and did excellent work. Without your informed decisions, you could have lost a bundle of money and still not have your new space. Your judgment and evaluation techniques were superb and paid off in ample savings.

These qualities all deserve recognition. Pat yourself on the back, you did a great job. This could be the beginning of a new life for you. With the experience you gained, you might be able to build a new career. You wouldn't be the first homeowner to turn into a professional contractor. Completing your first job successfully is the hardest step. They all get easier after the first one. From now on, adding a few shelves to the family room will seem like a walk in the park.

If you follow Dodge's remodeling rules, you will be on course to enjoying a rewarding remodeling venture. The experience will be much nicer, and the finished results will be exciting. The money you save will add to your happiness, not to mention your nest egg. I would wish you good luck, but luck doesn't enter into professional remodeling. Learn the skills I have outlined and you won't need luck. You will be well qualified to tackle any residential remodeling project.

Well, I guess it couldn't hurt to have a little good fortune on your side too, so good luck!

Appendices

DODGE'S REMODELING RULES

- Plan everything well in advance.
- Make contingency plans and have backup contractors available for each phase of work to be completed.
- Maintain clear, concise records from the beginning of the job.
- Predicting an accurate financial budget is vital to completing a successful job.
- Get everything in writing; everything you have in writing reduces your risks.
- Don't confuse an estimate with a quote.
- To understand which remodeling efforts are the most cost-effective, you must understand the appraisal process.
- Research the type of work you are planning before dealing with contractors.
- Get at least three quotes from each trade involved in your project.
- Always draw your plans and line drawings to scale.
- Protect yourself and your house at all times.
- Never allow a contractor to gain control of you.
- A good contract is an essential element to any remodeling job.
- Include a clause in your contract regarding damage to existing conditions and other contractors' work.
- Don't accept a post office box for an address; insist on a physical location for all people involved in your job.
- Include a clause in your contract setting a final completion date for each phase of work to be done.
- Include a clause in your contract charging a penalty for every day the work is not complete past the stated completion date.
- Include a clause in your contract allowing the use of backup contractors if the primary contractor is in contract default.
- Payment terms must be specific and should include provisions for your inspection and satisfaction of all work before payments are made.
- Insist on lien waivers being signed by all vendors being paid for services or material.
- Inspect all work thoroughly before advancing payments.
- Include a clause in your contract allowing you to hold a retainage with each payment made. The retainage should be at least 5% of the payment amount.
- Maintain strong financial leverage throughout the job.
- Good contracts and the right payment procedures keep you out of the judicial system.
- Use written change orders for every variance in the contract.
- Require all contractors to supply permits for their work as required by local and state building codes.
- Require copies of all approved code inspection certificates before releasing payments.
- Use detailed contracts with enforceable clauses and leave nothing to speculation.
- Confirm delivery and completion dates in writing.
- Ask all contractors for a certificate of insurance before any work is started.
- Request evidence of each contractor's state and

local licenses.

- Order materials early and check each shipment for accuracy and damage.
- When you put your job out for bids, give all bidders identical information and don't allow substitutions.
- Don't give a deposit at the signing of the contract; authorize payment of the deposit when materials are delivered and work is started.
- Keep deposit amounts to a minimum; they should not exceed 25% of the contract amount.
- Require detailed breakdowns for all labor and material prices quoted by contractors.
- Establish your budget based on the average bid price, not the lowest bid.
- Never allow a contractor to have more money than has been earned.

GLOSSARY

ABS PIPE — A type of plastic pipe frequently used in plumbing. The letters "ABS" are an abbreviation for Acrylonitrile Butadiene Styrene. The plastic is black and is most frequently used in the form of schedule 40 pipe.

ADJUSTABLE RATE LOAN — A loan with a flexible interest rate, tied to a common reference index. This index can be a Treasury Bill Rate, the Federal Reserve Discount Rate, or some other agreed-upon index. These loans typically start at a lower interest rate and escalate over a period of five years. After five years, most of these loans stay at a fixed rate for the remainder of the loan.

AIR GAP — The most common use of this term in remodeling is in reference to the device a dishwasher drain is connected to. These devices protect a dishwasher from the risk of back siphoning contaminated water from the drainage system into the dishwasher.

ANNUAL APPRECIATION RATE — The rate at which real estate values increase each year.

APPRAISER — An individual who determines the value of real estate. Appraisers may be certified or uncertified. In many states, appraisers are not required to pass stringent licensing requirements.

ARCHITECTURAL PLANS — Blueprints designed and drawn by an architect.

BAIT-AND-SWITCH SCAM — A frequently used unethical marketing ploy to make people respond to advertising. The advertising will entice an individual to come to the advertiser, but the advertised price or product will not be available. The advertiser will attempt to sell the consumer a different product or a similar product at a higher price.

BALLOON PAYMENT — A single lump-sum payment, frequently associated with real estate loans. These payments are generally due and payable in full after an agreed-upon time.

BAND BOARD — The piece of lumber running the perimeter of a building and attached to the floor joists. Normally, it is a wooden member of a size equal to the attached floor joists and placed on the outside wall end of the floor joists. A band board provides a common place for all floor joists to attach and maintains stability and proper alignment.

BASEBOARD TRIM — A decorative trim placed around the perimeter of interior partitions. Used where the floor covering meets the wall to create a finished and attractive appearance.

BID PHASES — The different phases or aspects of work to be performed and priced. Examples include: plumbing, heating, electrical, roofing, and all other individual forms of remodeling or construction.

BIDS — Prices given by contractors and suppliers for labor and material to be supplied for a job.

BLOCK NUMBER — One of the elements needed for a legal description of real property in areas segregated into blocks.

BLUEPRINTS — The common name of working plans; a type of plan printed in blue ink and showing all aspects of the construction methods to be used in building and remodeling.

BOILER — A type of heating system, usually designed to provide hot water heat from baseboard radiation.

BOW WINDOW — A window projecting outward beyond the siding of a home and supported by its own foundation or support beams. Sometimes referred to as a bay window.

BREEZEWAY — A covered and sometimes enclosed walkway from one point to another. Commonly used to connect a garage to a house when direct connection isn't feasible or desirable.

BTU — British Thermal Unit; an industry standard in the measurement of the amount of heat needed for an area. One BTU equals the amount of heat required to raise one pound of water one degree in temperature.

BUILDER-GRADE — A trade term meaning a product of average quality normally found in production-built housing.

CALL-BACK — A trade term referring to a warranty service call. A form of service call in which the contractor is not paid for the services rendered, due to the nature of the problem.

CANTILEVER — Refers to a building practice in which the wooden frame structure extends beyond the foundation. Cantilevers are created when the floor joists overhang the foundation.

CARDBOARD-STYLE CABINETS — A trade term referring to inexpensive production cabinets of low quality.

CARPET PAD — The support, generally foam, between the carpet and subfloor or underlayment.

CASEMENT WINDOW — A window with hinges on the outside and a mechanical crank to open and close the window. These windows open outward and are typically very energy efficient.

CAULKING — A compound used to fill cracks.

CEILING JOIST — Structural members providing support for a second story floor and a nailing surface for a lower story's ceiling.

CERAMIC TILE — A product used for floors, countertops, wall coverings, and tub or shower surrounds. The most common ceramic tiles are approximately 4 inches square and are made of a pottery-type material.

CERTIFICATE OF OCCUPANCY — These are issued by the local codes enforcement office when all building code requirements are met. They allow the legal habitation of a dwelling or business property.

CHAIR RAIL — A wooden member, of finished trim quality, placed horizontally at a point along the walls where chairs would be likely to come into contact with the wall. Chair rail serves some practical purpose but is most frequently used as a decorative trim in formal dining rooms.

CHANGE ORDER — A term applied to a written agreement allowing a change from previously agreed-to plans. Change orders detail the nature of the change and all pertinent facts affected by the change.

CHINA LAVATORY — A bathroom wash basin made of vitreous china. These lavatories provide a clean, non-porous surface for a wash basin and usually have a shiny finish.

CHRONOLOGICAL ORDER — The order in which events should happen, in planning a schedule of events or work to be performed.

CIRCUIT BREAKER — The modern equivalent to the old-style electrical fuses. These devices add protection from overloaded electrical circuits by shutting down the circuit if it is producing a dangerous electrical current.

CLOSE COUPLED FAUCET — Also referred to as a 4-inch center faucet, these faucets are produced as an integral, one piece unit. (The handles and the spout are molded from the same material, producing a faucet with all working parts molded together.)

CLOSED SALE — A closed sale is a consummated or settled sale. It is a completed transfer of the property being sold.

CLOSING COSTS — Expenses incurred to settle a loan transaction. They can include: legal fees, appraisal fees, survey fees, insurance, and other related expenses.

CLOUDED TITLE — When a title is clouded, there are unanswered questions about liens or against the title. These conditions can make the transfer of the property to another owner very difficult.

CODE ENFORCEMENT OFFICER — An authorized representative of the building code enforcement office. The individual responsible for the approval or denial of code inspections and the party responsible for issuing a certificate of occupancy.

COMMERCIAL GRADE CARPET — Normally a closely woven and very durable carpet, suitable for heavy traffic and abuse. This carpet is designed for easy cleaning and to handle the most demanding traffic without undue wear.

COMPARABLE SALES BOOK — Generally produced by Multiple Listing Services, these books reflect a history of all closed sales for the last quarter of a given year. These books are used to determine appraised values of the subject properties.

COMPARABLE SALES SHEET — A form used to compile information on real estate activity in an area, allowing an accurate appraisal of a property.

COMPETITIVE GRADE FIXTURE — A trade term referring to an inexpensive fixture, normally found in tract housing or starter homes.

COMPLETION CERTIFICATE — A document signed by the customer acknowledging all work is complete and satisfactory.

COMPRESSION FITTING — A type of fitting used to make a plumbing connection. Typically utilizes a brass body and nut with a ferrule to compress over the pipe, preventing water from leaking.

CONCRETE APRON — The section of concrete where a garage floor joins the driveway. Aprons allow for a smooth transition from a lower driveway to an elevated garage floor.

CONTRACT DEPOSIT — A financial deposit given when a contract is signed and before work is started.

CORNICE — A horizontal molding usually projecting from the top of an exterior wall to provide better water drainage.

COSMETIC IMPROVEMENT — An improvement with no structural significance, performed as an aesthetic enhancement to the property.

COST APPROACH — An appraisal technique used to determine a property value, based on the cost to build the structure.

COST ESTIMATE SHEET — A form designed to project accurately the cost of a proposed im provement.

COST INCREASE CAP — An amount of money set to limit the price increase of a future purchase.

CRAFTSMAN — A word used to describe a person working in a trade, who is experienced and proficient in the trade.

CRAWL SPACE — The space beneath a house, between the first story floor joists and the ground, surrounded by a foundation.

CROWN MOLDING — A decorative wood trim placed at the top of an interior wall, where the wall meets the ceiling.

CURB APPEAL — A term used in real estate sales referring to the exterior appearance of a property.

CUT SHEETS — Illustrated fact sheets providing detailed information on a product.

DAYLIGHT BASEMENT — A basement with windows allowing natural light to flow into the basement.

DECKING — The term decking can apply to the materials used to build an exterior deck or the material used to build interior flooring systems.

DEED DESCRIPTION — A legal description of a property as it is referred to in the registered deed to the property.

DEMO WORK — Demolition work; the process of dismantling or destroying existing conditions.

DENIAL NOTICE — A notice of rejection or turn-down for a requested service, such as a loan.

DIRECT MARKET EVALUATION APPROACH — An appraisal technique used to determine property value by comparing the subject property to other similar properties. All pertinent features of the subject property are compared to similar properties and financial adjustments are made for differences to establish a value for the subject property.

DISCRETIONARY INCOME — Income not committed to a particular expense. The amount of money an individual has to spend on anything he or she wishes.

DORMER — A projection built from the slope of a roof allowing additional room height and the opportunity to install windows.

DOWN-TIME — A period of non-productive or lost time.

DRAIN — A pipe carrying water or waterborne waste to a main drainage system.

DRYWALL — A term used to describe a type of wall covering made of gypsum.

DRYWALL MUD — Joint compound; the substance used to hide seams and nail or screw heads in the finished walls of a home.

DWV SYSTEM — Drain, Waste, and Vent system; the plumbing system used in a home for the drainage and venting of plumbing fixtures.

8-INCH CENTER FAUCET — A faucet designed to have the two handles spaced on an 8-inch center. These faucets are composed of separate elements for each handle and the spout; they are connected beneath the fixture's surface to allow the faucet to operate.

18-INCH TOILET — A special toilet designed for the physically restricted person. The seat of these toilets is higher than that of a standard toilet, allowing easier use without as much demand for physical strength.

ELECTRIC HEAT — A trade term referring to electric baseboard heating units attached permanently to the interior wall of a home. Electric heat can utilize other forms of heating equipment, such as a wall-mounted blower unit. Electrical current provides the source for producing heat.

ELECTRICAL SERVICE — A trade term referring to the size and capacity of a home's circuit breaker or fuse box. Older homes were equipped with 60 AMP electrical services. Modern homes have 100 AMP or 200 AMP electrical service as the standard.

ELEVATIONS — A term used with drafting and blueprints referring to illustrations on the blueprints. Examples are: picture drawings of the front of a house, the side of the house, and the rear of the house.

ESTIMATED JOB COST — The projected cost required to complete a job.

EXCLUSIONS — Phrases or sentences releasing a party from responsibility for certain acts or circumstances.

EXTERIOR FRAMING — The material or labor used in the construction of exterior walls and roof structures.

EXTERIOR IMPROVEMENTS — Improvements made outside of a dwelling. Examples are: garages, landscaping, exterior painting, and roofing.

EXTERIOR WALL SHEATHING — The exterior wall covering placed between the exterior wall studs and the exterior siding.

FAIR MARKET VALUE — The estimated

value of a property to the buying public in the real estate market.

FIBERBOARD — A composite sheet made from pressed materials bonded together for use as a wall sheathing.

FILL-IN JOB — A trade term for a job with no committed completion time. These jobs are often done at discounted prices because they allow flexibility for the contractor.

FINISHED BASEMENT — A basement that has been completed into finished living space. The walls, ceiling, and floor are all completed to an acceptable finished standard. The basement is provided with heat, electrical outlets, lights, and switches.

FIXED RATE LOAN — A loan with a fixed interest rate. The interest rate does not fluctuate; it remains constant for the life of the loan.

FLASHED — A trade term applying to the attachment of articles to houses or roofs and the penetration of roofs by pipes. When these conditions exist, they are flashed to seal the area from water infiltration. Plumbing pipes exiting through a roof are flashed with neoprene or some other material to prevent water leaks around the pipes. Where decks or bow windows are attached to a house, they are flashed with lightweight metal to prevent water damage behind the point of attachment.

FLOOR JOIST — A structural member or board used to support the floor of a house. Floor joists span foundation walls and girders at regular intervals to provide strength and support to the finished floor.

FLUORESCENT LIGHT — A lamp or tube producing light by radiant energy; a tube coated with a fluorescent substance giving off light when mercury vapor comes into contact with electrons.

FOOTING — A support, usually concrete, under a foundation, providing a larger base than the foundation to distribute weight. Footings are placed on solid surfaces and reduce settling and shifting of foundations.

FORCED HOT AIR FURNACE — A type of heating system producing warm air heat and forcing the warm air through ducts, with the use of a blower, into the heated area.

FORM CONTRACT — Standard or generic forms, available at office supply stores and stationery specialty vendors, intended for use as legal contracts when the blank spaces are filled in.

FOUNDATION — The base of a structure used to support the entire structure.

4-INCH CENTER FAUCET — Also known as a close coupled faucet. These faucets are produced as an integral, one-piece unit. (The handles and the spout are molded from the same material, producing a faucet with all working parts molded together.)

FRAMING — A trade term referring to the process of building the frame structure of a home to which siding, sheathing, and wall coverings are applied.

FUMIGATION — The process of exposing an area to fumes to rid the area of existing vermin or insects.

FUNCTIONAL OBSOLESCENCE — An appraisal term referring to the absence of common desirable features in the design, layout, or construction of a home. A kitchen without cabinets or a modern sink would be exhibiting functional obsolescence.

GENERAL CONTRACTOR — The contractor responsible for the entire job and the person who coordinates subcontractors in individual aspects of the job.

GRACE PERIOD — A term referring to the period of time a commitment may be unmet before enforcement action is taken.

GREENHOUSE WINDOW — A bow window unit designed to extend beyond the exterior wall of a house and made mostly of glass, including the roof portion of the window. The window is meant to allow additional lighting and provide a feeling of openness.

GROUND FAULT CIRCUIT INTERRUPTER OUTLET — An electrical outlet, used primarily in bathrooms and other areas where the outlet is near a water supply, with a safety feature to protect against electrical shock.

GROUT — The substance used to fill cracks between tile during the installation process.

HARD COSTS — Expenses easily identified and directly related to a job. Examples include the cost of labor and materials for the construction process.

HEAT LAMP/FAN COMBINATION — An electrical fixture commonly placed in the ceiling of a bathroom. The unit combines an exhaust fan with a heat lamp providing warmth and the removal of moisture.

HEAT PUMP — A device used for heating and cooling a home. Heat pumps are an effective heating and cooling unit in moderate climates and are being improved for use in extremely cold climates. They are energy-efficient and do not require a flue or a chimney.

HVAC — Heating, Ventilation, and Air Conditioning.

IN THE FIELD — A trade term referring to being out of the office and on the job.

INCANDESCENT LIGHT — A light using a filament contained in a vacuum to produce light when heated by electrical current.

INSULATED FOAM SHEATHING — A type of sheathing made from compressed foam and covered by a foil or other substance allowing its use as a wall sheathing with increased insulating value.

INTERIOR PARTITIONS — The walls located within a home dividing the living area into different sections or rooms.

INTERIOR REMODELING — Altering the condition of areas within the home.

INTERIOR TRIM — A trade term broadly referring to any decorative wood trim used within the home. Examples are: baseboard trim, window casing, chair rail, crown molding, and door casings.

JOB JUGGLING — A trade term referring to the practice of moving among multiple jobs at the same time. This practice is frequently used to describe ineffective work habits performed when a company has taken on too much work or has a slow cash flow.

JOINT COMPOUND — Also know as drywall mud, it is the substance used to hide seams and nail or screw heads in the finished walls of a home.

JOISTS — Supporting structural members, usually made of wood, allowing the support of floors and ceilings.

LIABILITY INSURANCE — Insurance obtained to protect the insured against damage or injury claims and lawsuits.

LIEN RIGHTS — The right of contractors and suppliers to lien a property where services or products are provided but not paid for.

LIEN WAIVER — A document used to protect property from mechanic's and materialman's liens. These documents are signed by the vendor upon payment to acknowledge the payment and to release their lien right against the property for which the products or services were rendered.

LINE DRAWING — A simple plan drawn with single lines indicating the area's perimeters and division into sections and rooms.

LINEAR FEET — A term used to describe a unit of measure, measuring the distance between two points in a straight line.

LOAD-BEARING WALLS — Walls supporting the structural members of a building.

LOAN COMPANY — Companies specializing in making loans but not offering the services of a full-service bank or savings and loan association.

LOT NUMBER — A number assigned to a particular piece of property on zoning or subdivision maps.

LOWBOY TOILET — A one-piece toilet with a low profile. These toilets have an integrated tank and the tank does not rise as high above the bowl as with a standard toilet.

MARKET ANALYSIS — A study of real estate market conditions used to establish an estimated fair market value for the sale of a home.

MARKET EVALUATION — A term used interchangeably with market analysis.

MARKETABILITY — A term used to describe the feasibility of selling a house on the current real estate market. Marketability is determined by the features and benefits of a home.

MATERIAL — A trade term referring to the products and goods used in building and remodeling.

MATERIAL LEGEND — An area on blueprints describing in great detail the type of materials to be used in the construction or remodeling of the proposed project.

MATERIALMAN'S LIEN — A recorded security instrument placed on the title of a property to secure an interest in the property until a legal dispute can be resolved. These liens are placed when a supplier has supplied material for a property and has been refused full payment. Liens create a cloud on the title and make transferring ownership of the property very difficult.

MECHANIC'S LIEN — A recorded security instrument placed on the title of a property to secure an interest in the property until a legal dispute can be resolved. These liens are placed when a contractor has supplied labor for a property and has been refused full payment. Liens create a cloud on the title and make transferring ownership of the property very difficult.

METES AND BOUNDS — The oldest method of describing the boundaries of a property. In this method the boundaries are described in detail using natural or artificial monuments and by explaining the direction and distance the property lines run.

MITER BOX — A small box with no top and slits in the top of each side to allow a saw blade to pass through the box and cut wood laid in the box. These slits are cut to guide the saw along a specific angle when the wood is cut. They are used for cutting angles on finish trim boards.

MORTAR — A mixture of lime or cement used between bricks, blocks, or stones to hold them in place.

MORTGAGE — A pledge or document securing a lender's investment and accompanying the note for the loan.

MORTGAGE BROKER — A liaison between a borrower and a lender. An individual who attempts to procure financing for a client for a fee.

MULTIPLE LISTING SERVICE — A service provided to real estate brokers combining a listing of all real estate for sale by the members of the service. Multiple listing books provide information on all homes for sale and sold during a given time by the participating members in the real estate profession.

NON-CONFORMING — A house or improvement dissimilar to surrounding properties in age, size, use, or style. An example would be a one-level ranch-style house in a neighborhood of two-story Colonial-style homes.

NON-STRUCTURAL CHANGES — Changes not affecting the structural integrity of a building. Examples are: replacing kitchen cabinets, installing new carpet, and painting.

OAK VENEER VANITY — A vanity constructed of plywood or particle board and covered with an exterior finish of oak.

ONE-PIECE TOILET — A modern style toilet with the tank and the bowl molded as a single element, creating a sleek appearance and an easy to clean surface. Standard toilets have the tank and the bowl as two separate pieces, joined together with brass bolts and nuts.

OPEN-END BILLING — A trade term referring to working on a time and material basis and billing for all labor and material involved in a job, with no limit on the total amount to be billed.

OUTLET PLATE — A trade term describing the cover placed over an electrical outlet and screwed to the center of the outlet.

OUTSIDE WALL — Any wall with one side meeting outside air space.

OVER-BUILDING — A term describing the practice of investing money in a home that is unlikely to be recovered, due to surrounding proper-

ties. An example would be adding three bedrooms to a home, for a total of six bedrooms, when surrounding houses only have three bedrooms.

PARTICLE BOARD — A composite of wood chips bonded and pressed together to create a sheet to be used for sub-flooring or sheathing.

PEDESTAL SINK — A bathroom sink with a china bowl hung on the wall and supported by a china pedestal. The pedestal adds support to the bowl and hides the plumbing connected to the sink and faucet.

PERMITS — Documents issued by the code enforcement office allowing work to be legally performed.

PLANS SCALE — A defined and constant unit of measurement for blueprints and drawings. An example: standard blueprints use a scale in which each ¼ inch on the blueprints equals 1 foot in the actual building.

PLUMBING STACK — A pipe rising vertically through a building to carry waste and water to the building sewer or to vent plumbing fixtures when it penetrates the roof of the building.

PLYWOOD — A wood product composed of multiple layers of veneer joined with an adhesive. Plywood usually has three layers but can have more, and it is always made of wood veneers in odd numbers. Typically, the grain of each veneer is joined at ninety degree angles.

POINTS — Also known as discount points, these are fees paid to a lender to increase the yield of a loan being offered by the lender.

POINT-UP — The procedure used to repair or replenish the mortar between bricks, blocks, stone, and tile.

POLYBUTYLENE PIPE — A modern type of flexible plastic pipe used for the distribution of potable water in a building.

POTABLE WATER — Water meeting the requirements to be considered safe for drinking, cooking, and domestic purposes.

POWDER ROOM — A trade term referring to a room containing a toilet and a lavatory, without a bathtub or shower.

PRE-FAB TRUSS SYSTEM — A manufactured roof system eliminating the need to stick-build a rafter roof. Trusses only need to be set into place and secured; they require no on-site cutting or building.

PREPAYMENT PENALTY — A penalty charged by a lender when a loan is paid in full before its maturity date. Prepayment penalties insure the lender's receiving the full yield of a loan, regardless of when it is paid off.

PRESSURE BALANCE CONTROL — A trade term used to describe a type of plumbing faucet. These faucets are considered a safety feature because they prevent the user from being scalded by hot water if there is a fluctuation in the cold water pressure.

PREVENTIVE IMPROVEMENT — Improvements designed to reduce costly repairs and replacements through routine maintenance.

PRIME FOR PAINT — The process of preparing a surface to receive paint. This procedure produces better results than when paint is applied without a primer.

PRODUCTION SCHEDULE — The agenda for events to be performed in the construction and remodeling process.

PROGRESS PAYMENTS — Periodic payments made as work progresses into defined stages, such as rough-in and final.

PUNCH-OUT — A trade term referring to the process of correcting deficiencies and making minor adjustments at the end of the job.

PVC PIPE — Poly Vinyl Chloride, a type of plastic pipe used in plumbing. Frequently used for drains and vents and occasionally used for cold water piping.

QUOTES — Firm prices given by contractors and suppliers for labor and material.

RAFTER CUTS — A trade term for the angles cut on rafter boards when stick-building a roofing system.

RAFTERS — Structural members, usually made of wood, supporting the roof of a building.

REGISTRY OF DEEDS — The place deeds are recorded and available for public inspection.

REHAB — Reconstruction or restoration of an existing rundown building.

REMODELING — The practice of altering existing conditions and adding new space to existing structures.

RETAINAGE — Holding back money owed to a contractor for an agreed-upon period of time, to protect the consumer from defective material or workmanship.

RIGID COPPER TUBING — Frequently called copper pipe, rigid copper tubing is a common material used in the potable water distribution system of residences. It typically comes in rigid lengths, 10 or 20 feet long, and can be cut as needed.

RIMMED LAVATORY — A drop-in style lavatory with a steel rim surrounding the lavatory bowl to hold it in place.

RIP-OUT — A trade term referring to the removal of existing items to allow the installation of new items. An example would be removing an old bathtub and surrounding tile, to allow for the installation of a new tub and surround.

ROOF SHEATHING — The material secured to the rafters or trusses to allow the installation of a finished roof. Plywood and particle board are frequently used as roof sheathing.

ROOFING FELT — A black paper-like product applied between the roof sheathing and the shingles. It reduces the effects of extreme temperature and moisture.

ROUGH PLUMBING — This term refers to the pipes and fittings of a plumbing system but does not include fixtures.

ROUGH-IN — A trade term referring to the installation of material prior to enclosing the stud walls. Examples would be for plumbing, heating, and electrical systems. The bulk of these systems must be installed before the wall coverings are applied, so this is considered rough-in work.

ROUGH-IN DRAW — A progress payment made when the rough-in work is complete.

ROUND FRONT TOILET — A toilet with a rounded bowl, as opposed to a toilet with an elongated bowl. Most residential toilets have round fronts.

SCHEDULE 40 PIPE — This is a rating for the thickness and strength of a pipe; it is the standard weight of plastic pipe used for residential drainage and vent plumbing systems.

SEAL FOR PAINT — When stains exist and must be painted over, a sealing agent should be applied to the stain before painting. This process prevents the stain from bleeding through the new paint.

SECONDARY MARKET — A financial term referring to markets where banks and other lenders sell their real estate loans. The original lenders normally continue to service these loans for a fee but are able to recycle their available lending funds by selling the loans to the secondary market. The secondary market is composed of individual investors, corporations, and organizations.

SECTION OF PROPERTY — A term used in providing a legal description of a property. The section of a property is typically referred to on zoning and subdivision maps.

SELLING UP — A trade term pertaining to selling a customer additional services and products. The act of enticing a customer to spend additional money, above and beyond the original contract amount.

SETBACK REQUIREMENT — A term relating to zoning regulations, in which a certain amount of unobstructed space must exist between properties. With setback requirements, owning the land does not mean you can build on all of it. These requirements establish a rule on how far a structure must be from each property line.

SHEATHING — The material applied to exterior studs and rafters to allow the installation of finished siding and roofing.

SHEET VINYL FLOORING — Also known as resilient sheet goods, these floor coverings are available in widths of 6, 9, and 12 feet. They are a common and widely accepted floor covering for kitchens and bathrooms.

SHIMS — Small pieces of tapered wood used to level construction and remodeling materials, such as doors, cabinets, and windows.

SHOWER HEAD ARM OUTLET — The female adapter located approximately 6'6" above the finished bathroom floor, in the center of the shower area. The location where a shower head arm is screwed into the adapter, allowing the use of the shower head.

SILL — The board placed on top of the foundation and beneath the floor joists.

SITE CONDITIONS — A term used when describing the conditions of a construction site. Examples would be: level, sloping, rocky, wet.

SITE WORK — Normally includes excavation, but always refers to the preparation of a site for construction.

SKYLIGHT — A glass panel located in the roof, allowing natural light to enter a space below it.

SLAB — Usually a flat interior reinforced concrete floor area.

SOFT COSTS — Expenses incurred in a project that are not directly related to construction or remodeling in the strictest sense. Examples are: loan fees, surveys, legal fees, and professional fees.

SPA — A bathing tub with whirlpool jets designed to hold and heat water indefinitely with the use of chemicals and an independent water heater. Spas are designed to be filled and drained with a garden hose.

SPECIFICATIONS — This term applies to a compilation of the services and products to be used in the completion of a project. Specifications can be addressed individually in a contract or may take the form of a separate collection of documents.

SQUARE FEET — This term is a unit of measure frequently used by contractors. To obtain the square footage of an area, you must multiply the length of two perpendicular walls together. In a rectangular space, this procedure will give you the total square footage of the area.

SQUARE FOOT METHOD — A appraisal technique in which a value is assigned for each square foot of space contained in a building. This method is reasonably accurate with standard new construction procedures but is rarely accurate or used in remodeling.

SQUARE YARDS — This term is a unit of measure most commonly used in floor coverings. To obtain square yardage you must take the square footage of an area and divide it by nine.

STANDARD-GRADE FIXTURE — This is a trade term used interchangeably with the term builder-grade fixture. A product of average quality, normally found in production built housing.

STICK-BUILD — A trade term meaning to build a structure on-site with conventional construction methods.

STORAGE CEILING JOISTS — Ceiling joists rated to carry an additional weight load for storage above the ceiling.

STRIP LIGHTS — Multiple incandescent lights mounted on a metal or wood strip. Common applications include three or four lights mounted on an oak strip for use in bathrooms.

STRUCTURAL INTEGRITY — The strength of a structure to remain in its planned position without fail.

STRUCTURAL MEMBERS — Structural members normally consist of wood and they support a portion of the building. Examples are: floor joists, rafters, and ceiling joists.

STRUCTURAL PLANS — Plans or blueprints detailing the materials to be used and the placement of these materials for structural additions or changes.

STRUCTURAL WORK — Work involving the structural integrity of a building. Examples are: adding a dormer addition, expanding an existing structure, or relocating load-bearing walls.

STUDS — Typically made from wood in residential applications, studs are the vertical wooden members of a wall. They are placed at regular intervals to allow support and a nailing surface for wall coverings and exterior siding.

SUBCONTRACTOR — A contractor working for a general contractor. Examples could be: plumbers, electricians, or hvac contractors. Called "subs" for short.

SUBFLOOR — Generally either plywood or particle board sheets attached to floor joists under the finished floor covering.

SUBSTITUTION CLAUSE — A common clause in contracts allowing a supplier or contractor to substitute a similar product in place of the specified product. These clauses should only be allowed when they are heavily detailed and clearly define the products to be substituted.

SUPPLIERS — A trade term referring to the companies supplying materials used in construction and remodeling.

SUPPORT COLUMNS — Vertical columns used for structural support. An example could be the columns found in basements or garages, supporting the main girder.

T & M — A trade term meaning Time and Material. A form of billing for all labor and material supplied with no limit to the billed amount.

TAKE-OFF — A trade term meaning an estimate of the materials and labor required to do a job. Take-offs are generally associated more with material than with labor.

TANKLESS COIL — An internal part of a hot water boiler heating system, also referred to as a domestic coil. The coil provides a source of potable hot water by heating water passing through a copper coil found beneath the boiler's jacket.

TAPED DRYWALL — A trade term denoting drywall that has been hung and taped. The tape is applied with the use of joint compound to hide the seams where sheets of drywall meet.

TEMPERATURE-CONTROLLED FOUNDATION VENTS — Modern foundation vents able to sense temperature and open or close automatically. These vents allow for better foundation ventilation throughout the year.

TEMPLATES — A trade term with multiple definitions. The first definition is a plastic stencil kit allowing draftsmen to draw consistent symbols of items for blueprints. Examples of these symbols are: toilets, doors, electrical switches, and sinks. The second use of the word is to describe a guide used for cutting countertops to allow the installation of kitchen sinks and other related work.

TENTED FUMIGATION — The process of enveloping an entire house in a tent to allow a total fumigation of all the home's wood-related products. This process is used to remove certain wood-infesting insects.

THRESHOLD — A trim piece connecting two flooring areas, usually made of wood, metal, vinyl, or marble. These serve to trim the seam between two different materials, such as a vinyl bathroom floor and the hall carpet.

TIME AND MATERIAL BASIS — Basically the same as open-billing; a form of billing for all labor and material supplied with no limit to the billed amount.

TITLE SEARCH — A function frequently preformed by attorneys to certify a title is clear of liens or other clouds preventing a satisfactory real estate closing.

TOILET BOWL — The part of a toilet to which the seat is attached.

TOILET TANK — The part of a toilet including the handle is for flushing a toilet. A reservoir tank holding up to five gallons of water to allow the toilet to be flushed.

TONGUE AND GROOVE PANELING — A type of paneling or siding with a groove on one side and a projection on the other. The projection is placed inside the groove of adjoining panels to form an attractive finished seam.

TRACT HOUSING — A trade term describing production or subdivision housing. The term refers to houses built on a tract of land.

TRIGGER POINTS — A sales term referring to the key words or actions resulting in a potential buyer agreeing to make a purchase.

TRIM — A trade term applied to any object, but usually wood, used to provide a finished look to a product or installation.

12-INCH ROUGH TOILET — A standard toilet with the center of the drain pipe located 12 inches from the finished wall behind the toilet.

TWO-PIECE TOILET — A combination of a toilet tank and bowl, connected by brass bolts and nuts, to form an operational toilet.

TYPE "K" COPPER TUBING — Type "K" copper is marked with a green stripe and has a thicker wall than type "M" or type "L" copper. It is the preferred choice of copper tubing for underground installations, but sees little use in above ground residential applications.

TYPE "L" COPPER TUBING — The type of copper refers to the thickness of the wall of the tubing. Type "L" copper is marked with a blue stripe and is approved for use underground and has a thicker sidewall than type "M" copper. It is becoming the most frequently used copper in residential water distribution systems.

TYPE "M" COPPER TUBING — The type of copper refers to the thickness of the wall of the tubing. Type "M" copper is marked with a red stripe and is frequently used for piping residential hot water heating systems. Until recently, it was a common carrier of potable water to plumbing fixtures. It is not approved in most locations for underground use; code revisions are phasing out type "M" as a potable water distribution pipe and requiring type "L".

UNDERLAYMENT — A trade term for a smooth sheet of wood applied between the subfloor and the finished floor. Underlayment is most commonly used when vinyl sheet goods are to be installed. It provides a smooth, even surface on which the vinyl rests.

UNFINISHED BASEMENT — A trade term describing a basement with a concrete floor and unfinished walls and ceiling. There are minimal electrical outlets and little to no heat in an unfinished basement.

VALANCE — A short curtain forming a border between a window and the ceiling or a short trim board connecting the top of kitchen cabinets to the ceiling.

VANITY — A trade term describing a base cabinet for a bathroom lavatory or sink.

VENT PIPE — A part of the plumbing system designed to allow the free circulation of air within the plumbing drain and vent system.

VENTED EXHAUST FAN — The two most common locations for vented exhaust fans are the kitchen and the bathroom. In the kitchen, the fan vents the fumes and gases from the range to the outside air. In a bathroom, the exhaust fan is designed to remove odors and moisture from the room. Both types of fans are vented to the outside air space with a duct or coiled hose.

VINYL SIDING — A type of exterior siding requiring little to no maintenance with a life expectancy of twenty years. The color is a part of the molded vinyl and will not fade or wear off under normal conditions.

WAINSCOTING — The procedure of installing wood on the lower portion of a wall, joined by a chair rail, to meet the upper wall, finished with paint or wallpaper.

WALK-IN CLOSET — A closet large enough to walk into and store or remove clothing.

WALK-OUT BASEMENT — A basement with a door on ground level allowing entry and exit from the basement to the outdoors.

WALL COVERINGS — Anything covering a wall, including: paint, wallpaper, drywall, wood, siding, and plaster.

WALL-HUNG LAVATORY — A bathroom lavatory designed to hang on the wall with no other support.

WASHER OUTLET BOX — A metal or plastic box designed to be recessed in an interior partition, allowing the connection of washing machine water hoses and providing an indirect waste for the washing machine discharge hose.

WATER DISTRIBUTION PIPE — A pipe carrying potable water to plumbing fixtures.

WATER SAVER TOILET — A toilet using three gallons of water or less each time the toilet is flushed.

WHIRLPOOL — A trade term describing a bathing tub with whirlpool jets. These tubs are equipped with faucets and a sanitary plumbing drain. They are designed to be filled and drained each time they are used.

WHIRLPOOL JETS — The devices found in whirlpool tubs and spas allowing jets of water to circulate the water contained in the bathing units.

WORKER'S COMPENSATION INSURANCE — A type of insurance protecting workers who are injured while performing their professional duties.

WORKING PLANS — Any set of plans adequate to allow tradespeople to perform their duties in a satisfactory manner.

Index